Contributions to Management Science

More information about this series at http://www.springer.com/series/1505

Jacobus (Kobus) Kok • Steven C. van den Heuvel
Editors

Leading in a VUCA World

Integrating Leadership, Discernment
and Spirituality

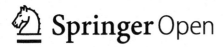

Editors
Jacobus (Kobus) Kok
Department of New Testament
Evangelische Theologische Faculteit Leuven
Belgium

Extraordinary Professor
University of Pretoria
South Africa

Research Associate (Classical Studies)
at the University of the Free State
Bloemfontein, South Africa

Steven C. van den Heuvel
Department of Systematic Theology
Evangelische Theologische Faculteit
Leuven, Belgium

Extraordinary Researcher at the
Faculty of Theology
North-West University
Potchefstroom, South Africa

ISSN 1431-1941   ISSN 2197-716X   (electronic)
Contributions to Management Science
ISBN 978-3-319-98883-2   ISBN 978-3-319-98884-9   (eBook)
https://doi.org/10.1007/978-3-319-98884-9

Library of Congress Control Number: 2018958921

This Springer imprint is published by the registered company Springer Nature Switzerland AG
The registered company address is: Gewerbestrasse 11, 6330 Cham, Switzerland

Preface

Revolutionary Times

We live in a particularly revolutionary time. To some it seems, in the words of W.B. Yeats' (1919) famous "The Second Coming" poem, that "[t]hings fall apart, the centre cannot hold."[1] "It is both the best and worst of times," to use the words of Charles Dickens (1859) in *A Tale of Two Cities*; our time could perhaps be called "A Tale of Twin Towers and Multipli-Cities." Many would agree that we live in one of the fastest changing times in history and that the change we experience now might be just as large and significant as the change between the Middle Ages and the modern world. We live amidst a digital and knowledge revolution, a knowledge worker economy of which the World Wide Web is its utmost symbol. We are connected globally like never before, but in a sense also disconnected in significant ways (De Wachter 2012). We are flooded with and have access to exponential knowledge, literally in the palm of our hand, but often realize that having that knowledge at hand does not always mean we acquire wisdom, character and discernment. We are constantly digitally connected and are expected to stay in contact and virtually online. We have shaped our tools but quickly realize that our tools inexorably shape us. This constantly digitally connected universe created a new form of morality, as we all realize when not answering our emails or WhatsApp's in what others consider to be a reasonable time. Thus, we are overflooded with incoming streams of communication on several platforms. Some people feel the need to announce their excuses on social media platforms if they will be "offline" for a couple of weeks and "take a break" from social media. The point is, we are overflooded with incoming information and impulses, and many do not have the luxury to stop and *think* or *discern* (Rosenberg and Feldman 2008).

---

[1]According to a particular analysis in 2016 by Factiva, this line was quoted more times in the first half of 2016 during Brexit and Trump's election, than the total amount of citation of it in the previous 30 years. See Ballard (2016).

Constant, disruptive and accelerating change is a phenomenon we experience all around us in different industries and even in our own societies. Steven Vertovec (2007) coined the term "superdiversity" to refer to diversity within diversity which is characteristic of our supermobile time. In the last few years, we have seen tremendous changes in immigration, multiculturalism and globalization. We could almost call this a "perfect storm" taking place which metaphorically could be related to a tornado sweeping over our global landscape, changing the very fabric of our sociopolitical and economic landscapes. The problem often is that we find ourselves entering a world which is wholly different than the world we knew and often discover that we are operating with an outdated cognitive GPS. We often come to realize that our old cognitive models do not fit this new world and what the new landscape demands of us. Covey (2004, p. 4) points out that in this complex era, people and organizations need to be *effective* on many levels and that this form of exceptional effectiveness is not optional, but rather a prerequisite for entering the game in the first place. Thus, we live in an extremely competitive environment, which demands more and more of people, requiring them to be agile and innovative. And for this to happen one needs engaged and passionate staff who feel fulfilled in their work and who feel that they make a significant contribution. What we need, says Covey (2012, p. 4), is a way to tap into the "higher reaches of human genius and motivation" and to tap into people's "unique personal significance" (Covey 2012, p. 6) to "serve the common good" (Covey 2012, p. 6). The language Covey uses here is deeply spiritual in nature, for he accentuates the importance of the whole person, encompassing *mind*, *heart* and *spirit*, just as Margaret Wheatley, Sharda Nandran and others like Louis Fry do. In our opinion, it is both fascinating and stimulating to see leading scholars and practitioners turning to "spirituality" in the context of business—this is one of the ways in which we can see the influence of new paradigms in anthropology, in which the old conception of the human being as a calculating, rational being (the *homo economicus* of classic economic thought) is being increasingly overcome.

Process of the Book

The idea for this book was kindled after a discussion between Jacobus (Kobus) Kok and some members of the Steering Committee of the Institute of Leadership and Social Ethics (ILSE), part of the Evangelische Theologische Faculteit, Leuven (Belgium), based on the book *Leadership, Innovation and Spirituality*, which was published in 2014. As we shared our mutual experiences in the global South and Europe alike, we soon realized that we all struggle with the same questions and sense a growing need for leaders to make sense of the complex environment(s) in which we live and the need for discernment on deeper levels of consciousness. Both in the West and in South Africa, many in recent years turned their attention to "spirituality" or "ancient wisdom," as can be seen in business books like those of Steven Covey (2004), Margaret Wheatley (2017), Sharda Nandran and Margot Borden (2010),

Louis Fry and Melissa Nisiewicz (2012) and others in the field of psychology like
J.O. Steenkamp (2018). Johan Beukes, CEO, of *in Harmonie*, which is located on
the picturesque La Motte wine estate, owned by Hanneli Rupert-Koegelenberg in
Franschhoek in the Cape, runs a spiritual retreat centre in which they want to
facilitate a space of rest, restoration and reconciliation where people could come to
terms and discern.[2] Similarly, the well-known business scholar and author Margaret
Wheatley (2017), after her retirement, established a programme of retreats for
business leaders to find "islands of sanity."[3] There are several reasons why leaders
and organizations from different continents in this specific time in history turn to
"spirituality" or "ancient wisdom" and do so within the denotative, connotative and
associative framework of "harmony" and "resonance." These phenomena reflect an
underlying need in our societies. There is a need to "come to terms," "rest," "be
restored," "become whole," "resonate," "reconcile," "retreat," "reflect" or "discern."

On 5 May 2017, a team of inter-and-transdisciplinary scholars and business
leaders convened by Jacobus (Kobus) Kok came together for an expert symposium
at the ETF in Leuven, the oldest university city in the Benelux in the heart of the
European Union.[4] This team consisted of scholars and practitioners representing
different countries ranging from South Africa, Germany, the Netherlands and
Belgium. During this expert symposium, it became clear that there is a need for
inter-and-transdisciplinary research and learning when it comes to the relationship
between leadership, spirituality and discernment. A follow-up meeting on 16 October
2017, again at ETF, helped to streamline the process—this effort was, among others,
supported by Louis W. Fry, of the International Institute of Spiritual Leadership. At
this meeting, the project "Roots and Wings: Building Bridges (in the spirit of rest,
restoration and reconciliation)" was launched. The aim of this project is to bring
diverse people together and discern on important socio-economic, political and
socio-religious matters in an effort to enhance social cohesion, or what Anton Rupert
referred to as "medebestaan" (co-existence).[5]

This book contains some of the papers which were presented at these expert
symposia and other papers of scholars and practitioners who were invited to make
contributions to this book. ILSE was deeply involved in this process, particularly
with Steven C. van den Heuvel coming on board as editor for the book.

---

[2]This retreat centre was the vision of Hanneli Rupert-Koegelenberg, daughter of the business
tycoon Anton Rupert.

[3]See http://margaretwheatley.com/ and also https://www.youtube.com/watch?v=LtaYNxp56gs
accessed on 28 March 2018. In the latter, Wheatley explains the background of her book *Who do
we choose to be?*

[4]These meetings were made possible by a research grant provided by the South African National
Research Foundation and the University of Pretoria.

[5]See the biography of Anton Rupert, written by Ebbe Domisse (2005, pp. 11–12, 13).

Acknowledgements

With all papers having undergone a rigorous double-blind peer review process, we as editors are deeply grateful to the many researchers who were willing to invest time and energy in providing us with thoroughgoing reviews, which in many cases have helped the authors greatly.

Dr. Prashanth Mahagaonkar, our editor at Springer, was gracious to accept the book into the series "Contributions to Management Science"—our thanks goes out to him as well as to other staff at Springer, who provided excellent editing service.

We dearly thank ILSE at ETF Leuven for financial support for the production of the book, which would not have been possible without their provision.

The Plan of the Book

The plan of the book is as follows. In the first, opening chapter, "The Metanarraphors we Lead and Mediate by: Insights from Cognitive Metaphor Theory in the context of Mediation in a VUCA World," Jacobus (Kobus) Kok and Barney Jordaan start off by further introducing the phenomenon of the VUCA world. They focus on the way in which the mediation and resolution of disputes takes place, in this context. In particular, they look at the way in which metaphor theory can contribute to this process. They argue that the metaphors used in a mediation context often remain unexplored—doing so, however, might empower the mediator as well as the parties in a dispute and mediation process. While written with regard to the particular context of mediation, the intra-and-transdisciplinary insights of this chapter will be highly relevant in other contexts as well.

The second chapter is written by Johann Kornelsen and is entitled "The Quest to Lead (with) Millennials in a VUCA-World: Bridging the Gap between Generations." Kornelsen argues that, especially in the West, there is a disconnect between the current generation of leaders on the one hand and the millennials on the other hand. In response, he argues that a new leadership approach is needed to bridge the gap—specifically, he calls for the development of "responsible leadership," a combination of qualities from transformational leadership, servant leadership and authentic leadership. This will lead to a certain reversal of roles, as current leaders will become the mentees of the millennials, who will help them adapt to the realities of the VUCA world.

The third chapter is entitled "Personal Leadership as Form of Spirituality." Written by Joke van Saane, this chapter argues that there is a paradox in contemporary leadership studies: on the one hand, situational theories flourish, while on the other hand, personality traits and personal skills are being asserted as crucial for leadership. Van Saane argues that this paradox can be overcome by taking into account spiritual concepts. She focuses on three in particular, namely (1) the way spirituality creates openings for growth and values in leadership theory; (2) the redefinition of traditional forms of religion, in religious leadership; and (3) the way that the concept of personal leadership brings in the crucial notion of "learning," in leadership theory. These strategies for bringing spirituality and leadership together are crucial ones and form important recommendations for leadership theory.

The fourth chapter is authored by Barney Jordaan, Professor of Management Practice, with a specialization in negotiation and dispute resolution. This background is clearly visible in the chapter he wrote, and which is entitled "Leading Organisations in Turbulent Times: Towards a Different Mental Model." He argues that the agility of an organization will help it survive and compete in the increasingly fast-changing VUCA world. He argues that this necessitates increasing collaboration in the organization—and therefore: trust. It is, however, precisely this trust that is often lacking in organizations, eroded as it is by the propensity to competition. Jordaan further investigates these obstacles to increased trust, in organizations, suggesting ways to increase trust and collaboration, as essential ingredients to organizational success in the VUCA world.

Anoosha Makka is the author of the next chapter, which is entitled "Spirituality and Leadership in a South African Context." She argues that the leadership models and practices that are dominant in South Africa have been strongly influenced by Western leadership theories. She argues for combining these leadership styles with the Afrocentric notion of "ubuntu," particularly in the context of South Africa. A possible contribution that this notion can make is the emphasis it puts on community and sociality. Makka's proposal is an important one—one dimension of the VUCA world is the increase in diversity; it is a marker of good leadership to identify this increase as positive and to seek to learn from it.

The sixth chapter is written by the South African scholars Calvyn du Toit and Christo Lombaard. In their chapter, entitled "Still Points: Simplicity in Complex Companies," they comment upon the tendency of organizations (and of social systems in general) to move to increased complexity. While the authors recognize the necessity of recognizing the complexity of today's social systems, they nevertheless make an argument for simplicity as a spiritual orientation to life. An example of such simplification is "waste management": the deliberate inclusion and ritualization of unstructured work periods, such as extended coffee breaks, in which unexpected connections can be made, and in which creativity can blossom. These "still points," argue Du Toit and Lombaard, are essential for people and organizations to thrive in a VUCA world.

The next chapter is entitled "How to Integrate Spirituality, Emotions and Rationality in (Group) Decision-making." In this chapter, Volker Kessler, the author, draws from the spirituality of Ignatius of Loyola, particularly to enhance the process of group decision-making. Volker explicates the three modes of decision-making that Loyola distinguishes, namely (1) immediate intuition, (2) emotional processing and (3) rational reasoning. Discerning parallels between these different modes and current management literature, he particularly seeks to assist in the integration of these Loyolan insights with the way in which managers can structure group decisions. In doing so, he further develops the concept of the "Six Thinking Hats," as described by Edward de Bono. This further development of what has become a classic model will be of relevance for the processes of leadership, discernment and spirituality in an increasingly VUCA world.

Jack Barentsen provides the eighth chapter, "Embodied Realism as Interpretive Framework for Spirituality, Discernment and Leadership." While he does not interact with the phenomenon of the VUCA world directly, he does provide a crucial building block for a new conceptualization for thinking through the nexus of spirituality, discernment and leadership, namely by seeking to overcome the conflict between two distinct ways of "knowing," one driven by science and the other by intuition. Barentsen argues that the conflict between these is overcome by the concept of embodiment, as it is being developed across a number of disciplines. In particular, a focus on embodiment is able to show that spiritual knowledge is not opposed to scientific knowledge, but that both forms of knowing are part of our human system of knowing, as it is fundamentally directed and limited by the way our bodies interface with the world in which we live. This insight is foundational for a renewal of leadership, discernment and spirituality in a VUCA world.

The South African scholar Stephan Joubert is the author of the next chapter, entitled "A Well-played Life: Discernment as the Constitutive Building Block of Selfless Leadership." This chapter argues that "discernment" is a crucial building block for especially selfless (or servant) leadership in the context of the VUCA world. In making this argument, Joubert asserts that discernment is not just a leadership skill for making the right decisions in the spur of the moment, but rather denotes a way of life, "a never-ending relational and rational process," as he calls it. This more comprehensive approach to discernment certainly is of value in the context of the all-encompassing VUCA world.

The tenth chapter is written by Nelus Niemandt. He is a professor of missiology, which is reflected in the title of his chapter: "Discerning Spirituality for Missional Leaders." As the title indicates, Niemandt addresses the question what kind of spirituality is needed, specifically for Christian missional leaders, particularly geared towards the South African context. To this end, he proposes to redefine spirituality, not seeing it as a process of "knowing and believing," but rather one that involves "hungering and thirsting," flowing from the recognition that longing and desire are at the core of our being. He argues that this new form of spirituality helps to give rise to a new form of discernment, which involves a trialogue between (1) church, (2) culture and (3) the Bible. While the particular focus in this chapter is the renewal of the spiritual process of Christian missional leaders, in the face of challenges in the VUCA world, the redefinition of spirituality will be relevant for a broader public as well.

Steven C. van den Heuvel is the author of the next chapter: "Challenging the New 'One-Dimensional Man': The Protestant Orders of Life as a Critical Nuance to Workplace Spirituality." In this chapter, it is argued that while the renewed call for "spirituality in the workplace" is to be lauded as a good and necessary emphasis, there are certain risks and problems connected to it as well. Van den Heuvel focuses on three of these in particular: (1) the danger of instrumentalization and narcissistic misdirection, (2) the pragmatism often opted for in solving conflicts between different spiritualities in the workplace and (3) the dominance of radical social constructivist approaches to workplace spirituality. In addressing these problems, he reappropriates the Protestant theological concept of the "different orders of life," specifically as this concept has been developed by Dietrich Bonhoeffer. He identifies different ways in which this concept can help address the problems he identified with the contemporary emphasis on workplace spirituality. This chapter is a necessary correction to some of the problems with the current emphasis on spirituality, in the business world—it draws attention to the "dark side" connected to it, seeking ways to overcome these.

The twelfth and last chapter is written by Patrick Nullens. Like Johann Kornelsen, he too writes about "responsible leadership": his chapter is entitled "From Spirituality to Responsible Leadership: Ignatian Discernment and Theory-U." Like Van Saane, in her chapter, so too Nullens is concerned with renewing current leadership theory—in particular, he seeks to connect the emphasis on a leader's self-awareness with the call for ethical leadership. In making this connection, he—like Volker Kessler, in chapter seven—draws on the spirituality of Ignatius of Loyola, which emphasizes the importance of humility, silence and detachment, among other things, as avenues into increased self-awareness. He brings his Ignatian spirituality in dialogue with Theory-U, as developed by Otto Scharmer. This results in an enriched understanding of the process of spiritual discernment, which can be beneficial to leaders in the current VUCA world.

Together, the chapters in this volume present a variety of contributions to the interrelated processes of leadership, discernment and spirituality, as well as to their integration, and with a particular view on the VUCA world. It is our express hope that as such, this volume will prove to be a timely and helpful resource, not just for academics, but also for practitioners in various fields.

Leuven, Belgium   Jacobus (Kobus) Kok
Leuven, Belgium   Steven C. van den Heuvel
March 31, 2017

References

Ballard E (2016) Terror, Brexit and U.S. election have made 2016 the year of Yeats. Wall Street J. https://www.wsj.com/articles/terror-brexit-and-u-s-election-have-made-2016-the-year-of-yeats-1471970174. 23 Aug 2016
Covey S (2004) The 8th habit. FranklinCovey
Dickens C (1859) A tale of two cities. Chapman & Hall, London
Domisse E (2005) Anton Rupert: 'n Lewensverhaal [Anton Rupert: a Biography]. Tafelberg uitgewers, Kaapstad
De Wachter D (2012) Borderline times. LannooCampus, Leuven
Fry, Louis W, Nisiewicz, Melissa Sadler (2012) Maximizing the triple bottom line through spiritual leadership. Stanford University Press

Nandram, Sharda S, Borden, Margot E (2010) Spirituality and business: exploring possibilities for a new management paradigm. Springer-Verlag, Berlin Heidelberg

Rosenberg H, Feldman CS (2008) No time to think: the menace of media speed and the 24-hour news cycle. Bloomsbury, London

Steenkamp JO (2018) SHIP: an integrated theory & psychotherapy for trauma-spectrum manifestation. SHIP, Pretoria

Vertovec S (2007) Super-diversity and its implications. Ethn Racial Stud 30:1024–1054

Wheatley M (2017) Who do we choose to be? Berrett-Koehler

Yeats WB [1919] (1921) 'Poem: the second coming' In Michael Robartes and the dancer, Cuala Press. Online open access at http://www.theotherpages.org/poems/yeats02.html

---

The original version of the book was revised: Editor affiliation in Copyright page has been updated. The erratum to the book is available at https://doi.org/10.1007/978-3-319-98884-9_13

Contents

List of Contributors

Jack Barentsen (Ph.D.) is Full Professor and Head of the Department of Practical Theology at the Evangelische Theologische Faculteit, Leuven (Belgium), as well as Senior Research Fellow of the Institute of Leadership and Social Ethics. He is also Extraordinary Associate Professor of New Testament and Practical Theology in the Faculty of Theology at the North-West University in Potchefstroom, South Africa.

Calvyn C. du Toit is a Ph.D. candidate in Christian Spirituality at the University of South Africa and a Research Associate in the Department of Dogmatics and Christian Ethics at the University of Pretoria, South Africa.

Barney Jordaan (Ph.D.) is Professor of Management Practice at Vlerick Business School (Belgium).

Stephan Joubert (Ph.D.) is Extraordinary Professor of Contemporary Ecclesiology at the University of the Free State, South Africa.

Volker Kessler (Ph.D., D.Th.) is Director of the Akademie für christliche Führungskräfte and Dean of the GBFE. He is also Professor Extraordinarius at the Department of Philosophy, Practical and Systematic Theology, University of South Africa.

Jacobus (Kobus) Kok (Ph.D) is Full Professor and Head of the Department of New Testament Studies at the Evangelische Theologische Faculteit, Leuven (Belgium). He is also an Extraordinary Professor and NRF Y1 Rated Researcher at the University of Pretoria, and Research Associate in Ancient Greek at the University of the Free State, South Africa.

Johann Kornelsen is managing partner of 3D Leaders and the co-owner and CEO of an investment company. He is also a doctoral student at Regent University, USA.

Christo Lombaard (Ph.D., D.D.) is Research Professor of Christian Spirituality at the University of South Africa, in Pretoria, South Africa.

Anoosha Makka (Ph.D.) is Senior Lecturer in Management at the Johannesburg Business School of the University of Johannesburg, South Africa.

CJP (Nelus) Niemandt (D.D.) is Professor in Missiology and Head of the Department of the Faculty of Theology at the University of Pretoria, South Africa.

Patrick Nullens (Ph.D.) is Full Professor of Systematic Theology and Ethics at the Evangelische Theologische Faculteit, Leuven (Belgium), as well as Extraordinary Professor of the Faculty of Theology at North-West University, South Africa.

Steven C. van den Heuvel (Ph.D.) is Postdoctoral Researcher in Systematic Theology and Ethics at the Evangelische Theologische Faculteit, Leuven (Belgium), as well as Extraordinary Researcher in the Faculty of Theology at North-West University, South Africa.

Joke van Saane (Ph.D.) is Professor of the Psychology of Religion and holds the chair of Education Theology and Religious Studies at the Faculty of Religion and Theology of the Vrije Universiteit Amsterdam, the Netherlands.

The Metanarraphors We Lead and Mediate by: Insights from Cognitive Metaphor Theory in the Context of Mediation in a VUCA World

Jacobus (Kobus) Kok and Barney Jordaan

Abstract We live in a superdiverse and supermobile world which is Volatile, Uncertain, Complex and Ambiguous (VUCA). Diversity management, social cohesion, mediation and negotiation skills are needed in such times. In all discourses, within the context of leading and facilitating the resolution of disputes metaphorical frameworks of meaning are created. The challenge for the mediator is to become aware of, and keep in mind how metaphors affect the process of mediation and the mediator's own role in it. Those unaware of the dynamics of metaphor theory might implicitly be limited in the mediation process due to the socio-cognitive confines and frames of the metaphors being used in a given mediation context. By becoming aware of the dynamics of metaphor, by means of critically reflecting on metaphor theory, that which is often overt in the mediation dynamics, could be reflected upon covertly. This in turn will empower not only the mediator, but also the parties to a conflict or dispute as they reflect critically on the "metanarraphors" (meta-narratives and metaphors) they mediate or are influenced by.

The original version of this chapter was revised. A correction to this chapter is available at https://doi.org/10.1007/978-3-319-98884-9_13.

J. (Kobus) Kok (✉)
Department of New Testament, Evangelische Theologische Faculteit, Leuven, Belgium

Extraordinary Professor, University of Pretoria, Pretoria, South Africa

Research Associate (Classical Studies) at the University of the Free State, Bloemfontein, South Africa
e-mail: kobus.kok@etf.edu

B. Jordaan (✉)
Management Practice, Vlerick Business School, Ghent, Belgium

University of Stellenbosch Business School, Cape Town, South Africa
e-mail: barney.jordaan@vlerick.com

1 Introduction and *Status Quaestionis*

1.1 Structure of the Chapter

The structure of the chapter will be as follows. In the first section of the chapter the need for the essay and a cursory *Status quaestionis* will be provided. Secondly the conceptual and technical framework of the paper will be sketched, by providing a theoretical discussion of metaphor theory in which we will specifically draw on the insights of Lakoff and Johnson (2003) who are considered world leaders in conceptual metaphor theory. Within the context of the research group/book, and the intersection between leadership, spirituality and discernment, we will provide some perspectives from research on the phenomenon (and philosophy) of hope, drawing on Richard Rorty's insights, and its possible relation to mediation.[1] Thirdly, these insights will be brought into dialogue with mediation as academic discipline within jurisprudence, i.e., how metaphors (of hope) and the underlying philosophy of hope, could influence the mediation process. Since the social-constructivist epistemology is used, the meta-theory of language and meaning being used here serves as the conceptual frame underlying the scientific approach of the argument. Secondly, from an epistemological point of view, spirituality[2] and the perspective of hope serves within the post-foundational[3] frame of reference of the authors and their

---

[1]See the renewed interest in some circles of business to reflect on hope. See Borman's (2016) "The world book of hope" and also Van den Heuvel and Nullens' (2018) book "Driven by hope: Economics and Theology in Dialogue."

[2]The term "spirituality" has a wide range of definitions (see Nullens and Barentsen 2014). For us spirituality is defined within the awareness of our embodied realism and embodied cognition which calls for the Other to extend our cognition and participate relationally with others (or the Divine Other) in a process of co-creation of meaning, significance and values, growth and transformation (see Waaijman 2002). A Hermeneutic of hope, which we will discuss at the end of the chapter, is thus a form of spirituality.

[3]For the definition and understanding of post-foundational, and also for inter-and-transdisciplinary approaches, see Van Huyssteen (1997). We understand it as an epistemology that is hesitant to build on an assumed authority, but rather in dialectical fashion argue in favour of a certain rationale for acts denoting a rejection of an assumed or given authority for a specific belief or action but arguing, in dialectical fashion, for a rationale for action or belief in a social-constructivist context. This includes in our view also a sensitivity to contexts in which dialogue should take place and inclusivity be promoted. This does however not exclude the multi-facetness of identity of the researcher(s) who might from a Dialogical-Self Theoretical perspective (see Hermans and Hermans-Konopka 2010) embody certain forms of social identity which might adhere to values within certain socio-religious groups. The construction of narratives play an important role in discourses and identity. Within narratives, one also finds metaphors that guide and shape the discourse of a narrative and for that reason some even speak of "narraphor" [see the term used by Nelus Niemandt (2018), influenced by Sweet (2014, p. 91)]. "Narraphor" is understood as "At the core of who we are, we crave a narraphor. A narraphor is a story made with metaphors that help us understand the world, ourselves, each other and our community." Subsequently, I (J. Kok) have coined the term "metanarraphor" which will be discussed below. [One of the blind peer reviewers of this article made the following remark which is worth noting for further discussion and research: "Freud, and most recently Steenkamp, point out how much metaphors (and what you call

Fig. 1 Inter-and-
transdisciplinary dialogue

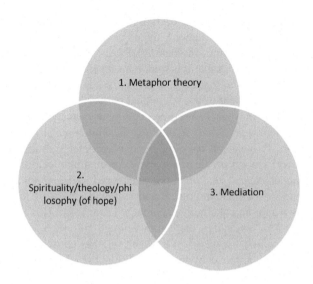

trans-disciplinary engagement. Subsequently, attention is turned to the discipline of
mediation with an example of a concrete case study which will be discussed with the
aforementioned theoretical presuppositions. Graphically the inter-and-transdisciplinary[4] structure of the article could be illustrated as follows (Fig. 1).

1.2 Lifelong Learning Organizations: From Unconscious Incompetence to Unconscious Competence

In Business management and in other disciplines like theology, in this case, learning
organizations (a term coined by Peter Senge)[5] aim to *continuously facilitate transformation and growth* of their staff.[6] The research gap this article wants to address

---

narraphors) are inter-translators of trauma-induced psychological content. It is evidential, and I
agree with the formulation 'that we crave a narraphor'. The craving, though, signals a projection.
Describing metaphors being 'at the core of who we are' to me expresses the observation of the
prevalence of trauma in the human condition, but would not be an ontological statement of human
nature"].

[4]By inter-disciplinary we mean discussions between different subfields within on discipline, for
instance theology. This would entail discussions and collaboration between systematic theologians
and practical theologians for instance. Transdisciplinary discussions would for instance entail
engagement between practical theologians and neuroscientists or quantum physicists—disciplines
that would normally not work together on a particular research question. In this article, the authors
bring several disciplines in dialogue with each other.

[5]See Senge's (1990 and 2006) book on *The art and practice of the learning organization* and also
Senge's insights in *The Firth Discipline* (2006).

[6]As one of the peer reviewers of this article remarked, organizational psychologists point that out
that it is important for leaders, and in this case mediators, to do sufficient self-work to understand
their own shadows and emotional triggers to ensure countertransference is limited. In this regard see

lies on the theoretical basis of the inter-and-transdisciplinary dialogue between jurisprudence (mediation), theology and philosophy, and social science about the topic of mediation. Jordaan (2013, ad loc),[7] following Burch's four stage learning model,[8] remarks that it is important for mediators and negotiators to become aware of their *unconscious incompetence*, i.e., the fact that they are not always necessarily explicitly aware of the theoretical basis of their negotiation and mediation practice and that they could become even better and more effective in what they do. The problem here is that *unconscious incompetence* also limits the growth of the mediator. By means of ongoing practice and inter-and-transdisciplinary dialogue, exposure to a proper learning cycle, a mediator could enter a stage of *conscious incompetence*, i.e., when one is exposed to deeper knowledge and confronted with one's own epistemological and theoretical basis of mediation and aware of one's own gaps and alternative approaches available.[9] This entails a phase of "deconstruction."[10] When one then goes through this stage, one could eventually become *consciously competent*, i.e., when one has consciously learned and practiced new methods, approaches and ways of thinking (theory) about mediation. Then, eventually one moves into the stage of becoming *unconsciously competent*, i.e., when one has integrated the newly acquired skills and theory by means of reflection and constant practice.[11]

In the next section of the paper we will reflect on theory, that is, to stimulate a process of becoming conscious of their incompetence.

1.2.1 Inter-and-Transdisciplinary Discernment in a Superdiverse and Supermobile World

Sketching the Backdrop/Relief/Setting the Scene

We live in one of the fastest changing times in history, amidst a digital, communication and travel revolution which some consider to be as significant as the transition

---

Kegan (1982) who could be considered to be in the constructive-developmental tradition (vias a vis humanistic and existential-phenomenological [like Buber, Rogers, etc] and the neo-psychoanalytic tradition [like Anna Freud, Erik Erikson, etc]). Kegan (1994) was very much influenced by dialectical philosophy and psychology.

[7]These perspectives of Jordaan (2013, ad loc) was taken from his insights in the "Maximizing Value in Negotiations Programme" hosted at the Graduate School of Business at the University of Cape Town. See https://youtu.be/poiST7IpZpw accessed on 02 February 2018.

[8]See Davis, Leary (2012). Competence as Situationally Appropriate Conduct: An Overarching Concept for Lawyering, Leadership, and Professionalism. *Santa Clara Law Review* 52(3):725–793. Available at https://digitalcommons.law.scu.edu/cgi/viewcontent.cgi?referer=https://www.google.be/&httpsredir=1&article=2715&context=lawreview.

[9]See Kegan (1982, 1994) for the stages of ego development.

[10]On the importance on generalizations and the "pictures" or "mental models" we create and according to act from, and the necessity to become personally aware of these and communicate these effectively to co-workers, see Senge's (2006) book Third Discipline.

[11]E.g. keeping e.g., a negotiation ad mediation journal, and over a long time practicing the newly acquired theory and practical skills consciously until it becomes integrated and part of the *unconscious competence* skill set.

between the middle ages and the modern word or the dawn of the industrialized world. Our time is characterised by superdiversity and supermobility, which in Business Studies we refer to as resulting in a VUCA (Volatile, Uncertain, Complex, Ambiguous) world (Barentsen and Kok 2017, pp. 7–10; Van den Broeck and Jordaan 2018, p. 12).[12] The term "superdiversity," a term which originated in the social sciences, was coined by Steven Vertovec[13] in 2005 and appeared for the first time in an academic article in 2007. His 2007 article on *Ethnic and Racial Studies,*[14] and the term superdiversity has since been used widely in different fields.[15] Superdiversity refers to diversity *within* diversity (Barentsen and Kok 2017, pp. 7–8). Thus, a form of "diastratification"[16] appears within one and the same family for instance, where some members were born in a different country, have a low competency to speak the local language of the host country while others within the same family might have been born and socialized within a liberal democracy and embody a Western conceptual framework as part of their social identity complexity.[17] After some years they may be highly educated and earn a high income over and against some of their family members who might be dependent on the host country's social system, for instance. The implication is often that the legal statuses between family members might be different. This is what Vertovec means by superdiversity—which is diversity and complexity *within* diversity (and complexity). In this latest book Geldof (2016) correctly argues that diversity within diversity will increase and be characteristic of the twenty first century. The latest research Geldof (2016) points out, that has been done on population composition in the EU capital Brussels for instance, indicates that circa 66% of residents have a migration background. Soon to follow the statistical tendency is Antwerp where the majority of citizens will soon be those having a migration background. Thus, we will increasingly find Europe to be a context of "Ethnic-cultural (super)diversity." This will of course shape the future of our society and the need for skills to mediate and negotiate conflict will grow.

Against the background of a VUCA world characterised by superdiversity, scholars and practitioners increasingly become aware of the need for inter-and-transdisciplinary research. Rather recently (2011) the Carnegie Foundation reported on research that has been done on the need for inter-and-transdisciplinary intersection between Business Studies and other disciplines in a study "Rethinking

---

[12]Van den Broeck and Jordaan (2018), *The Agile Leader's Scrapbook,* LannooCampus, Leuven.

[13]Vertovec was at the time involved at the *Max Planck Institute for the Study of Religious and Ethnic Diversity.* See http://www.mmg.mpg.de/departments/socio-cultural-diversity/research-focus/ retrieved 22 February 2018.

[14]Vertovec, Steven (2007). "Super-diversity and its implications." *Ethnic and Racial Studies.* 30(6): 1024–1054. On 22 February 2018 the article had been cited 2951 times, which proves the impact factor of the article. On a Google search the term super-diversity reported 190 million hits on 31 March 2018.

[15]Geldof, Dirk (2016), *Superdiversity in the heart of Europe,* Acco Uitgewerij.

[16]Jennifer Slater, from UNISA was the first person who made me aware of the term "diastratification" at a conference in Leuven on 29–30 April 2016.

[17]On social identity complexity theory, see Roccas and Brewer and also Kok (2014) on social identity complexity.

Undergraduate Business Education: Liberal Learning for the Profession" (Colby et al. 2011). One of the outcomes of the research was that a significant amount of business schools in the United States tend to focus on "one-dimensional and specialised courses of study." After the international economic crisis in 2008, scholars and practitioners reflected on the "need (for) entrepreneurs (to) consider the consequences of their activities and who understand the connections between business activities and society." Consequently, the influential Carnegie Foundation deliberately aims to include in their business curriculum, perspectives and insights from human/social sciences. This tendency is also seen in the "European Haniel Program in cooperation with HSG and CBS," and others like the Copenhagen Business School follow educational programs and curricular design that aim at inter-and-transdisciplinary research.[18]

In the field of mediation and negotiation studies, and in the courses presented in the MBA programs in Europe and the U.S. these challenges are inter alia addressed by engaging in inter-and transdisciplinary research, conferences, expert seminars and joint publications.[19] From the perspective of mediation, this development has proven fruitful for scholars from different disciplines and for practitioners alike.

Below we will provide some examples and further reflect on metaphor theory and a philosophical approach to hope and how it could help mediators to enrich their theoretical approach and skillset.

2   Insights from Metaphor Theory in Mediation

Mediation could be defined as a *social process* whereby a third party (mediator) assists and facilitates individuals or groups in a context of conflict to find win–win solutions.[20]

At the world's leading[21] Dispute Resolution Program hosted at Pepperdine's Strauss Institute for Dispute Resolution,[22] scholars and practitioners have for some years already mentioned the importance of narratives[23] and metaphors in

---

[18]Source: https://www.haniel-stiftung.de/en/promoting-future-generations/the-european-way accessed 19 February 2018.

[19]See for instance the research project on hope between the Erasmus University Rotterdam and the Institute of Leadership and Social Ethics in Leuven (see https://www.etf-ilse.org/our-projects-and-research/ accessed on 08 March 2018).

[20]See Noce et al. (2002).

[21]See https://law.pepperdine.edu/straus/ for the announcement of the 2018 award for the best U.S. dispute resolution program accessed 01 March 2018.

[22]See https://law.pepperdine.edu/straus/ accessed 1 February 2018.

[23]Hansen (2004, p. 1) remarks "In mediation, the conflicting parties' stories act like 'theories of responsibility,' which construct the logical, causal linkages between actors, their actions, and outcomes." "People can actually be said to think in terms of stories and their constituent parts (the themes, roles, and plots), which work together to create a system of meaning around particular

mediation.[24] Thomas Smith (2005, p. 343), a mediator from Colorado, is correct
when he argues that metaphor:

> [O]perates covertly to gain tacit agreement on direction, means, and ends without full
> description or rationale. It constrains a discussion, focusing on certain concerns while
> masking others. Becoming consciously aware of the metaphors commonly used during
> negotiation offers valuable insights into meanings not overtly discussed. This awareness
> helps reveal intentions and implicit evaluations while also illuminating obvious areas for
> mutual gain.

He is also correct in suggesting that the dynamics of metaphor could be particularly helpful "to reinforce rapport, to persevere in negotiating, to reflect and query
usefully, and to explore and propose different options" (Smith 2005, p. 343).

It is of utmost importance that a mediator as leader in a process of mediation not
only develops the ability to understand the dynamics or structural properties of
metaphor but also ways in which to construct and deconstruct meaning by means
of analysing the way in which particular metaphors *frame* a discourse and also
determines the boundaries within which possibilities could be created.[25] Furthermore, in negotiation an important skill to master is the (psycholinguistic) ability to
analyse and clarify meaning behind the words of discourse participants in an effort to
ascertain implicit concerns and ways in which possibilities for mutual gain (win–win
situations) could be negotiated. In this regard, inter-and transdisciplinary insights
from conceptual metaphor theory, promises to provide valuable insights.[26]

In a recent business meeting one of us observed the following metaphorical frame
in the discussions between discourse participants referring to Brexit:

> The unfortunate divorce between us and England
>   also effects the relationships with the in-laws.
> I suppose we would not be enjoying tea in the garden soon.
> The relationship is stuck and we are parting ways—there is simply no hope on the
> horizon.

It is interesting to note that the particular person interpreted Brexit within the
metaphorical frame of a divorce between a husband and a wife and the subsequent
estrangement of relations involved in the process. From a socio-cognitive and
critical-discourse analytical perspective it could be argued that the discourse participant in this meeting *projected* certain dimensions, and the frame of a divorce *unto*

---

people and events. The stories that one constructs fit into a wider web of stories relating to other
stories created by the same individual, to stories created by members of one's social network, and
even to cultural stories on a societal level." See Hansen (2004).

[24]See Lynne J. Cameron (2007, pp. 197–222 accessed from http://journals.sagepub.com/doi/abs/
10.1177/0957926507073376?journalCode=dasa). In her article, Cameron "investigates emergent
patterns of metaphor in reconciliation talk. . ." and also the "identification of linguistic metaphors
and works recursively between levels of discourse, revealing how micro-level negotiation of
metaphors contributes to emergent macro-level metaphor systems."

[25]Discourse is understood as a *social practice* in linguistic form (We dó things through words).

[26]See https://www.haniel-stiftung.de/en/promoting-future-generations/the-european-way accessed
19 Feb 2018.

the diplomatic (and economic) context. One problem with this metaphor is that it immediately frames the negotiations as adversarial. The frame is likely to impact on the negotiators' approach to the process—i.e, positional rather than collaborative; their tactics or behaviors during the process of negotiation and thus also on the quality of the outcomes they achieve (if any).

The question of course is whether this particular metaphorical frame is at all adequate and whether it will not perhaps *limit* the possibilities of the negotiation process and influence the discourse between the leaders. Instead of simply uncritically engaging within the frames of this particular discourse and the metaphor being used here, the negotiators and leaders around the table could perhaps consider to reflect critically on the use of this metaphor in this situation. Secondly, by becoming aware of the dynamics of metaphor, leaders, mediators and negotiators could use insights from metaphor theory to build rapport with discourse participants and also steer the direction of discourses in the negotiation process in a more informed (and sophisticated) manner. Different cultures embody different values, and that is often expressed in deep and surface (cultural conventional) metaphors. As described above, in a context of superdiversity and supermobility, which is characteristic of the VUCA world we live in, the negotiator and mediator's ability to reflect critically on language use and meaning by discourse participants becomes even more desired, if not essential.[27]

In the following section we will discuss some salient conceptual and theoretical aspects to buttress the aforementioned scenario and need for deeper understanding of metaphor theory.

3   Conceptual and Theoretical Discussion

3.1   Understanding the Social-Constructive and Socio-Cognitive Critical Discourse Nature of Language

Some (like Rooney 2015) go so far as to argue that "[T]he mediator is the most powerful person in the room, given his or her control over the process. The mediator's process calls (e.g., whether to meet in private or plenary sessions only); the terminology he or she uses; proposals he or she might make to the parties all have the potential to alter the course of a dispute." This makes it even more important for mediators to be aware of their role, their frames (about the problem, people and process aspects of the dispute) and how these might affect the course of a dispute and, ultimately, the parties themselves. Rooney puts it as follows: "The mediator's presence in the room changes the dynamics in the relationship between the parties. . .

---

[27]On superdiversity and supermobility, see Barentsen, Van den Heuvel and Kessler (2017), especially on "Increasing Diversity: Loss of Control or Adaptive Identity Construction" and the dynamics thereof.

The challenge is to work internally on ourselves for it is through this endeavour that we have the most profound effect on those around us both professionally and privately. We cannot afford to be blind to this power."[28]

Specialists in socio-cognitive critical discourse analysis like Fairclough correctly illustrate that when discourse participants utter words in an effort to communicate meaning, they *draw from/on social cognitions or mental maps*. We could thus speak of a form of *intertextuality of discourse*, i.e., that we not only draw from different layers of meaning "out there" but that our utterances are also multi-layered in particular contexts on the level of *interdiscursivity*. The latter term wants to express the reality that we dialectically draw on *multiple discourses* and that in our micro-expressions, we take part dialogically in larger macro-socio-political discourses. Thus, there is a *dialectical process* taking place as we engage with different layers of discourses in society or in a group. In other words, as we take part in the construction of meaning through words, we not only *produce* but also *consume* texts by means of drawing from *shared and assumed knowledge in our culture which is based on our habitus*. Habitus is defined as the system(s) of embodied dispositions, tendencies, etc., which we have internalized from our social world and have become a form of *sensus communis*. As Bourdieu has argued, it manifests in our *hexis* (body posture, mannerisms, accent, taste, habits, perceptual schemes and mental habits, etc). The point here is that from a socio-cognitive perspective, what we say draws from existing social maps of knowledge which we in some form *reproduce* through our communicative actions.[29] Furthermore, as Bourdieu has showed, communicative action is mostly "contaminated" by power dynamics, i.e., that by our words and our metaphors, we *position ourselves* vis a vis another, in a particular way. A mediator should in other words also have the heuristic tools to be sensitive to the manner in which power relations are structured, embodied, maintained/sustained or transformed in the process of negotiation.[30] Fairclough (1992, pp. 65, 126, 124–130) has shown that particular power interests are either *reproduced* or *transformed* in and through the way we use language and discourse in a given context. As we enter as patients the consulting room of a medical specialist, the mere context *positions us in a certain hierarchical relational dynamics*. We draw on our *habitus* and play our respective roles in that discourse context. The social system and the context in other words *determines* and *shapes* the nature of the discourse and relations. People aware of this might decide to either *reproduce existing discourses and social (power) positioning* or decide to *challenge and transform the social power relations and meaning*. The mediator leads a process of negotiation, and for this reason, he/she needs to be skilled in analysing these

---

[28]Rooney (2015).

[29]See in this regard also Steenkamp (2018, p. 81) for the way in which social maps which we internalize from an early age, are created and "directly shape the neurobiological state of our infant brain" from an early age with implications for the way we shape our identity and habitus.

[30]See in this regard Fairclough's work on Language and Power (1989), Discourse and Social Change (1992), etc.

complex discursive elements in a given discourse context and aim to become aware not only how people intertextually draw on existing "mental maps" (Fairclough 1992, p. 82) but also wise in how to steer discourses into the direction of a win–win outcome.

3.2 Understanding the Dynamics of Metaphor

The study and critical reflection on metaphor is an ongoing process. Classic scholars for instance provide helpful insights on Aristotle, who wrote extensively on the nature of metaphors. In his contribution to the debate, negotiator Thomas Smith (2005) remarks: "Writings at least as old as Aristotle define metaphor as talking about one thing in terms of another." But here Smith lacks depth in his approach probably due to the fact that he mainly makes use of secondary sources and have not consulted Aristotle as primary source directly. However, already in ancient times, a difference was pointed out between a metaphor, a simile, a comparison and a symbol. Also, they reflected critically on the *function of words* by the speaker. Functionally speaking, there is a difference between a surface metaphor and a deep metaphor. There is a difference between [see Lyons[31] (1986, p. 216)][32] the understanding of the *functional* dynamics of metaphor and figurative meaning, between a metaphor and a so called proper comparison.

Let us provide the following examples from a recent case[33] where an employee claimed constructive dismissal.[34] The mediator played an important role in the resolution of the dispute with a successful (win–win) outcome for all parties *inter alia* by means of his/her use of metaphor theory and socio-cognitive discourse analysis[35]:

---

[31]Lyons as referred to by Van der Watt (2009, p. 305).

[32]Van der Watt (2009, p. 306).

[33]All persons fictitious disclaimer: "The story, all names, characters, and incidents portrayed in this (re)production are fictitious. No identification with actual persons (living or deceased), places, buildings, and products is intended or should be inferred."

[34]See http://www.legislation.gov.uk/ukpga/1996/18/contents. The employee had some knowledge of employment law [and the terms of constructive dismissal (see Employment Rights Act 1966 section 95(1)c)] and therefore was aware of certain forms of unethical behaviour/discrimination occurring in the workplace based on emotional interpersonal conflict between the respective employee and his/her superior. This was also evidenced in the negative performance evaluation process, although the employee outperformed set targets. An oral negotiation process in the recruitment phase, was also not honoured by the employee, leading to damage or breach in trust because of unilateral contract changes by the employer [see ERA96 s98(4)]. Since this constituted a legitimate dispute, a mediator was called in.

[35]The term "constructive dismissal" is a *terminus technicus* used in employment law to refer to the voluntary resignation of an employee, as a direct result of what he/she experiences as an hostile environment, created by an employer. This might include the experience of unfair treatment, unreasonable work-related demands, or possible intention by an employer to force an employee

#a. Employee before and during mediation: "Barry, my boss, is stubborn like a horse with blinkers/blinders. I try to talk to him but gained no ground and in the process he attacks my integrity and underestimates my experience. How dare he refer to me as an 'African' and that 'Up here' we do it the 'European' way. Or the fact that I am not 'integrated' well enough. It is blatant racism and discrimination, especially when put in an email copied to colleagues, or discussed around the staff room. I feel that the time has come for our paths to separate, for I have no hope."

#b. Employee after mediation [endorsement]: "The mediator was a catalyst.[36] He/she created a positive effect in restoring the trust and power balance."

Within these two extract examples one finds several metaphors which need to be deconstructed. In example (a) the "point of comparison" framework is more closely determined than example (b). The point being made is the "stubbornness" of the "opponent" and in the process of conveying this message functionally, the boss (tenor) is compared to a blinded horse[37] (vehicle), with the *function* of communicating the point of "stubbornness." Also note that there is a certain power dynamics at play here, because the parties in this process are *hierarchically* positioned in a lower and higher position in the particular context *from the perspective of their* discourse. The employee experiences that the employer views his/her African identity as inferior to that of the Westerner and that he/she is discriminated against and feels powerless against the "inflexibility" or "obstinacy" of the employer. The metaphorical frame of implicit "distance" and difference in class, is underlying the use of the words "up here" and "down there." Below we will show how this way of speaking is a performative act in which power is exercised and some positioned "lower" than others on the level of competency or quality based on what we will refer to as "metanarraphor."

---

to resign. If this is proven, it would technically constitute a case of constructive dismissal (See Kennedy 2015). If the claim is valid, the employee could make legal claims against the employer. In the case of the UK, constructive dismissal is explained and defined in the Employment Rights Act 1996 section 95(1)c. "The notion of constructive dismissal most often arises from a fundamental breach of the term of trust and confidence implied in all contracts of employment. In order to avoid such a breach *'[a]n employer must not, without reasonable or proper cause, conduct himself in a manner calculated or likely to destroy or seriously damage the relationship of trust and confidence between the employer and the employee.'* Whilst a breach can be of the implied term of trust and confidence, a fundamental breach of any of the express or implied terms of a contract of employment is sufficient." http://www.legislation.gov.uk/ukpga/1996/18/contents visited 22 Feb 2018.

[36]"The negotiator is a catalyst" is a copulative metaphor [negotiator is tenor (tenor is the lexical item which one can take literally and "on which the metaphorical meaning is applied"); Catalyst is the vehicle, (i.e., the "lexical item generating the metaphorical meaning") See Van der Watt (2009), p. 309]. Van der Watt also makes use of (and prefers) "focus" and "frame," i.e., *"frame* refers to the literal situation, while *focus* refers to the word(s) that generated the metaphorical meaning."

[37]This could be seen as an intergenerational and cross-cultural metaphor. One still see this image when tourists are visiting Brugge in Belgium or Vienna in Austria alike. In South Africa, for instance this image and metaphor is also used and was influenced by the use of blinkers for horses in (British) colonial times.

On the other hand, example (b), is much more complex in nature. The reason is that from an inter-discursive perspective (especially from a socio-cognitive level discussed above), there are multiple ways, and thus a complexity of possible semantic qualities/relations between the lexical items in which the source domain and the target domain are compared. In a VUCA world characterised by superdiversity and supermobility with clients representing diverse backgrounds, this could become a complex analytical task. According to Van der Watt (2009, p. 308), one can think of explaining the relationships between these items by means of the image of a "semantic sieve," looking at all the qualities of both lexical items that "fall through" and are related/overlap. By looking at these shared qualities one can discern the dynamics of the points of interaction which Van der Watt calls "the system of associated commonplaces" which form the *analogical* basis by which means interpretation is made and meaning constructed. In most cases, there would be points where a target and source domain share qualities or "simultaneous similarity" and where they do not "simultaneous dissimilarity" (Van der Watt 2009, pp. 308–309). Important to note is how the meaning of metaphors used by discourse participants are to be understood? For metaphors are in nature relatively "open" as discourse participants draw comparative connections.

For this reason, one should carefully also look at the *cohesion* within a body of literature or in a discourse structure by looking at the following (here we are following/drawing from Van der Watt 2009, p. 313):

- Words which are *thematically related*, for instance, sun, light, sunrays, dawn, dusk, dew, etc.
- *Repetition of words* which indicates that the author is building on and expanding a particular image.
- *Stylistic features*, for instance chiasmus, parallelism etc.
- *Contextually related coherence* within a particular frame, for instance in hospitals where you have sick people, doctors, ambulances, waiting rooms, operating theatres, nurses, scrubs, etc.

By means of these methods one could also determine the nuances and explore the "emotional meaning carried by the metaphor" (Van der Watt 2009, p. 313).

Lakoff and Johnson (2003) explained some of the results of research that has been done in cognitive neuroscience and the relation to metaphors. The latter points out that metaphors are always embedded in a particular frame of reference and also *ipso facto* a result of an *embodied experience*.

Lakoff and Johnson (2003) and Lakoff (2009) often uses the following examples: Firstly, it is important to note the importance of *frames*. For instance, when entering a hospital, that space/frame would be associated with reception desks, nurses, doctors, operating rooms and scalpels. Discourse participants would know that something is wrong from the perspective of the accepted frame if a patient is given a scalpel and asked to operate on a doctor. It simply does not fit the frame. Apart from frames, metaphors are also related to embodied experiences, and there is a significant amount of similarity between cultures because of this embodied experiential reality. When a container is filled with water, we observe the content being filled from outside *into* the container which makes it full. Thus, more water means that we observe vertical increase in level: Thus, more is up and less is down. Accordingly, as Lakoff points out, we would speak of "stock prices going through the roof" with the presupposition of vertical increase. Secondly, the metaphors we use for expressing whether someone is a "warm" person is directly related to experience of physical warmth in close relationships. We also use metaphors to explain emotions like "I am boiling" (for anger) which has a *biological experiential basis*. Anger is related to the physical increase in blood pressure which leads to increase in body temperature, within the embodied experience of the body as container. Lakoff also often refers to the following example, from his time at Berkeley as this theory was developed. The expression: "Our relationship is stuck and we are parting ways" is embedded within the frame of relationships as journeys with destination(s). The conceptual framework of relationships as journeys, is embedded within the framework of linear thinking of movement from point a to point b. Within this frame of "love is a journey" it is thus possible to combine several ways of expressing metaphors and images related to this frame. For instance, "The relationship is on a bumpy road; the wheels are spinning; from here on it will be downhill; hope is on the horizon, etc." These are all examples in which the root metaphor "relationships are journeys" are expanded within the frame of conceptual mapping made possible by the root metaphor.

Metaphors can also function by means of analogy. For instance, if V is to W as Y is to Z and A is to B like V to W, then W could be analogical to Z and V to A. We could argue that old age (V) stands in a relationship to life's journey (W) as winter (Y) stands to seasons (Z), or dusk (A) to day (B). Thus, we could speak of old age as the dusk of life's journey, or winter as day's dusk. "My journey is entering the chill of days' dusk" is an analogical metaphorical expression that combines the frames of "life as journey" and embodied experience of winter/cold and the slowing down of "life" within the perspective of a linear frame of distance and movement in time from young to old.

The power of metaphor is that the interaction between a source domain and a target domain leads to a creative process of bringing together elements which are not normally brought together in a particular way, creating a new force of meaning. On the other hand these metaphors share particular frames which are rather generic and the apparent connections between communities expressing these metaphors perhaps not that significant. Halstead (2003, p. 83) remarks: "Metaphors are both motivated by and constrained by common patterns of bodily experience and experience of the social and natural environment. . ." Metaphors are thus a "fusion of the imagination and embodied experience. . ." and "grounded in human embodied experience. . ." Johnson (2005, p. 159)[38] also agrees and points to the importance of empirical data, illustrating that core analogies "typically come from *basic-level-experiences* that are

---

[38]Mark Johnson (2005) in "Why metaphor matters for philosophy", *Metaphor and Symbolic activity* 10, 3, pp. 157–162.

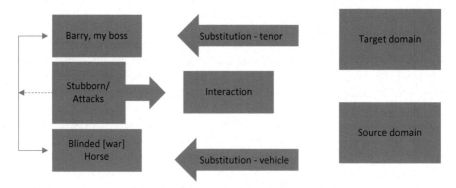

Fig. 2 Schematic representation of dynamics of metaphor

shaped by human beings because of their *shared bodily and cognitive makeup* and because common features of the environments with which people interact."[39]

The metaphorical structure, and transference of meaning from a source domain unto a target domain in the above mentioned examples could be expressed as follows (Fig. 2).

The Mediator as Catalyst of Hope and Win–Win Scenarios

Mediation is both an art and a science (Jordaan 2013, ad loc). The role of a mediator is *inter alia* to serve as a catalyst and create trust for a positive win–win situation for both parties in a dispute (Jordaan 2017). Some scholars might criticize the field of mediation for not having a theoretical consensus, but that does not mean that those scholars and practitioners in the field do not have, or take serious various theoretical perspectives in a rather sophisticated manner.[40] In the process of mediation between the employee and the employer the negotiator facilitated a process in which all the parties could express their feelings by means of what we call "metanarraphor." This term is understood as follows:

> We continually construct our identity inter-discursively on macro-meso and micro levels by telling narratives about ourselves in relation to the world at large and the groups we belong to and use metaphors to bind these narratives into coherent meta-narratives about the self-in-the-world. Thus the term "metanarraphor in mediation."

This definition draws on several presuppositions, which range from knowledge of Social identity and Self-Categorization Theory,[41] Dialogical Self Theory,[42]

---

[39]Halstead (2003, p. 83) also quotes Johnson in a similar argument.

[40]See Noce et al. (2002).

[41]This theory was developed by Tajfel and Turner (see Kok 2017) and illustrates that in-group and out-group dynamics often occur in contexts of conflict and competition. Some people are more loyal to the in-group and will often hold negative views of the out-group. Stereotyping of the out-group is a result of social identity construction.

[42]Dialogical Self Theory (DST) was developed by Hermans and Hermans-Konopka (2010). This theory has shown that "the self" is not monolithic, but pluriform in character. There are different aspects of the self. Thus, myself as academic, myself as son of my father, myself as a negotiator, etc. Sometimes, these different dimensions or parts of the self could be in conflict with one another. The

Ethnicity Theory,[43] Socio-Cognitive Discourse Analysis, Narrative Counselling techniques, Psychology, etc., which the negotiator had in his/her back pack/tool set.

With regard to dispute resolution, Hansen (2004, p. 2) correctly observes: "For mediation to effectively use the storytelling metaphor and create a cooperative climate among disputants, it becomes necessary to destabilize those 'theories of responsibility' which simultaneously serve to legitimate one's point of view and de-legitimate the point of view of the other party. This leaves conflicting parties with a previously 'closed' interpretation (their story) open to new possibilities and interpretations. This new climate of openness can lead to the genesis of a new account and mutually satisfying interpretations and outcomes."

The analytical tool kit of the negotiator will enabled him/her not only to analyze different discursive elements in the discourse structure of the employee's words, but also to enable him/her to ask certain questions to the employee in a process to facilitate a non-judgmental space of trust between himself/herself and the client.

The mediator for instance became aware that the employee holds on to an underlying meta-narrative (or metanarraphor) in which he/she implicitly believes that Europeans consider Africans to be inferior (refer to "up here" and "down there") which is part of an *interdiscursive dominating race discourse*.[44] Lakoff and Johnson have illustrated that the notions of "up here" and "down there" are a result of certain embodied metaphors which connotatively and associatively link "up" with better/ stronger and "down" with weaker. In his/her embodiedness, in his/her habitus, he/she carries "African" ethnic identity. There is sufficient research that shows the problematic nature of the subjective lived experience of "African bodies" being discriminated against,[45] with the (unfortunate) result of what some in the Benelux in the form of an eponym refer to as a calimero-complex. The employee also had many stories that he/she could tell of previous experiences where existential (discrimina-tory) trauma was experienced. In his latest book on Trauma-Spectrum Manifestation, Steenkamp, a South African Clinical Psychologist, pointed out that trauma is "stored" in the body like pearls to a necklace and past trauma experiences (and memories) are activated in certain circumstances. Steenkamp (2018, p. 181) remarks:

---

self could also have a distance relationship with aspects of the self from the past, viewing the self from the past as another. Thus, this theory shows that although we embody and belong to different social groups and have different social roles and social identities, these identities are in dialogue with one another. Thus, we embody aspects of the society to which we belong *within ourselves*. The debates in society are also often debates within the self. This leads to a dialogical self which is not static, but grows and develops over time.

[43]Ethnicity theory, in combination with Social Identity theory (SIT) holds that a particular ethnic group, which is often characterised by a shared language, history, phenotypical characteristics, customs, etc., tend to show favouritism to the in-group in contexts of conflict and change (Kok 2017).

[44]On the interdiscursive "dominating race discourse," see Andreassen and Vitus (2015).

[45]See in this regard the work of Fanon (1967) and the experience of Black people in the West or in African countries with colonial histories in his well-known book "Black Skin, White Mask." Also important in this regard (on the experience of the Black body and decolonialization) is the work of Mignolo (2000, 2007, 2011).

> When we have internal trauma we will be subjected to potential reactivation through
> futuristic (usually adulthood) external associative activators that are cues reminiscent of
> previous trauma-activating events. Stress enhances amygdala function, and seeing that the
> amygdala is involved in implicit memory for emotionally charged events, stress enhances
> implicit emotional memory for traumatic events.

It is thus deducible that the employee could in fact theoretically easily be *activated* by words and gestures of his/her European employer which *ipso facto* entails an emotional response which is extremely complex, for it not only deals with interdiscursive societal discourses on topics like migration and integration, but also with personal trauma which the employee experienced and is *reactivated* in the current conflict in the workplace. In the process of the mediation, the employee revealed that the employer also reminded him/her of his/her father who was very abusive, strict and stubborn and that he/she vowed never to be the victim again of abuse and oppression. Clearly then, there is a problem behind the problem, and trauma behind the trauma on macro (societal), meso (family) and micro (personal) levels. In this case, several interdiscursive (meta)narratives of trauma, and the emotionally linked metaphors associated with it (narrametaphors) intersected and culminated into a conflict situation in the workplace. As employee and employer we bring our *whole selves* and therefore conflict also needs to be understood as a multifaceted and nuanced phenomenon. Those sensitive to these complexities can only benefit in the long term.

From the perspective of the words used by the employee, it was clear that another root metaphor, namely that of "argument is war" has been used. Notice the subtle nature of the implicit metaphorical nature of the words "attack" and "gain no ground" in the employee's utterance in #a. above. Lakoff and Johnson (2003, ad loc) remark:

> We saw in the ARGUMENT IS WAR metaphor that expressions from the vocabulary of war,
> e.g., attack a position, indefensible, strategy, new line of attack, win, gain ground, etc., form a
> systematic way of talking about the battling aspects of arguing. It is no accident that these
> expressions mean what they mean when we use them to talk about arguments. A portion of the
> conceptual network of battle partially characterizes the concept of an argument, and the language
> follows suit. Since metaphorical expressions in our language are tied to metaphorical concepts in
> a systematic way, we can use metaphorical linguistic expressions to study the nature of
> metaphorical concepts and to gain an understanding of the metaphorical nature of our activities.

Naturally then, one could assume that in such a situation of a *destructive*,[46] *dysfunctional*[47] *emotional*[48] *conflict* situation (*vis a vis* constructive, substantive

---

[46]In Organizational Psychology dysfunctional conflict is often refer to as *destructive conflict* which leads to interpersonal animosity and hostility (see Schermerhorn et al. 2011, p. 234 in *Organizational Behavior*).

[47]In organizational psychology a distinction is made between functional (constructive) and dysfunctional (destructive) conflict: the former refers to healthy conflict that leads to discussions, creativity and individual and team performance, and creative change and development, etc., whereas the latter refers to conflict that break social cohesion, lead to employee disengagement, mistrust, etc. (see Schermerhorn et al. 2011, p. 234 in *Organizational Behavior*).

[48]In management literature a distinction is made between substantive and emotional conflict: The former refers to disagreements in functional aspects between workers related to work related aspects like strategy, allocation of sources, etc., whereas emotional conflict refers to feelings of mistrust, resentment, animosity towards fellow workers or superiors (see Schermerhorn et al. 2011, p. 232 in *Organizational Behavior*).

conflict) the primitive fight/flight response of the brain is activated by the parties involved. In this state of hyper-arousal and acute stress response, logical thinking and problem solving do not take place efficiently.[49] There are many Physiological changes induced by the sympathetic nervous system that show mediators that clients are in a state of hyper-arousal, one being the dilation of the pupils, shaking, flushed cheeks, etc., which are results of catecholamine hormones (e.g. adrenaline and noradrenaline) which prepare the body for fight or flight.[50] For that reason the mediator can play a significantly positive role in facilitating the client into a safe (r) space where more logical and problem solving reasoning could take place and where the client is "shifted" through the different "stages" of the (primitive) brain.[51] This is inter alia done by asking open ended questions and asking the client questions that help them to connect with their "metanarraphors," the narratives and the metaphors they live by. The research of Steenkamp (2018) and others have shown that the creation of a *non-judgmental space*, where narratives and metaphors of clients could be told, has the potential to facilitate a space of "healing" and "integration."

In a superdiverse and supermobile world, social relationships will increasingly be sources of potential conflict as persons from *short-term cultures* (like the US) and *long-term cultures* (like Japan); *high-power-distance* cultures (Japan) and *low-power-distance cultures* (Western Europe/e.g. Netherlands) work together (Jandt 1998). In this particular case study, the difference between African values and Western values were also underlying in the conflict. When employers and employees do not understand or have knowledge of these differences, it would lead to conflict and dysfunctional multicultural teams. On the other hand, when these differences are understood and managed from the perspective of adaptive change and constructive conflict, it could be a source of diversity, innovation and creative solutions (Schermerhorn et al. 2011, p. 236).

Often the narratives and metaphors (metanarraphors) we live and lead by limit our possibilities, sense of self, creativity and vision of hope for the future. By understanding metaphorical theory, and by means of the above mentioned toolkit at his/her disposal, the mediator helped the client not only to voice emotions, but also to penetrate deeper levels of past trauma that have been experienced in his/her life. In the process the client was "activated" into a "healing space"[52]—a space in which he/she is confronted with the way in which he/she construct and is constrained

---

[49]See https://www.linkedin.com/pulse/negotiation-brain-game-peter-thompson/ accessed 22 Feb 2018. See Steenkamp (2018, pp. 81–82) for brain physiology and trauma or conflict as well as the work of Damasio (2000, 2010).

[50]See https://courses.lumenlearning.com/boundless-ap/chapter/functions-of-the-autonomic-ner vous-system/ accessed 08 March 2018.

[51]See https://www.healthline.com/health/brain-anatomy accessed 22 Feb 2018.

[52]For the understanding of the terms "activated" and "healing space" in this context, consult the work of Steenkamp (2018, p. 194).

by their narratives and metaphors and how some form of projection is being made on the employer in this particular case.

After the successful mediation process, the employee remarked: "The mediator is a catalyst.[53] He/she created a positive effect in restoring the trust and power balance."[54]

Here the copulative metaphor of the "mediator as catalyst" is interesting. The mediator is said to have restored trust and balanced the power dynamics. This is a complex metaphor with many inter-discursive layers of meaning. When trust and power imbalance is felt to have been "restored," a form of hope for collaboration in future is created.

4 Breaking Bread: A Hermeneutic of Hope and Possibility for Solidarity

Thus far we have critically reflected on the metanarraphors [(meta)narratives and metaphors] of the employee and the employer in the dispute mentioned as an example case study to illustrate the importance of metaphor theory for mediation. But perhaps it is also important, within the context of this book, with its focus on the nexus between leadership, spirituality and discernment, to reflect also on the metanarraphors that implicitly influence the mediator and the mediation process. Within mediation theory, there are different perspectives and approaches which range for instance from "transformative self-determination" [cf. transformative mediation movement (Baruch Bush and Folger 1994)] and the "mediator as problem solving expert" (see Rooney 2015, pp. 8–9). The broad approach, role and view of the respective mediator will also influence and determine the metanarraphor the mediator will use in his/her general approach to dispute resolution.[55]

Above we have already mentioned that Rooney (2015) argues: "[T]he mediator is the most powerful person in the room, given his or her control over the process. The mediator's process calls…; the terminology he or she uses; proposals he or she might make to the parties all have the potential to alter the course of a dispute." Here we want to further argue that from the perspective of metanarraphor, the mediator's

---

[53] As mentioned above also: "The mediator is a catalyst" is a copulative metaphor [negotiator is tenor (tenor is the lexical item which one can take literally and "on which the metaphorical meaning is applied"); Catalyst is the vehicle, (i.e., the "lexical item generating the metaphorical meaning") see Van der Watt (2009), p. 309]. Van der Watt also makes use of (and prefers) to "focus" and "frame," i.e., "*frame* refers to the literal situation, while *focus* refers to the word(s) that generated the metaphorical meaning."

[54] Note the important remark by Greg Rooney (2015, p. 2) that "neutral" facilitative mediation and principles like "balanced power" simply do not exist in pure form, but only in theory—and for that reason mere aspirations.

[55] The "Riskin Grid," for instance, illustrates the different roles the mediator can play in a dispute. See Riskin (2003).

hermeneutics of hope might also have a significant influence on the mediation process.[56] There are different theories of hope, and that also influences one's meta-approach.[57]

Rooney (2015, p. 3) makes a strong case, and rightly so, that no mediator is neutral, and that "[Y]ou cannot take the mediator's physical, mental, emotional and spiritual presence in the mediation session out of the relationship equation." In this sense, Rooney (2015, p. 3) points out, in following Ogden (1994), that the mediator as third party in a dispute is the "analytic third" which inevitably has an intersubjective influence on the whole. Ogden (1994) states:

> The analytic third is a metaphor for the creation of a mind that has an existence of its own and is capable of thinking in ways that neither contributor to the creation of the third subject is capable of generating on its own
> (Ogden 1994; Quoted by Rooney 2015, p. 3).

This by implication means that within the context of mediation, the thoughts, intention and presence of the mediator about the success of the mediation "affects this communal mind" or dimension of the "analytic third" (Rooney 2015, p. 3). Thus, perhaps we need to think about the very metaphors we mediate by and the role that hope plays in the process of leading a process of mediation, in which the mediator is an "equal player in the mediation process" (Rooney 2015, p. 9).

Moti Mironi, experienced mediator and arbitrator and professor of Law at Haifa University always commits to "Breaking Bread" with the parties in a dispute, both as prerequisite for entering into the process and concluding the process, irrespective of the outcome.[58] Mironi's approach as mediator, as an "analytic third" and his metaphorical notion of "breaking bread" at the start and end of the mediation process, leads to a certain intersubjectivity and creates a "third space" between the parties and the field which is created whenever they share that dialogical space (Ogden 1994; Rooney 2015, p. 3).[59] The power and dynamics of this metaphor is understandably rather influential in the whole (meta)process as the mediator and the parties co-create mediating moments and movements.

Jordaan (2017) recently observed the importance of hope theory after having been exposed to the work of Snyder (2002), Luthans and Jensen (2002), Cohen-Chen et al. (2014) and Bar-Tal (2001). After a careful study he came to the following conclusion:

> My ultimate conclusion from delving into this fascinating subject was that hope theory is in fact intimately connected with what we do as mediators and conflict management

---

[56]There are different theoretical approaches to hope like Snyder, from a positive psychology perspective and others like Rorty from a more philosophical perspective which differs from others like Bloch.

[57]On the theories of hope, see Stanford Encyclopedia referenced above and in the bibliography.

[58]Email exchange on 08 March 2018. Mironi is well-known for using this metaphor in his mediation practice and also in training in the subject. Mironi is a colleague of Jordaan.

[59]Rooney (2015) "Rebooting mediation by detaching from the illusions of neutrality," available at http://ssrn.com/abstract=2564035.

practitioners. Further, I believe that by applying the concept consciously in our work we could potentially enhance the impact of what we do.
    Jordaan (2017, ad loc).[60]

Cohen-Chen et al. (2014) illustrated in their research that hope played an important role in the willingness of Israelis and Palestinians to engage in peace talks and fear played an important role in inhibiting possibilities for creative engagement [cognitive freezing; see Cohen-Chen et al. (2014) and Jordaan (2017)].

Jordaan (2017, p. 4) is correct when he remarks that: "As mediators we are in a particularly privileged position to help disputing parties develop a hopeful disposition with respect to their current conflict and so reap some of the benefits... (e.g., improvement in relationship quality and the management of negative emotions and stress; improved creativity, cognitive flexibility and greater ability to engage in integrative problem–solving").

Rorty on the Hermeneutics of Hope

As mentioned above, there are many approaches to the theory and philosophy of hope which range from positive psychological perspectives like that of Martin Seligman (2011), Charles R. Snyder[61] and others (from another angle) like Richard M. Rorty's[62] hermeneutics of hope. We are inspired by the insights Rorty who worked with "hope as a central element of a hermeneutic" and not *per se* as an epistemological approach based on certainty and knowledge.[63] Rorty (1979, p. 318; quoted by Stanford Encyclopedia [SEP] 2017, p. 26) states:

---

[60]Jordaan (2017, ad loc) https://www.linkedin.com/pulse/hope-theory-implications-conflict-man agement-barney-jordaan/ accessed on 08 March 2018.

[61]Charles R. Snyder (1944–2006) was a positive psychologist at the University of Kansas. He is well known for his work on positive psychology in fields of personal feedback, transgression excuse drive and later specialized in research on hope from the perspective of positive psychology.

[62]Richard M. Rorty (1931–2007) was a philosopher at universities like Princeton and Stanford and was educated at Yale and Chicago Universities. He developed strongly the notion that subjective thinking does not equate reality outside of the self. Thus, Rorty did not believe that *knowledge represents correctly* that/the world which is wholly outside of and independent of the interpreting subject. In this regard he is well-known for his book Philosophy and the Mirror of Nature (1979). He advocated American Pragmatisms (neopragmatism). Later work of Rorty (1989) engage with hope and solidarity, although he was known to be, and heavily criticized for being an "ironist" and radical sceptic.

[63]Of course Rorty disagrees with Bloch on some points, but it is the opinion of the authors of this article that Rorty's view does not in principle exclude in its entirety the notion of Bloch's "*Erwartungsaffekte*" (expectant emotions like hope and fear) based on his "processual metaphysics" which bases hope on a free human act of "future directed anticipation" (Bloch 1986). The strength of Bloch is that he views open ended "objective tendencies and possibilities in reality" as interacting in some way with "closed" matters of fact, "such that the moment of potentiality surpassing into actuality always opens up *opportunities* for the interventions of active decision making" (Bloeser and Stahl 2017, p. 19). For that reason he also speaks of the correct way to relate to these "Front" opportunities as nothing less than "militant optimism," i.e., expecting that the "future directed anticipation" could indeed be realized (Bloeser and Stahl 2017, p. 19). Thus, Bloch's notion moves into the domain of what we would call "spiritual," in the sense that a "militant optimism" towards "future directed anticipation" of desires, beliefs and expectations is a form of

> Hermeneutics sees the relations between various discourses as those of strands in a possible conversation, a conversation which presupposes no disciplinary matrix which unites the speakers, but where the hope of agreement is never lost so long as the conversation lasts.

Against Rorty as radical ironist and atheist, we would like to argue (by using his own words) that hope is a form of a spiritual/faith/ethical value, which is not always in the first place grounded in knowledge or probabilities, but rather seen as "an attitude by which interlocutors express both their commitment to certain forms of future interaction and their belief in its possibility" (SEP 2017, p. 20). It is a firm belief and "ability to believe that the future will be unspecifiably different from, and unspecifiably freer than, the past" (Rorty 1999, p. 120 as quoted by SEP 2017, p. 20). This opens up the dimension of spirituality mentioned in the beginning of this essay, namely that for us spirituality is defined within the awareness of our embodied realism and embodied cognition which calls for the Other to extend our cognition and participate relationally with others (or the Divine Other) in a process of co-creation of meaning, significance and values, growth and transformation. A Hermeneutic of hope, which we will discuss below, is thus a form of spirituality and transcends the self.

For Rorty, and for the author(s) of this article, hope has an ethical dimension in the sense that it *ipso facto* entails intersubjective communication and that we are called to dialogue with each other even as "liberal ironists"[64] in our projected "selfish hopes" in such a way that we witness to the hope and active belief that it is possible to reach agreement and that this form of expectation of future (im)possibility is a reflection of "the liberal virtue of civility" (see Rorty 1979, p. 318) and a source of (possible) mutual solidarity (Rorty 1989, p. 93, 1999, p. 87). In this sense, such a mediator's hope might even be seen as "unjustifiable" due to the fact that it does not require objective foundations (See Rorty 2002, p. 58; SEP 2017, p. 21). Important to note is that Rorty points out that "hopelessness is always based on the absence of a narrative of political progress" which means by implication that "if such a narrative is available this seems to provide rational support for political hope" (SEP 2017, p. 21). This brings us back to the notion of metanarraphor, i.e., the way we think about life and the metanarratives and metaphors we construct and live by. A good

---

"metaphysical possibilities in the world and part of a range of human capacities that make it possible to relate to that which is not yet, but which is already prefigured in the objective potentials of reality" (Bloeser and Stahl 2017, p. 19). See Bloeser and Stahl (2017), "Hope," *The Stanford Encyclopedia of Philosophy* (SEP) (Spring 2017 Edition), Edward N. Zalta (ed.), URL = https:// plato.stanford.edu/archives/spr2017/entries/hope/.

[64]Rorty differentiates the "liberal ironist" from the "liberal metaphysician." The latter "expects social cooperation to be based on scientific or philosophical insight that penetrates individual idiosyncrasy and aims at the adoption of a universal, final vocabulary that then leads to solidarity" (See Bloeser and Stahl 2017, p. 20 in the *Stanford Encyclopedia of Philosophy* [from here on SEP]); (see Rorty 2010, p. 93). The "liberal ironist" on the other hand does not hold on to the idea of "a final vocabulary" or some form of intrinsically, universally human communality or basis (SEP 2017, p. 20). Rather, in continuing dialogue and in our "selfish hopes" we may/will find and co-create solidarity being born from shared experiences and shared interests (Rorty 1999, p. 87; Bloeser and Stahl 2017, p. 20).

mediator, even the disillusioned-liberal-ironist legal practitioner often functioning as a mediator, has the ethical (and spiritual) duty to fight for hope as "an expression of the liberal virtue of civility" (Rorty 1979, p. 318). Only when the mediator's own metanarraphor witnesses to the attitude and belief in hope as a sacred space of potential change, does he or she do justice to the insights of modern political philosophy that give hope a central and rightful place in their respective mediatory (and political) thought and actions. For this reason, this fundamentally important attitude and hermeneutics of hope of the mediator in the context of a dispute resolution process is a form of discernment and a form of leadership which is guided towards the possibility of facilitating moments where bread could be broken and communal solidarity be created. The "open" way in which Rorty conceptualizes hope is in other words helpful for mediation as an open ended process. But of course there are many other, even more valuable and applicable conceptions of hope (see e.g. Jordaan 2017). Riskin (2003) calls the mediator the most powerful person in the room. Perhaps that is an overstatement, perhaps not. Be as it may, for the mediator as leader, facilitator and empowering facilitator of disputants in a dispute resolution process, it is wise to be able to discern several options and approaches available.

5 Conclusion

In this paper we argued that we are living in one of the fastest changing times in history—a time which is characterised by superdiversity and supermobility. This leads to a VUCA environment which challenges us to become even more sophisticated in conflict management, dispute resolution and discernment. Latest trends in Business Studies and some MBA programs illustrate an increasing need for inter-and-transdisciplinary engagement to such an extent that we find courses like Spirituality and Entrepreneurship being offered at Business schools in Europe.[65] In this paper we argued that mediators will benefit themselves and the parties to a conflict or dispute if they are equipped with inter-and-transdisciplinary insights like metaphor theory, narrative approaches to counselling (metanarraphor) and insights from philosophers on aspects of hope. This is where leadership, spirituality and discernment engage in creative exchange of possibilities for constructive change towards communal solidarity and conflict management. Not only could those disciplines like theology who are concerned with the "spiritual" and "metaphorical" dimensions learn from those in the discipline of mediation and dispute resolution, but also *vice versa*. Thus, this chapter wanted to contribute to mediation theory and to the ongoing

---

[65]See for instance https://www.nyenrode.nl/faculteit-en-onderzoek/faculteitsleden/p/sharda-nandram website visited on 1 March 2018. Prof. Sharda Nandram specialises in Spirituality and Entrepreneurship within the context of the Center for Entrepreneurship & Stewardship. See Nandram et al. (2010). Others like the well-known Luk Bouckaert in Bouckaert and Zsolnai (2011). Both Bouckaert and Nandram are on the board and steering committee of the European SPES (Spirituality, Economics, Society) Institute (see http://eurospes.org/ visited 09 March 2018).

inter-and-transdisciplinary dialogue between the disciplines mentioned in the article, with the hope that it would stimulate further engagement and research.

References

Barentsen J, Kok J (2017) Leadership, (super)diversity and identity construction. In: Barentsen J, Van den Heuvel S, Kessler V (eds) Increasing diversity: loss of control or adaptive identity construction? vol CPLSE 5. Peeters, Leuven

Andreassen R, Vitus K (2015) Affectivity-and-race-studies-from-Nordic-contexts. Routledge, Surrey

Baruch Bush RA, Folger JP (1994) The promise of mediation: responding to conflict through empowerment and recognition. Jossy Bass, San Francisco

Borman L (ed) (2016) The world book of hope. Lannoo, Tielt

Bloch E (1986) The principle of hope. vol 3, translated by N. Plaice, S. Plaice and P Knight, MIT Press, Cambridge

Bloeser C, Stahl T (2017) "Hope", The Stanford Encyclopedia of Philosophy [SEP] (Spring 2017 Edition). Zalta EN (ed), https://plato.stanford.edu/archives/spr2017/entries/hope/

Bouckaert L, Zsolnai L (eds) (2011) The Palgrave handbook of spirituality and business. Palgrave Macmillan, Basingstoke

Bar-Tal D (2001) Why does fear override hope in societies engulfed by intractable conflict, as it does in Israeli society? Polit Psychol 21(3):601–627

Cameron LJ (2007) Patterns of metaphor use in reconciliation talk. Discourse Soc 18(2):197–222. Available http://journals.sagepub.com/doi/abs/10.1177/0957926507073376?journalCode=dasa. Accessed 31 March 2018

Cohen-Chen S et al (2014) The differential effects of hope and fear on information processing in intractable conflict. J Soc Polit Psychol 2(1):2915–3325

Colby A, Ehrlich T, Sullivan WM, Dolle JR (2011) Rethinking undergraduate business education: liberal learning for the profession. Jossy Bass, San Francisco

Damasio A (2000) The feeling of what happens: body, emotion and the making of consciousness. Vintage, London

Damasio A (2010) Self comes to mind: constructing the conscious brain. Vintage, London

Davis L (2012) Competence as situationally appropriate conduct: an overarching concept for lawyering, leadership, and professionalism. Santa Clara Law Rev 52(3):725–793 Available at https://digitalcommons.law.scu.edu/cgi/viewcontent.cgi?referer=https://www.google.be/&httpsredir=1&article=2715&context=lawreview

Fairclough N (1992) Discourse and social change. Polity Press, Cambridge

Fairclough N (1989) Language and power. Longman, London

Fanon F (1967) Black skin, white mask. Translated by Charles Lam Markmann, Grove Press, New York

Geldof D (2016) Superdiversity in the heart of Europe. Acco Uitgewerij, Leuven

Halstead JM (2003) Metaphor, cognition and spiritual reality. In: Carr D, Haldane J (eds) Spirituality, philosophy and education. RoutledgeFalmer, London, pp 81–94

Hansen T (2004) The narrative approach to mediation. Pepperdine Disput Resolut Law J 4(2): Collaborative Law Article 10

Hermans HJM, Hermans-Konopka A (2010) Dialogical self theory: positioning and counter-positioning in a globalizing society. Cambridge University Press, New York

Jandt F (1998) Intercultural communication. Sage, London

Johnson M (2005) Why metaphor matters for philosophy. Metaphor Symb Act 10(3):157–162

Jordaan B (2013) "Maximising value in negotiations programme" hosted at the Graduate School of Business at the University of Cape Town. Available https://youtu.be/poiST7IpzZpw. Accessed 02 Feb 2018

Jordaan B (2017) Hope theory: implications for conflict management. https://www.linkedin.com/pulse/hope-theory-implications-conflict-management-barney-jordaan/. Accessed 08 March 2018

Kegan R (1982) The evolving self: problem and process in human development. Harvard University Press, Cambridge

Kegan R (1994) In over our heads: the mental demands of modern life. Harvard University Press, Cambridge

Kok J (2014) Social identity complexity theory as heuristic tool in new testament studies. HTS Teologiese Stud/Theol Stud 70(1):9 Art. #2708. https://doi.org/10.4102/hts.v70i1.2708

Kok J (2017) Drawing and transcending boundaries in the DRC. University of Pretoria UPeTD, Pretoria

Kennedy G (2015) 'Negotiation', Edinburgh Business School MBA module in Negotiation, Heriot-Watt University. Available https://www.ebsglobal.net/EBS/media/EBS/PDFs/Negotiation-Course-Taster.pdf. Accessed 09 March 2018

Lakoff G, Johnson M (2003) Metaphors we live by. University of Chicago Press, Chicago

Lakoff G (2009) https://www.youtube.com/watch?v=Eu-9rpJITY8. Accessed 1 July 2017

Luthans F, Jensen SM (2002) Hope: a new positive strength for human resource development. Hum Resour Dev Rev 1(3):304–322

Mignolo W (2000) (Post)occidentalism, (post)coloniality, and (post)subaltern rationality. In: Afzal-Khan F, Seshadri-Crooks K (eds) The pre-occupation of postcolonial studies. Duke University Press, Durham, pp 86–118

Mignolo W (2007) Delinking. Cult Stud 21(2–3):449–514

Mignolo W (2011) The darker side of western modernity: global futures, decolonial options. Duke University Press, Durham

Niemandt N (2018) Competing narraphors in the post-Zuma landscape. Lecture delivered at the opening of the Faculty of Theology, University of the Free State (19 Feb 2018)

Nandram S, Borden S, Margot E (eds) (2010) Spirituality and business exploring possibilities for a new management paradigm. Springer, Heidelberg

Noce DJ, Baruch Bush RA, Folger JP (2002) Clarifying the theoretical underpinnings of mediation: implications for practice and policy. Pepperdine Disput Resolut Law J 1. Available http://digitalcommons.pepperdine.edu/drlj/vol3/iss1/3. Accessed 1 March 2018

Nullens P and Barentsen J (2014) (see source at http://www.peeters-leuven.be/boekoverz.asp?nr=9491)

Ogden TH (1994) The analytic third: working with intersubjective clinical facts. Int J Psychoanal 75 (Pt 1):3–19

Riskin LL (2003) Who decides what? Rethinking the grid of mediator orientations 9 No. 2 Dispute Resolution Magazine 22, 22 (Winter 2003) and also http://www.adrtoolbox.com/library/riskins-grid/. Accessed 09 March 2018

Rooney G (2015) Rebooting mediation by detaching from the illusions of neutrality. Available http://ssrn.com/abstract=2564035. Accessed 08 March 2018

Rorty R (1979) Philosophy and the mirror of nature. Princeton University Press, Princeton

Rorty R (1989) Contingency, irony and solidarity. Cambridge University Press, Cambridge

Rorty R (1998) Truth and progress (Philosophical papers, vol 4). Cambridge University Press, Cambridge

Rorty R (1999) Philosophy and social hope. Penguin Books, Middlesex

Rorty R (2002) Hope and the future. Peace Rev 14(2):149–155. https://doi.org/10.1080/10402650220140166

Seligman MEP (2011) Flourish. Free Press, New York

Senge PM (1990) The art and practice of the learning organization. The new paradigm in business: emerging strategies for leadership and organizational change, 126–138

Senge PM (2006) The fifth discipline: the art and practice of the learning organization. Doubleday, New York

Schermerhorn JR, Hunt JG, Osborn RN, Uhl-Bien M (2011) Organizational behavior. Wiley, Hoboken

Smith TH (2005) Metaphors for navigating negotiations. Negot J 21(3):343–364

Snyder CR (2002) Hope theory: rainbows in the mind. Psychol Inq 13(4):249–275

Steenkamp J (2018, forthcoming) Trauma spectrum manifestation. SHIP, Pretoria

Sweet L (2014) Giving blood: a fresh paradigm for preaching. Grand Rapids, Zondervan

Van den Broeck H, Jordaan B (2018) The agile leader's scrapbook. LannooCampus, Leuven

Van den Heuvel SC, Nullens P (eds) (2018) Driven by hope: economics and theology in dialogue, vol CPLSE 6. Peeters Press, Leuven

Van der Watt JG (2009) Reading new testament imagery. In: Du Toit A (ed) Focusing on the message. Protea, Pretoria, pp 305–340

Van Huyssteen JW (1997) Essays in postfoundationalist theology. Eerdmans, Grand Rapids

Vertovec S (2007) Super-diversity and its implications. Ethn Racial Stud 30(6):1024–1054

Waaijman K (2002) Spirituality: forms, foundations, methods. Peeters, Leuven

Internet Sources Consulted

See Jordaan B (2012) https://www.youtube.com/watch?v=poiST7IpZpw&feature=youtu.be. Accessed 01 March 2018

See Nandran S https://www.nyenrode.nl/faculteit-en-onderzoek/faculteitsleden/p/sharda-nandram website visited on 1 March 2018

See Lakoff G (2009) https://www.youtube.com/watch?v=Eu-9rpJITY8. Accessed 09 March 2018

See https://courses.lumenlearning.com/boundless-ap/chapter/functions-of-the-autonomic-nervous-system/. Accessed 08 March 2018

See https://www.haniel-stiftung.de/en/promoting-future-generations/the-european-way. Accessed 19 Feb 2018

See https://en.wikipedia.org/wiki/Constructive_dismissal visited 22 Feb 2018

See https://www.healthline.com/health/brain-anatomy. Accessed 22 Feb 2018

See https://law.pepperdine.edu/straus/ for the announcement of the 2018 award for the best U.S. dispute resolution program. Accessed 01 March 2018

See https://www.etf-ilse.org/our-projects-and-research/. Accessed on 08 March 2018

See http://eurospes.org/. Accessed on 09 March 2018

See http://www.legislation.gov.uk/ukpga/1996/18/contents. Accessed 29 March 2018

Jacobus (Kobus) Kok (Ph.D; Ph.D) is Professor and Head of Department New Testament Studies at the Evangelische Theologische Faculteit Leuven in Belgium, Extraordinary Professor in New Testament at the University of Pretoria and Research Associate in Greek at the University of the Free State. NRF Y1 rated research associate at the University of Pretoria, South Africa. Kok is also an experienced corporate trainer and facilitator and head of coaching and mentoring at ETF Leuven. He serves on the editorial boards of the Institute of Leadership and Social Ethics, Neotestamentica, Verbum et Ecclesia, In Luci Verbi, etc. Kok authored or edited nine books on topics mainly revolving around social cohesion—the latest being "New Perspectives on Healing, Restoration and Reconciliation in John" published with Brill.

Barney Jordaan (Ph.D.) holds a doctorate in law from Stellenbosch University, South Africa. He is currently professor of management practice (negotiation and dispute resolution) at Vlerick Business School, Belgium. Jordaan is also an Extraordinary Professor at the University of Stellenbosch Business School. Prior to moving to Belgium in 2014 he held a number of academic appointments in South Africa. These included 14 years as professor of law at Stellenbosch University and thereafter as professor of negotiation and conflict management at the University of Stellenbosch Business School and the Graduate School of Business, University of Cape Town. In conjunction with his academic involvement, Barney also practised as human rights lawyer in South Africa during the apartheid era before co-founding a consulting firm in 1998 which advises corporate clients on conflict management strategies, negotiation and related matters. He has been involved in the mediation field since 1989 as practising mediator, trainer and coach. He is an internationally certified as mediator with, amongst others, the Centre for Effective Dispute Resolution (CEDR, UK) and the International Mediation Institute in The Hague.

The Quest to Lead (with) Millennials in a VUCA-World: Bridging the Gap Between Generations

Johann Kornelsen

Abstract Western workplaces are currently experiencing a leadership challenge that relates to a conflict between the senior leaders in organizations and the so-called Millennial generation. This has resulted in traditional leadership approaches being less effective in a "dynaxic" (dynamic and complex) world. The purpose of this chapter is to help senior leaders better understand the essence of the conflict between Millennials and the previous generations. It is an attempt to increase understanding of the conflict and solve the problem by suggesting a leadership approach that could work for both generations and help organizations survive in a VUCA world. After the nature of the conflict is described, a relatively new leadership approach—responsible leadership—is suggested, in combination with mentoring. Responsible leadership combines the essential qualities of three well known leadership styles: transformational, servant, and authentic. The transformational aspect of responsible leadership relates to encouraging teamwork, setting high performance targets, and encouraging out-of-the-box thinking among followers. As servants, responsible leaders put the interests of subordinates and organizations first to create an empowering experience for followers. An authentic leadership approaches ensures learning agility, flexibility, and the participation of others. Through mentoring, Millennials may come to identify with their mentees and even adopt some of their values and attitudes. So-called reverse mentoring may provide a very valuable double function: increasing Millennials' involvement within their organizations while at the same time engaging and educating Baby Boomers.

Leadership is typically influenced by three component factors which are leader, follower, and context (Yukl 2013). Effective leadership is displayed when these three dimensions are appropriately aligned. Currently, the Western world is experiencing two challenges in the context of this triangle: the first one concerns leader-follower work relationships and the other arises from current challenges in the environment of the corporate world. One central challenge is the conflict between

J. Kornelsen (✉)
Regent University, Virginia Beach, VA, USA
e-mail: johann@kornelsen.biz

© The Author(s) 2019
J. (Kobus) Kok, S. C. van den Heuvel (eds.), *Leading in a VUCA World*,
Contributions to Management Science, https://doi.org/10.1007/978-3-319-98884-9_2

senior leaders in organizations and the so-called Millennials, the emerging leader generation born between 1980 and 2000. This cohort, known as Generation Y, will account for 50% of the global workforce, and will outnumber their Generation X predecessors quite quickly (PwC 2011). For many employers and senior leaders, Generation Y presents a leadership challenge. The concerns and criticisms of parents and leaders stretch from a claim that this generation is dumber than previous generations, to the assertion that it is narcissistic or has no work ethics (Tapscott 2009). Gelbart and Komninos (2012) argue convincingly that workforce managers always struggle with new generations and their different world views and values, and Gesell states that the current generational mix of Baby Boomers, Gen X, and Gen Y makes leadership more complex. The large difference between the generations results in traditional leadership approaches being less effective. Acknowledging this, authors such as Ferri-Reed suggest that contemporary employers need a transition "from a 'boomer-centric' workplace to a 'millennial-centric' workplace" (Ferri-Reed 2014, p. 13). As Kilber concludes, the conflict between the generations needs to be solved through embracing the different approaches that come with the new generation. Such an attitude will get the most out of this new generation for the benefit of the organization (Kilber et al. 2014). Even if senior leaders find a leadership approach that fits the needs of the Millennials, the organizational environment still poses further challenges. Therefore, a leadership approach aimed at making Millennials more effective is not enough: the approach applied must also address the challenges of the environment. Currently, the term most frequently used to describe organizational environment is VUCA. The acronym VUCA, originally coined by the US Army, refers to an environment that is volatile, uncertain, complex, and ambiguous. Since all of these characterize our corporate world today, traditional approaches to leading organizations no longer work (Nick Horney et al. 2010). The combination of these two leadership challenges [Millennials changing the way that relationships are formed, and therefore how work is carried out and knowledge transferred (Rodriguez and Rodriguez 2015), and the prevailing characteristics of the VUCA world] demands enormous wisdom and a completely new leadership approach. This applies especially to senior leaders in contemporary organizations. The purpose of this chapter is to help senior leaders better understand the essence of the conflict between Millennials and the previous generations, and to explore the challenges that the current organizational environment poses for organizations. Its ultimate purpose is to determine whether there is a leadership approach that can help lead Millennials more effectively and can support organizations in facing a "dynaxic" (dynamic and complex) world.

1   The Conflict Between Generations

To understand the conflict between senior leaders and Millennials we need to understand the world views and values of the Millennial generation. Pinzaru et al. suggest that the theory regarding the difference in generations is based on the idea of cohorts. A generation is a group of people going through similar experiences in a certain period of time. External forces, including "media, economic and social events, popular culture, values shared by families and friends and used as guidance in action," shape a generation and create unique sets of values (Pinzaru et al. 2016). In this context, a generation may be seen as an "approximation of the collective set of attitudes, behaviors, ideals, memories, and life expectations that will certainly affect work-life" (De Campo et al. 2011). The so-called Baby Boomers (born between 1946 and 1964), Generation X (1965–1980), and the Millennials are the three generations currently in the workplace. The term that is also used for the Millennials is Generation Y, where the "Y" comes from the English word youth, representing the first wave of a digital generation, born into a world of technology. Being aware that every attempt at delineating the characteristics of any generation will be open to debate, Rodriguez and Rodriguez have summarized the most important characteristics of Millennials to help senior leaders understand and lead this generation better. They are (Rodriguez and Rodriguez 2015, pp. 856–857):

- Tech-savvy: Millennials are familiar with technology and use it as a key method for knowledge transfer in organizations.
- Informed: Since all kind of information is available for this generation at any time from the internet or social networks, this generation believes that they must be heard. This may lead to them being over-confident in their own abilities.
- Diverse: Millennials are tolerant to diversity and put a high value on teamwork in a collaborative, informal context.
- Multitaskers: Millennials perform tasks simultaneously, believing that they excel at this.
- Autonomous: Millennials tend to have less respect for hierarchies, especially if actions are not well structured.

In general, this generation prefers to sacrifice high incomes for leisure time.

It also believes that education is the key to success and is considered the best-educated generation ever, especially with regard to the demands of a globalized world (Kilber et al. 2014). Millennials want to learn, develop their potential, and do meaningful work (Müller 2013). Buying into the mission of an organization is also important for this generation, considering great benefits and state-of-the-art technology as important factors for an ideal work environment (Christensen 2017). In general, they value personal relationships in private and professional contexts (Balda and Mora 2011). Optimism, civic duty, confidence, and achievement are considered to be the core values of this generation (Al-Asfour and Lettau 2014).

While Millennials have many strengths, there are also traits that are considered weaknesses or seen as negative from the perspective of other generations. There are some terms that are used in discourse about Gen Y (Rodriguez and Rodriguez 2015, pp. 857–858):

- Plaintiffs Reward for activities rather than for achievements is an expectation. Immediate gratification is often demanded, while commitment can be very shallow.
- Lightning Speed: This generation has no tolerance for delays and expects feedback, results, promotions, and much else as soon as possible.
- Over-watched: Since many Millennials were planned from birth, their parents expect them to achieve a lot of (their parents') goals. Many individuals from this generation have not learned to set their own goals and pursue them with discipline. They expect others to set the goals for them and to explain why things must be done. This may also result in high dependency on their parents, even after reaching adulthood.
- Grasshoppers: Like grasshoppers, Millennials stay with groups and organizations for a relatively short time. They move because staying still could mean losing other opportunities. Thus, they are skeptical of long-term commitment.
- Sailboats: While Millennials complete multiple tasks at the same time and process large amounts of information by using the newest technology, they reveal a lack of profundity in knowledge and synthesis. Therefore, their critical thinking is sometimes questioned.
- Fragile: The ability to recover from setbacks and failures is less pronounced than in previous generations. While Millennials may be adept at creating and managing the impression they want to give, and also at getting jobs, they are not very good at keeping jobs or maintaining relationships.

Millennials are sometimes considered to be naïve and not prepared for the world of work (Pinzaru et al. 2016). At the same time, they are overly self-confident. According to Hines, Millennials are "ready to lead now and are confident in their ability to make things happen and change the world" (Hines 2011). This leads to the paradoxical combination of self-trust and dependency on others at the same time (Pinzaru et al. 2016). Pinzaru even considers narcissism to be the central characteristic of this generation. Gen Y members want the organizations they work with to offer them many opportunities but "they want things to develop only as they wish and they have a sense of entitlement, which is obvious in their demands." Leading Millennials is therefore a challenge because of their strong drive to succeed while wanting little supervision and guidance (Hines 2011). Since almost all information is available for Millennials at any time, they no longer have a need for senior leaders as content experts, weakening the influence and authority of those leaders. Flat hierarchies are taken for granted, resulting in free-flowing and bidirectional communication regardless of position (Balda and Mora 2011).

In order to understand the conflicts between the generations, we need to have a summary understanding of the different values and world views that distinguish the cohorts. Baby Boomers are very often seen as competitors who have dedicated their lives to their jobs (DelCampo et al. 2011). For researchers, it is therefore not clear which stance this generation really takes on teamwork (Bencsik et al. 2016). Many have developed career ambitions and, where they are parents, this has given rise to personal struggles and to an increase in the divorce rate. While being idealistic, this generation did not have the necessary free time to achieve the many goals they had set for themselves (DelCampo et al. 2011). In terms of relationships and communication, this generation puts personal communication first (Bencsik et al. 2016). The Boomers' main goal is a stable existence, realized through conscious, long-term career building. The main traits of this generation are patience, soft-skills, respect for traditions, and hard work (Ibid.). Bencsik et al. add that this generation accepts and uses hierarchies to lead. More negative characteristics could be exaggerated modesty or arrogant inflexibility, passivity, cynicism, or disappointment (Ibid.).

Naturally, the values and world views of the Boomers as outlined here may collide with the preferences of the Millennials in many organizational contexts. While Generation Y is skeptical of hierarchies, Boomers rely on them and expect people to accept the flow of authority and information according to defined hierarchies. In that context, Generation Y believes strongly in an eye level communication, common effort, and teamwork that is independent of hierarchies. Boomers might feel less respected, and even offended, by that attitude on the part of the younger generation, especially, if it is bolstered by strong self-confidence in a relatively inexperienced person. Ferri-Reed notes that "Millennials respond best when communication is direct, honest, and without hidden agendas. The quickest way to lose the loyalty of Millennials is to withhold information or restrict it to a selected few individuals" (Ferri-Reed 2014, p. 16). There is yet another area of conflict related to the work ethic because Boomers believe that those who openly display strenuous effort and spend more time at the office actually possess a stronger work ethic. This may be the reason for Millennials reporting that their own work styles do not seem to fit within the effort-focused paradigm of work ethics. In general, Millennials are more result than effort oriented. Boomer managers sometimes express the view that Millennials want the honors of the workplace without making the sacrifices that earn them, the same sacrifices that the Boomers made in order to achieve their goals. Therefore, while Boomers rely on patience, effort, and position-based authority, the Millennials question these values. Nevertheless, it must be admitted that the desire for independence, when combined with a lack of respect for tradition, and occasional arrogance, is not something to be proud of. This conflict, then, is a result of different world views and lack of appreciation and understanding of each other. Where there is an inflated self-esteem on the Gen Y side, there is also a rigid, closed-minded, overbearing attitude on the Boomer side. This rigidity, and unwillingness to take the discussion further, produces an inability to cope. HR expert Linda Gravett describes her experience with some Boomers as follows: "Many boomers are not coping well. I've had so many boomers say to me, I'm not going to learn how to text, I want to talk to someone face-to-face, doggone it, and I'm going to track them down till I find them face-to-face" (Huffington Post 2011). The consultant suggests to that generation that if they want to communicate with people of all age groups they will need to learn how to text and how to use instant message, instead of demanding face-to-face communication as often as possible (Ibid.). In a poll conducted by the Society for Human Resource Management (SHRM), 47% of younger workers complained that senior managers were resistant to change and had a tendency to micromanage, something that Gen Y does not like at all (Huffington Post 2011). This creates another area of conflict, because Gen Y is open-minded, accepting of diversity, and unafraid of change. What this generation obviously demands are leaders acting as coaches instead of bosses. But while there are conflicts and opposing world views, there is also common ground that may help to bring the generations together and increase understanding and appreciation. As Anderson et al. conclude, Millennials and Boomers are similar in the way they see work. Both generations value meaningful and challenging work.

The relationship between Gen X and Gen Y is different, and seemingly less conflictual. According to Lissitsa and Kol, many members of the Gen X generation grew up when both parents were working or in divorced households. As a result, Gen X members seem to be more independent than the average Millennial (Lissitsa and Kol 2016). The childhood background they describe may also result in insecurity and a minimal sense of tradition. This generation may lack the social skills of its parents, but it was the first generation to develop stronger technical skills (Ibid.), giving them a connection to the tech-savvy Millennial generation. It may even be stated that in terms of multiculturalism and global thinking, Gen X was a forerunner (Ibid.). Here, again, we can see Gen X as a transition generation and a link between the Boomers and Gen Y. Regarding relationships, Gen X prefers a mixture of personal and virtual communication (Bencsik et al. 2016). While this generation shows openness to diversity and is curious about new ideas, it still values hard work. This generation is known for its practical approach to getting things done very quickly, effectively, and efficiently (Lissitsa and Kol 2016). But, as is the case with every generation, Gen X has its negative aspects. From time to time this generation can be materialistic and can choose to abide by the rules. What unites it with Gen Y is having less respect for hierarchy than the Boomers. Nevertheless, it tends to abide by the rules (Bencsik et al. 2016). To conclude, it is not surprising that there is much more literature on the conflict between Gen Y and Baby Boomers than about the relationship between Gen Y and Gen X. The characteristics mentioned show that Gen X is most likely to get along with the other generations at the workplace. Having appreciated the nature of the conflict between Baby Boomers and Millennials, especially, it is in this context that we should observe the current VUCA environment with its challenges, and its risks of generational conflict.

2 The VUCA World and Its Challenges

The term VUCA was developed by the US Army War college to describe the current world, being volatile, uncertain, complex, and ambiguous (Horney et al. 2010). Volatility stands for the speed, magnitude, and dynamics of change, while uncertainty describes the unpredictability of issues and events. Complexity stands for the chaos that surrounds all organizations, and ambiguity describes "haziness of reality and the mixed meanings of conditions" (Ibid.). Rodriguez and Rodriguez show that contemporary organizations must face both sudden and continuous change all the time. For instance, Millennials do not remain in one workplace for more than a few years, because someone who stayed too long would be considered a failure. According to the authors, in such a world, most decisions seem to be based on emotion instead of reason (Rodriguez and Rodriguez 2015). Further, the uncertainty of the future makes personal and organizational identities fluid and the "ethical radar" is used to make decisions. The complexity in our world produces confusion. Even when all routes seem to be equally valid, the result is even greater confusion and perplexity (Ibid.). Finally, in an ambiguous world, "every decision taken presents a series of ambiguous dilemmas" and affects both the individual's ethics and organizational core values (Ibid.).

According to Sarkar critical factors for success in a VUCA world are as follows (Sarkar 2016):

- Sound business fundamentals;
- Innovation;
- Fast-paced response;
- Flexibility;
- Change management;
- Managing diversity at local and global level;
- Market intelligence; and
- Strong collaboration with all relevant stakeholders including employees, customers, suppliers, shareholders, and society.

Horney et al. emphasize the aspect of strong collaboration in the context of organizations (Horney et al. 2010). As the authors argue, the leadership challenge of the current phase is to balance relationship management and task achievement. Leaders will need to deploy user-friendly technology to involve people from different parts of the world, and from different generations, in sharing knowledge and information. Agile, successful leaders of the future need to learn how to infuse collaboration into work processes, job roles and monitoring, and rewards and development systems, thus generating changes in mindsets and behavior (Ibid.). Difficult VUCA times demand shared effort and collaboration between generations because in an ambiguous world, where single leaders sometimes seem to be overwhelmed, collective effort in heterogeneous groups is needed for wise decision making. Millennials are willing to make collaborative decisions, but if vanity on both sides leads to a stand off because of generational differences, appropriate decision making cannot happen. Today's leaders need strong discernment, which may be defined as the "ability to regulate one's thinking in the acquisition and application of knowledge to make decisions that are right, fair, and just" (Traüffer 2008, p. iii). Excellent discernment in a VUCA world is a result of joint decision making in heterogeneous teams. One crucial factor for organizational survival and success is, therefore, successful collaboration, especially between Baby Boomers and Millennials. The future of organizations in a VUCA world is related to whether these two generations can resolve their conflict and get on with shared leadership.

3 Interim Conclusion and Solution Finding

Further reflection on the facts sheds more light on the nature of the conflict. Some may ask why the experienced and so far successful Baby Boomer generation should change their approach and adapt to the needs of the Millennials. It seems the arguments for adapting to the ways of this generation are strong. In a recent opinion poll, 62% of 186 German high-level managers said they believed that in the next year, young leaders would climb the career ladder faster than older generations (Jumpertz 2017). The Millennials have the appropriate attitudes and skills for success in the new world of VUCA: there is an openness to change, to taking risks, a willingness for collaboration, and a strong confidence that they can achieve success. While sounding almost arrogant, the Millennials are the best educated generation so far, and operate in a more developed international context than either of the previous generations. As Bishop states, they "possess skills, knowledge, and abilities that far exceed those of previous generations" (Bishop 2014, p. 54). Last but not least, their tech-savviness is of enormous help to them in dealing with the challenges of a digitalized world. The fit of Gen Y's strengths with the characteristics of the new world is the strongest argument for relying on that generation. The world is changing so fast that many of the experiences and skills of the previous generations are no longer an asset. Many senior leaders in German small and medium enterprises (SMEs) are unable to estimate the consequences of digitalization on their companies. In addition, they do not have a positive approach in facing an uncertain future. In Germany, we can see that defensiveness is an attitude that tends to intensify blindness when it comes to dramatic change. Germans tend to be more pessimistic about the future and have an external locus of control. Even the media displays a disparaging reaction to trends from the US, especially from Silicon Valley (Keese 2016). The challenges of digitalization confront a world view where things need to be controlled and in which well-tried Christian working values, including diligence, persistence, and fidelity are sufficient. This is not enough in times of digitalization, where the rules of the game have changed and where the upcoming wave will destroy formerly successful traditional businesses. On the other hand, we have shown that Millennials are not easy to lead and that they display some negative attitudes, including naivety and exaggerated self-confidence. While corrective feedback is often required, it can cause Millennials to become defensive because they see receiving praise as a birthright (Hall 2016). Further, the tendency of Gen Y members to switch organizations frequently creates a further challenge for their leaders. All in all, it is not surprising that conflict flares up especially between Baby Boomers, who stand for reliability and patience, and Gen Y.

Baby Boomers typically react to conflict in two ways: they either devalue Gen Y to inflate their own significance, or they exaggerate their praise of the generation. Swaim provides an example of the former in a discussion of leading US Millennials (Swaim 2016). The author tries to show exhaustively that in terms of literacy and numeracy skills, Millennials are less skilled than previous generations. Further, he tries to show that their general knowledge of history, and of other subjects that

Swaim deems important, is generally inadequate. He also cites the tendency of Gen Y to marry later, or to live with their parents longer than previous generations did. Swaim finishes by stating that there is no need for "Millennial experts" to tell the world how to lead Millennials because our current organizational needs are not really different from before and what we need is simply one consistent leadership style for all generations in the workplace (Ibid.).

The alternative view is put forward by Smith in the preface to a book about the Millennials (DelCampo et al. 2011, pp. xv–xvi):

The Millennials have expertise and knowledge that we do not—for example, they understand technology and use it like no other appendage. They are not afraid of new ideas. They have grown up with diversity in their classrooms and their activities, and they welcome it now. They are quick to laugh and quick to critique, not automatically accepting the status quo as the only way to get things done. Yes, they demand a lot, but look what they have accomplished in their short lives. (. . .) The Millennials are poised to become our greatest generation yet. They work together. They embrace groups and collaborate. They are forward-thinking, positive, and achieve what they set their sights on. As the authors aptly attest, the Millennials are the heroes of the workplace today.

Both stances are most likely extremes. While Swaim fails—does he even want to try?—to integrate the VUCA environment into his considerations, Smith virtually glorifies Gen Y. Nevertheless, Swaim represents a significant portion of the Baby Boomers who display a kind of ignorance and arrogant inflexibility, cynicism, and perhaps even disappointment. Their anger may be a result of frustration: some Baby Boomers unconsciously feel overly challenged or no longer respected. And here is the contribution of the younger generation that—in its exaggerated self-confidence—does not see the strengths of the older generation. Their respective vanities, and the conflicting negative emotions involved, endanger organizations because they impact greatly on decision making. As Goleman has shown, positive moods often lead to better decisions by individuals and teams. Distress, instead, erodes mental abilities. Effective leaders have learned to understand their own emotions and are able to control negative ones. However, they can speak openly about their emotions and are even able to "attune to a wide range of emotional signals" in a person or group (Goleman et al. 2004, pp. 253–256). In a VUCA world, where joint decision making is key, the unsolved conflicts and the negative emotions involved are a threat to organizations. Therefore, while some Baby Boomer leaders may doubt whether they have something to offer, Millennials should recognize that this generation does have strengths and should honor these strengths in order to build well-rounded teams for the benefit of their organization. Millennials need to understand that their passion for meaningful work gives them a real connection with Baby Boomers, who may also provide role-models in terms of work ethic and workplace commitment. Senior leaders will have experienced many storms and will have gained a great deal of experience in dealing personally with difficult times, changes, conflicts, and organizational politics. Millennials need to understand that their own drive and their own skills can be made more effective when used in conjunction with the wisdom of seniority.

The goal of this chapter is to present a leadership approach that may be helpful to those facing a complex business environment and it may help to connect senior leaders and Millennials for the benefit of their organizations. The suggestion is to adopt a relatively new leadership approach—responsible leadership—in combination with mentoring. Responsible leadership helps to meet the demands of followers and their organizations, while mentoring, as will be demonstrated, is helpful for strengthening the ties between senior leaders and Millennials.

4   Responsible Leadership as Part of a Solution

As already demonstrated, the VUCA world demands a particular style of leadership—agile leadership that fosters collaboration and unbiased communication between generations. This kind of collaborative leadership allows organizations to be more innovative, flexible, and fluid, and enables them to make sound decisions in an ambiguous world. In addition, the Millennials' preferred leadership style can be characterized as a polite relationship with authority, based on personality. Leaders who pull people together are appreciated, since this generation believes in collective action (Al-Asfour and Lettau 2014). Responsible leadership is a relatively new field of research and seems to meet the demands of Millennials within an organizational environment. According to Doh and Quigley, the focus of responsible leadership is a leader's exchange with followers, team, organization, and society at large (Doh and Quigley 2014). Leadership in a global, complex, uncertain, and interconnected environment results in a need "to reduce complexity and uncertainty for people and provide a desirable future, which is shared by the people they lead. Leaders need to have a sense of purpose and a guiding vision, which help bundle individual and 'organizational energy'" (Maak and Pless 2006, p. 99). The new context, according to Maak and Pless, should affect the mindset, the roles and responsibilities of leaders, which "simultaneously change, become more complex and multi-faceted, expand from an internal leadership perspective to a broader world view, from a shareholder mindset to a stakeholder orientation with respect to the leadership role" (Ibid, p. 100). Contemporary leaders need to win the mandate to lead by using a relational leadership approach based on inclusion, collaboration, and co-operation with all stakeholder groups, including employees, clients and customers, business partners, the social and natural environment, and shareholders (Ibid, pp. 100–101). Responsible leadership may be best understood by using the metaphor of a weaver, where the responsible leader acts from the center, not the top, focusing more on building relationships than developing power (Ibid, p. 104). Maak and Pless show that a responsible leadership has these central value-based roles (Sarkar 2016, p. 10):

- Visionary: involving stakeholders in the process of future thinking,
- Steward: acting as a defender of the organization's most precious resources, including vision and relationships,

- Servant: developing a vision that aligns with stakeholder needs and goals,
- Citizen: acting as integral part of the community which is committed not only to business matters but to civic matters,
- Coach: facilitating the relational process, development and learning,
- Architect: building a culture where diverse people find meaning, feel respected, recognized, and included,
- Storyteller and Meaning Enabler: creating shared systems of meaning, through sense making and dialogue,
- Change Agent: initiating change that will establish a value-conscious and sustainable business.

As Sarkar sums it up, responsible leadership combines the essential qualities of three well known leadership styles: transformational, servant, and authentic leadership. The transformational aspect of responsible leadership relates to encouraging teamwork, setting high performance targets, and encouraging out-of-the-box thinking among followers. As servants, responsible leaders "put the interests of subordinates first, over and above their own self interests. This creates an empowering experience for followers" (Ibid.). Empowerment leads to increased creativity at work, which is one of the most important factors of success in a VUCA world. Authenticity in a leader ensures learning agility, flexibility, and the participation of others, because the leader integrates diverse perspectives in decision making (Ibid.). Finally, Sarkar argues that the "all-inclusive leadership approach of responsible leadership is bound to make change management seamless" (Ibid, p. 11), and that building relationships can enhance employee performance and promote a democratic community for the benefit of an organization. The author finishes with a strong statement:

An individual's own self-reflection combined with an organization's vision, mission and practices also plays a major role in shaping the responsible leader who is self-aware, can subdue his/her self-interest for a greater cause and is committed to serving the broader interests of relevant stakeholders. Responsible leadership embraces societal issues and concerns based on sound ethical judgment, which ensures the long-term sustainability of any organization in the VUCA world.

5 Mentoring

While an appropriate leadership approach is helpful mid- and long-term, a mentoring approach could serve as a transitional solution to bridge the gap between Millennials and Baby Boomers because Millennials are very open to being mentored. As Ferri-Reed put it, in order to help Millennials succeed in the workplace one should "give them the big picture, help them find the 'me' in the team, and mentor them on career-building behaviors" (Ferri-Reed 2014, p. 18). Today, nearly all big companies have established mentoring programs that aim at developing a mentee through a personal relationship with a more experienced mentor (Biemann and Weckmüller 2014). In business, a mentor's task is usually to motivate one or more individuals to advance their careers by helping them to learn and work to their potential, and to find new perspectives and meaning in their jobs (Wells 1997). In many organizations a mentor is less likely to be an immediate supervisor, but may be found at a higher level or outside of the organization. Within a mentoring relationship, mentors provide their protégés with "sponsorship, exposure, and visibility, coaching, counseling, protection, friendship, and challenging assignments" (Bass and Bass 2008, p. 1092). Bass & Bass add that mentors also act as role models and as a source of acceptance and confirmation. They may also increase the visibility of their protégé by informing other leaders about the young professional's great potential. Research on the topic shows that, in that way, mentoring provides both a psychosocial (acceptance, encouragement, coaching, counseling) and a career-facilitation function (sponsorship, protection, challenging assignments, exposure, and visibility) (Yukl 2013). Although coaching is very often mentioned as a part of mentoring (which it is), there is a difference between coaching and mentoring. Clutterbeck suggests that "coaching in most applications addresses performance in some aspect of an individual's work or life; while mentoring is more often associated with much broader, holistic development and with career progress" (Clutterbuck 2008). Latest research also emphasizes that mentoring should be seen as reciprocal and collaborative, with benefits for mentors including job satisfaction, organizational commitment, and job performance (Ghosh and Reio 2013). Thus, mentoring is suggested as a tie that could help the generations to overcome their conflicts. By utilizing each generation's skills, mentoring brings the generations together. Kilber highlights that, perhaps unconsciously, these two generations may even seek each other out naturally, because many Baby Boomers have Generation Y children. Most Boomers report that Gen Y members look to them for advice and prefer them to Gen X colleagues as advisors (Kilber et al. 2014). Since building meaningful relationships is a basic human need, mentoring relationships could greatly increase the collaboration between generations for the benefit of organizations. As Neufeld shows, bonding is developed through a relationship where people are valued and unconditionally loved. Further, where there is bonding, a human being has no need to act rebelliously (Neufeld 2006). Thus, the first step towards unity between generations is the unconditional acceptance and appreciation of Gen Y members by Boomers. This can be a significant challenge because the expectations of the Millennials are difficult to meet. Since mentoring may typically have a negative connotation for Millennials, some authors even suggest labelling it differently—as career advising or organizational support (Kilber et al. 2014).

If one wants to go further, reverse mentoring may be a social exchange tool for keeping Boomers engaged and Millennials committed. Reverse mentoring is defined as mentoring of older employees by younger employees. Murphy states that the benefits of reverse mentoring include "building the leadership pipeline, fostering better intergenerational relationships, enhancing diversity initiatives, and driving innovation" (Murphy 2012, p. 550). The main focus of reverse mentoring is to help older generations acquire technological knowledge and to know how it can be used, for instance, to collaborate with customers or generate new contracts. Without reverse mentoring, this may be knowledge they would not acquire. Inevitably within this process, and this is where both organization and Boomers benefit, there will be occasions when seniors give feedback or advice to young associates, resulting in a mutual relationship. Furthermore, Millennials may come to identify with their mentees and even adopt some of their values and attitudes. Finally, reverse mentoring programs also result in higher retention of Millennials (Murphy 2012). This kind of mentoring has a double function: it increases Millennials' involvement within their organizations while at the same time engaging Baby Boomers.

6   Conclusion and Further Research

The VUCA world throws up challenges for contemporary organizations and highlights the conflict between senior leaders and Millennials. Strong discernment in intergenerational teams is needed to align organizations to a continuously changing world. The conflict between Baby Boomers and Millennials is a threat to organizations in the Western world. It hinders the parties involved from combining their strengths for the benefit of the organization. Humility and realistic self-evaluation are critical in order for members of both generations to work together in unity. This chapter is an attempt to increase understanding of the conflict by suggesting a leadership approach that could work for both generations and at the same time help organizations survive in a VUCA world. Leading Millennials is a challenge and, if we think of the characteristics of this generation, almost sounds like an oxymoron. But organizational success will only be achieved with Millennials and their strengths. Good relationships and appreciation are crucial to ensuring that responsible leadership and mentoring are successful. The era of typical hierarchical organizations with structures of power that demand military-type obedience are most likely over. Standardized approaches and norms no longer help in navigating VUCA contexts. Western leaders need to start dreaming, thinking, and trying new scenarios and approaches without knowing the outcome. This is the basic definition of playing. Leaders can only succeed if they are sufficiently humble to try things out and to fail within a safe environment. The new credo is: "I either win or learn." Sedlacek highlights that the world is not a chessboard with only limited opportunities for action (Sedlacek 2013). Instead, most of the strong and dynamic solutions will probably be found outside of the common playground. This is where Millennials can help, and this is also what many of them are excited about. The first step in making a joint effort is to overcome vanity on both sides and develop an authentic appreciation of each other.

Acknowledgment I would like to thank Kay Caldwell for her help with the language editing of this chapter.

Bibliography

Al-Asfour A, Lettau L (2014) Strategies for leadership styles for multigenerational workforce. J Leadersh Account Ethics 11:58–69

Balda JB, Mora F (2011) Adapting leadership theory and practice for the networked, millennial generation. J Leadersh Stud 5:13–24

Bass BM, Bass R (2008) The bass handbook of leadership: theory, research, and managerial applications, 4th edn. Free Press, New York

Bencsik A, Tímea J, Horváth-Csikós G (2016) Y and Z generations at workplaces. J Compet 8 (3):90–106

Biemann T, Weckmüller H (2014) Mentoring: wann nützt es und wem nützt es? Pers Q 66(2):46–49

Bishop WH (2014) Structure? We don't need no stinkin' structure! J Strateg Leadersh 5:48–58

Christensen S (2017) Millennials rewrite workplace rules. Signal 71(9):13

Clutterbuck D (2008) What's happening in coaching and mentoring? And what is the difference between them? Dev Learn Organ 22(4):8–10. https://doi.org/10.1108/14777280810886364

DelCampo RG, Haggerty LA, Knippel MJA (2011) Managing the multi-generational workforce. Taylor & Francis, Farnham

Doh JP, Quigley NR (2014) Responsible leadership and stakeholder management: influence pathways and organizational outcomes. Acad Manag Perspect 28(3):255–274

Ferri-Reed J (2014) Millennializing the workplace. J Qual Particip 37(1):13–14

Gelbart N, Komninos J (2012) Who? where? Y? Charter J 84(7):20–23

Gesell I (2010) How to lead when the generation gap becomes your everyday reality. J Qual Particip 32(4):21–24

Ghosh R, Reio TG Jr (2013) Career benefits associated with mentoring for mentors: a metaanalysis. J Vocat Behav 83(1):106–116. https://doi.org/10.1016/j.jvb.2013.03.011

Goleman D, Boyatzis RE, McKee A (2004) Primal leadership: learning to lead with emotional intelligence. Harvard Business School Press, Boston, pp 253–256

Hall A (2016) Exploring the workplace communication preferences of millennials. J Org Cult Commun Confl 20:35–44

Hines A (2011) A dozen surprises about the future of work. Employ Relat Today 38:1–15

Horney N, Pasmore B, O'Shea T (2010) Leadership agility: a business imperative for a VUCA world. Hum Resour Plan 33(4):32–38

Huffington Post (2011) Boomers vs. generation Y: bridging the generation gap at the office. Retrieved from http://www.huffingtonpost.com/2011/11/18/bridging-the-generation-gap_n_1102396.html

Jumpertz S (2017) Chancen für Jung Manager. managerSeminare 231:8

Keese C (2016) Silicon Valley: Was aus dem mächtigsten Tal der Welt auf uns zukommt. Penguin, Munich

Kilber J, Barclay A, Ohmer D (2014) Seven tips for managing generation Y. J Manag Policy Prac 15(4):80–91

Lissitsa S, Kol O (2016) Generation X vs. generation Y – a decade of online shopping. J Retail Consum Serv 31:304–312

Maak T, Pless NM (2006) Responsible leadership in a stakeholder society: a relational perspective. J Bus Ethics 66(1):99–115

Müller EB (2013) Innovative leadership: Die fünf wichtigsten Führungstechniken der Zukunft. Haufe Verlag, Freiburg

Murphy W (2012) Reverse mentoring at work: fostering cross-generational learning and developing millennial leaders. Hum Resour Manag 51(4):549–573

Neufeld G (2006) Hold on to your kids: why parents need to matter more than peers. Ballantine Books, New York

Pinzaru F, Vatamanescu E-M, Mitan A (2016) Millennials at work: investigating the specificity of generation Y versus other generations. Manag Dyn Knowl Econ 4(2):173–192

PwC (2011) Millennials at work: reshaping the workplace. https://www.pwc.com/en_M1/m1/ services/consulting/documents/ millennials-at-work.pdf. Accessed 23 May 2017

Rodriguez A, Rodriguez Y (2015) Metaphors for today's leadership: VUCA world, millennial and 'cloud leaders'. J Manag Dev 34(7):854–866

Sarkar A (2016) We live in a VUCA world: the importance of responsible leadership. Dev Learn Organ 30(3):9–12

Sedlacek T (2013) Die Ökonomie von Gut und Böse. Munich, Goldmann

Swaim R (2016) Peter Drucker on leading millennials. Retrieved from https://www. managementmattersnetwork.com/strategic-leadership/columns/peter-drucker-on-leading-millennials

Tapscott D (2009) Grown up digital, now the net generation is changing your world. McGraw-Hill, New York

Traüffer HCV (2008) Towards an understanding of discernment: A 21st-century model of decision making. Doktoral Dissertation, Regent University Virginia Beach, VA. Published at Proquest LLC. UMI-No: 3325539

Wells S (1997) From sage to artisan: the nine roles of the value-driven leader. David-Black Publishing, British Columbia

Yukl G (2013) Leadership in organizations. Pearson Education Limited, Harlow

Johann Kornelsen is managing partner of 3 D Leaders, a European HR-consulting and headhunting network, and the co-owner and CEO of an investment company that invests in e-commerce-based businesses. His pioneering networking approach in Germany connects Christian entrepreneurs and investors with the aim of developing a new generation of generous entrepreneurs for the benefit of society. Previously, he worked in strategic development as the assistant to the president of a private university and was founder and CEO of a consulting company with a focus on HR development. Having finished his MA in strategic management in Germany in 2011, Johann is currently finishing his Ph.D. dissertation at Regent University (USA). His topic is organizational leadership, focusing on entrepreneurship and leadership education through mentoring. Passionate about pioneering and networking, Johann enjoys traveling for business and voluntary work, connecting people in new initiatives, and speaking at international conferences about issues of organizational leadership and leadership development. Johann and Helena Kornelsen have been married since 2003 and have two sons aged 12 and 8.

Personal Leadership as Form of Spirituality

Joke van Saane

Abstract In theories on leadership a paradoxal development can be perceived. The growth of social constructionist theories on leadership with a strong focus on both leaders and followers goes hand in hand with a call for strong leadership with a focus on skills and traits of the leader. Situational and reciprocal theories on leadership flourish as much as theories on effectiveness of leadership in relation to personality traits and leadership skills. This paradoxal development can be overcome when the paradigms of spirituality are taken into account. In this chapter three perspectives are discussed: the impact of spiritual concepts on leadership, the contemporary developments within religious leadership, and the connection between leadership and learning in the concept of personal leadership. Spiritual concepts open the domain of leadership to growth and values. Contemporary developments in religious leadership reveal the redefinition of traditional forms of religion and the impact on leadership. Personal leadership brings in the notion of learning, and offers a promising way of connecting contemporary needs in a complex world to sources of spirituality.

1 Introduction

In theories on leadership a paradoxal development can be perceived. The growth of social constructionist theories on leadership with a strong focus on both leaders and followers goes hand in hand with a call for strong leadership with a focus on skills and traits of the leader. This paradoxal development can be overcome when the paradigms of spirituality are taken into account. In this chapter three perspectives are discussed: the impact of spiritual concepts on leadership, the contemporary developments within religious leadership, and the connection between leadership and learning in the concept of personal leadership.

J. van Saane (✉)
Faculty of Religion and Theology, Vrije Universiteit Amsterdam, Amsterdam, The Netherlands
e-mail: j.w.van.saane@vu.nl

J. (Kobus) Kok, S. C. van den Heuvel (eds.), *Leading in a VUCA World*,
Contributions to Management Science, https://doi.org/10.1007/978-3-319-98884-9_3

43

2 Paradoxal Paradigms in Leadership

Traditional and authoritative forms of leadership have failed in the last few decades. It is a broadly and globally shared experience that traditional leadership has led to a deep moral crisis and at the same time to a need of sustainable and credible forms of leadership. The economic crisis, the lack of morality within the financial system, the rise of popular politics are in the newspapers and other media easily connected to the failure of leadership.

Leadership in our times sometimes even seems an impossible task. In many domains, both in the public and in the private sector, leaders experience a great need for charismatic leadership. People want to be inspired; people want to be taken by a bigger story. A story that frees one's own life above the limitations, and gives meaning tot it. This perceived need for powerful leaders sometimes seems to be at odds with what is said in many dominant theories about leadership. In these modern theories (see e.g. Yukl 2010) the emphasis is placed on reciprocity between leader and followers, rather than on strong personalities as leaders. An increasing number of authors stress the importance of the interaction between the leader and follower, above the importance of the properties and personality traits of the leader. This leads to different concepts of leadership. The work of Yukl (2010) is prototypical for this change. Yukl (2010, p. 26)—defines leadership as follows:

> Leadership is the process of influencing others to understand and agree about what needs to be done and how to do it, and the process of facilitating individual and collective efforts to accomplish shared objectives.

This widely used definition focuses on leadership as a process. It is about the dynamics of leadership: leader and followers influencing each other. It is not about the leader convincing others smartly based upon a certain set of characteristics or skills, in this definition leadership shows up as a reciprocal interaction process. In this view on leadership, three dimensions interact: (1) the person of the leader, (2) the individual followers, and (3) the structure of the group or organization as a whole. Variables in each of these dimensions have an impact on the effectiveness of leadership. This means that a particular set of properties of the leader is no longer decisive for effective leadership. A particular leader can be successful in one group, but fail in a different context. This model of situational leadership is originally described by Hersey and Blanchard (1977), and expanded and specified by Yukl. This emphasis on interaction meant a paradigm shift in leadership theories. For a long time, all the attention has been focused on the qualities of strong, successful leaders, in the hope of further developing and teaching these qualities. In contemporary paradigm, however, leadership is the process in which leader and followers influence each other, and certainly not (exclusively) focusing on strong leaders or manipulating your group as smartly and efficiently as possible.

This new perspective appears to be a fruitful perspective on leadership. By looking for reciprocity, justice can be done to the ambitions of the leader, the needs of individual followers and the structure and organization of the group.

This shift is already taking place since the nineties. Haslam et al. (2011) calls this *the new psychology of leadership*. It is therefore striking that the need for inspiration and meaningfulness seems to be opposed to this emphasis on reciprocity within leadership. Inspiration by the leader assumes a form of charismatic leadership, with the leader in the foreground. Reciprocal leadership brings the person of the leader more to the background, while the followers become more central. This development in leadership theories is essential to understand contemporary debates on leadership (van Saane 2018).

The paradox in leadership theories can now be seen. The dominance of situational leadership theories does not match with the popular and societal call for charismatic leadership. Situational and reciprocal leadership should shift the focus from the leader to the followers and the contextuality of leadership. This shift takes place, but at the same time a strong and persuasive leader tends to be attractive. In fact, this can be seen as a return to older views about leadership. After all, the attention to personality traits of the effective leader is not new. On the contrary, isolating personality traits and skills to provide predictors of successful leadership has a long history in leadership theories. In some cases, these theories are very detailed. The work of Nauss can be seen as an example. Skills for successful predecessors and leaders of interest are identified by Nauss (1996) as no fewer than 65 variables in 56 dimensions. The most important ones he isolated seemed to be: persuasion, relationship orientation, task orientation, teamwork ability, and stress tolerance. It is in other words, successful leadership has to do with communication skills, social skills and the appropriate cognitive skills. Besides, skills—in contrast to personality traits—can be taught, learned and developed.

This development towards new dominance for the leader's role in the leadership process is confirmed by research of the Center for Creative Leadership (Van Velsor et al. 2010). This center conducts research into leadership in all sorts of domains and concludes in its handbook that there are characteristics that are of importance to every leader: emotional stability, integrity, self-defense, sense of responsibility, interpersonal skills and the right cognitive or technical skills. According to CCL, these traits are predictors for effective and successful leadership in different domains, both in the profit as in the non-profit sector. Training programmes on leadership should focus on strengthening these traits and skills. Leaders in all types of organizations appear to be more effective if they have these characteristics than leaders who score low on these traits. And that seems to be rather obvious. Emotionally stable leaders are leaders who can handle pressure well and remain calm in times of crisis. This is expressed in predictability: these leaders remain consistent in their behavior and choices, which increases the perceived reliability of leadership. Emotional stability includes the ability to take responsibility for one's own behavior, even if mistakes are made. Effective leaders learn from their mistakes and are able to change. In addition to emotional stability, effective leaders are characterized by integrity. Integrity is a concept that is fulfilled in various ways in the research into leadership (cf van Saane 2012; Bass and Steidlmeier 1999; Brown and Trevino 2006). However, it always has to do with the commitment between leader and group. Integral leaders act from that commitment, and do not allow personal interests to prevail over group interests. This can be reflected in the fulfillment of promises, being open about personal ambition and not having a hidden agenda or hidden financial transactions. Emotional stability and integrity are character traits, characteristics that belong to a person's personality and do not or hardly change over time. In addition to this type of characteristics, successful leaders also distinguish themselves with certain skills. Unlike personality traits, skills are easy to learn and develop. Key skills in leadership appear to be social skills and specific cognitive skills. Social skills, interpersonal orientation, provide the leader to be able to make contact easily, not only with the members of the own group, but also with the outside world. Interpersonal skills improve both external and internal relationships and the right substantive skills and knowledge elements give authority, again both inside and outside the organization (Yukl 2010; Mintzberg 1973; Quinn et al. 2007, 2011).

Obviously, this frame is constructive because of its clearness. Within this frame, the effectiveness of leadership can easily be increased: if we know which traits and skills are good predictors of effective leadership, training programs and selection procedures can become far more efficient.

3 Spirituality and Leadership

So, the call for charismatic, persuasive leadership reveals the paradox within leadership theories. On the one hand, a strong focus on personality traits seems to be constructive. On the other hand, the whole leadership paradigm shifts from the personality of the leader to interactive and reciprocal influencing processes between leader and followers. This apparent contradiction can be overcome when the paradigms of spirituality are taken into account within the domain of leadership. This can be shown by elaborating on some essential concepts of spirituality. After all, the call for strong leaders is in many cases the call for inspiration, for trust, for meaning and for perspective. Spirituality is pre-eminently the domain of meaning and inspiration; a domain that has a very long history here. Despite this long history, theories and models of spirituality have sometimes become somewhat invisible amid the dominance of secular models of leadership and organization. It is true, the theories on Servant Leadership (Greenleaf 1977), Spiritual Leadership (Fry 2003) and Transformational Leadership (Burns 1978; Bass 1996) have become part of the canon of leadership theories, but the mainstream of textbooks on leadership (cf van Vugt and Ahuja 2010; Day and Antonakis 2012) have a different focus. That is unfortunate, because the discipline of spirituality offers plenty of opportunities to make an essential contribution to the experienced need for charisma and meaning within leadership. This need for a form of leadership that meets responsibility for the whole and for perspective, can lead to the domain of spirituality. Therefore, the question is how can leadership be inspired by fundamental concepts from religious or spiritual traditions? Inspiration and meaning can easily become empty concepts. Spiritual traditions and models of spirituality, on the other hand, can provide words and concepts that give meaning to these concepts, so that they actually contribute to the quality of leadership that demands high standards.

How can leadership be inspired by concepts from religiosity and spirituality? First of all, we need some clarification of definitions (see also van Saane 2014). Although religion, spirituality and worldview are interconnected, for the purpose of relating spirituality and religion to leadership we need a broad definition of spirituality, which can be linked to a variety of religious and philosophical traditions. For the definition of spirituality, I follow the philosopher Roothaan, who defines spirituality as an attitude of openness, attention and consciousness (Roothaan 2007, p. 65). This attitude can be based on a philosophical or religious worldview, but that is not necessarily the case. Spirituality can be rooted in more secular worldviews as well.

Spirituality is the constant search for meaning, from an open attitude, with a focus on sustainability and credibility, rooted in self-knowledge and in the desire for growth and development. From this description of spirituality follows a number of characteristic aspects, which are useful to explore when we relate spirituality to leadership.

Spirituality is about the search for meaning. Spirituality is connected with morality, with norms and values that set the satisfaction of one's own needs against the public interest. This may be related to a traditional form of religion, but that is of course not necessary.

Within spiritual traditions, truth can only be personal truth. The truth that one seeks is uncertain in nature, flexible. This truth should not only be found, but also constructed by the seeker. Personal truth offers a renewed perspective or someone's life, a consciousness from which life can be interpreted in different ways. Constantly, the truth must be involved in one's own life and in one's own context. Abstract truth as such is meaningless. This process of construction and connection is in principle infinite, one never reaches the point that the search can be stopped.

From this follows that searching is more important than finding. In many traditions spirituality is conceptualized as a journey or a road, often with a mystical variant as an exemplary highlight. The journey as a search for destination and goals in life can take a lot of time. The difficulties and challenges faced are more important than achieving the goal in itself.

Dealing with difficulties requires a certain openness; openness for the self, for the other, for complexity, for hidden motives. Openness requires a lot of learning and experience. Within spirituality one can grow in attention and awareness. Increasing openness can lead to growth and continuous transformation. A high ideal in many traditions is the acceptance of the inevitable.

What is needed to be able to experience leadership as a form of inspiration and trust? The spiritual traditions offer a number of building blocks to answer this question. From the above description of spirituality the following building blocks can be distilled.

In the first place, a leader should feature a rather high amount of self-knowledge. He needs to know what his own strengths and weaknesses are, where the pitfalls lie and how personal experiences influence behavior. Lack of self-knowledge will result in lack of knowledge of the other; knowing yourself leads to knowing the other. However, self-knowledge is not the only contribution from spirituality. In the second place, spirituality makes clear that a leader benefits from self-confidence. Self-confidence is self-knowledge in combination with acceptance of yourself. Within spiritual traditions this is an important element, because self-confidence is part of perception of yourself through the eyes of the Other. The perspective of the Other also leads to a third element of spirituality in connection to leadership: norms and values. Failing leadership is leadership that results in immoral behavior. In that case, the standards for right choices are lacking, resulting in prevalence of individual interests instead of the general interest and humanity as a whole. In almost all spiritual traditions it is a recurring refrain: do good, take care of the other person, put the other person before yourself. If the leader, in the fourth place, is an open and learning leader, an opportunity for inspiration and trust can arise. The leader must be able to reflect upon himself and learn from the choices made. However, learning is more than that: it is openness to new experiences and perspectives, so that within leadership process growth and development (of the leader, of the followers, of the organization) are stimulated. The last core element of spirituality as building block for inspirational leadership is very much needed to strengthen the openness: imagination. Leaders with imagination are able to rise above the everyday perspective, they can imagine the apparent impossible, and they are capable of acting from this ideal and visionary perspective. Imagination flourishes from irrational forms of knowledge; imagination is creative and intuitive thinking. Leaders who do not limit themselves to the purely rational reality, leaders who give space to their intuition, those leaders are inspiring and innovative for their followers (Van Saane 2012, 2014; Verstraeten 2003).

4   Religious Leadership

Leadership in relation to spirituality takes two forms: inside and outside religious communities. Above, spirituality has been connected to secular forms of leadership. However, it is also important to focus on leadership within religious communities. This is a different way of connecting leadership and spirituality, besides the input of concepts of spirituality on leadership models as outlined above. Can religious leadership reveal fruitful insights on the relation between spirituality and leadership?

Traditionally, the main task of the leader within a religious organization was keeping the community on course, both in terms of theological conviction as social organization. The core of spiritual leadership consisted of taking care of the believer's soul life. This conception of religious leadership was supported and validated by theologies or ministry that connected the authority of the leader with the divine calling of the leader and its confirmation by the official religious institutions (Barentsen 2011).

This typical theological interpretation of religious leadership fits in a traditional religious context of rather stable religious communities practicing their different dimensions of religion: rituals, social relations, religious experiences, diaconal services to each other and to society. This theological interpretation of religious leadership, however, falls short of the contemporary changing religious landscape. To be clear, these changes are not unambiguous of nature.

The number of registered members of organized religious institutions is decreasing more and more. This applies to the mainstream Protestant churches, to the Roman Catholic churches, and also to the mosques. It is no longer obvious that children follow in the religious footsteps of their parents. It is no longer entirely self-evident that children take over the religious practices of their parents. The result is that religious institutions lose power and influence. Religious communities are no longer a natural conversation partner of governments and other organizations or companies. This development has had consequences for the position of religious leaders. More pressure arised on them, as a result of which burnout and exhaustion are relatively common in the professional group of religious leaders (Brouwer 1995; Evers and Tomic 2003). Less financial resources, more pressure to perform, more complicated constructions with volunteers: religious leadership offers less authority and more risk than before. At the same time, for those who choose to join or remain within a religious group, membership has become a conscious act that usually goes along with high expectations. If you belong to a religious community, entirely from a free choice, it should be rather attractive, meeting high standards. One seeks high-quality celebrations, balanced rituals, an elaborate narrative, fulfillment of the need for meaning and the availability of appropriate norms and values. Usually, the standards are high. The leaders of these modern religious communities are not always fully equipped for this new context. Within the Muslim community in the Netherlands, for example, a professionalization trajectory for imams is currently under construction, focusing on imams who have had a traditional education, usually in the countries of origin of Muslim immigrants. The governmental expectations from the imams with respect to issues like radicalization, conversion and integration go far beyond the boundaries of that traditional education—with much attention to the conduct of prayer and other ritual acts. The professionalization trajectory is aimed to fill the gap between contemporary expectations and traditional education. This casus reveals a first field of tension: the importance of organized forms of religion, and thus of traditional forms of religious leadership, is decreasing, while at the same time the importance of leadership for believers only increases, due to the personal motives underlying religious commitment.

A second field of tension within the religious context comes next to the first one. Leadership is under pressure, in the individualized and secularized modern Western society. Religion is no longer a matter of self-evidence, the religious leader is no longer an authority a priori. Although in the secularized Western European context, such as in the Netherlands, different ways have been developed to respond to this— developing for example religious entrepreneurship and missionary leadership, or connecting new individual spiritual questions with old religious traditions—, faith communities fail to have constructive and sustainable answers to these societal developments in society, while those answers are really asked for.

5   Leadership and Spirituality in a VUCA World

The super-diverse modern Western societies no longer provide for coherent "big stories" leading to social cohesion and stability with their shared values and convictions. On the contrary, modern society is referred to as a VUCA world: volatile, uncertain, complex and ambiguous. The world is rapidly changing, within uncertain conditions and with ambivalent outcomes. Society is fragmented and diverse in many different ways, which are not always easy to interpret. For example, polarization goes hand in hand with nationalism, global awareness with a tendency towards the local community. Secularisation goes hand in hand with an increasing need for meaning. And strangely, individualisation and de-institutionalization seem to be just as important as the societal impact of an organization.

Van de Berg (2016, p. 92) describes some of these contradictions with reference to Van der Woud (2015), complicating the interpretation of the global context. He points out the role of freedom. Freedom is seen as perhaps the highest value in contemporary society. At the same time and in contradiction, people hope for powerful and authentic leadership that solves their problems. And the freedom to develop yourself exists in addition to the social pressure to succeed. The need for freedom is accompanied by the need for security. In other words, people are looking for open-ended connectedness.

In short, people experience a lot of fear and uncertainty. Old structures such as traditional religion, extended families and geographical proximity are rapidly disappearing. Everything is constantly changing, the politics are fleeting, news reports catch each other at a frightening pace, and can still be fake news as well. People experience a lack of control. As a result, people feel scared, insecure and isolated. Anxiety, insecurity and isolation if fundamental and basic human needs are not met properly. In psychology three basic needs of people are distinguished: the need for solidarity with others, the need for control over reality and the need for self-enhancement. If these three needs are not met, isolation, insecurity and anxiety arise. This pattern leads to the comprehensible urgent need for meeting, solidarity and self-affirmation in the contemporary fragmented and individualized society (McAdams and Bryant 1987). This need can be an opportunity for spiritual values in leadership.

In this context, I especially point out the meaning of rituals. New forms of interdependence can very well take the form of rituals. Rituals help people in times of crisis, tension and transition by satisfying basic needs. In sorrow and crisis these needs are temporarily under pressure, but in modern society one sometimes experiences that these needs are permanently under pressure. Attempts and initiatives to bring people together will work well if they meet the requirements of a good ritual (van Saane 2010; Post et al. 2002). One of these requirements concerns togetherness. Performing a ritual on your own does not contribute much, within the ritual one has to experience being part of a larger whole and being supported by a relevant social group. The ritual should also give space to emotional experience. A proper ritual offers people the space to complain, to cry, to be angry, to be sad or to show joy. Bringing people from different groups together and instructing them to bridge the differences only works if they also have the opportunity to show their emotions about the other person. If the emotions are channeled and thus stripped of their disruptive function, space is created to learn from each other. Good and valid rituals offer sufficient space for the individual experience without limiting the ritual to the individual emotions entirely. Within the ritual context, the individual experience is always mirrored to a different and often broader perspective.

In this confusing context full of paradoxes and tensions, more and more calls are made to religious or spiritual communities to participate in and contribute to society, with inspiration and vision, with modern traditions, with meaning (Post et al. 2002). For example, religious communities are expected to be able to bring different generations into dialogue, to bridge diversity, to endeavour civic participation. The question is whether that is possible, and what the impact of modern religious leadership can be in secular society as a whole.

As outlined above, the global development of de-institutionalisation puts traditional forms of leadership under severe pressure. Paradoxically, however, this trend does not mean that the role of the leader is getting smaller, but rather bigger. The disappearance of frameworks and meaning systems makes the process of social identification and construction increasingly important. The experience that everything can be deconstructed is a dominant one, there are no fixed truths anymore. This playing field creates room for personal and individual experience, for less rational aspects of human existence, and for inspiration through leadership. In the dynamic interaction between leader and followers, meaning and interpretation arise, as a reciprocal process in which mutual influence ensures continuous transformation.

The conceptualization of leadership as a dynamic process fits into the scientific paradigm of *social construction*. In this paradigm, meaning is not only an attribute of an object, but also something that is created in the perception by the subject. Meaning is subjective, and occurs in the interaction between the subject and his or her environment.

Leadership as social construction is not so much about the personality of the leader anymore, the social perception and reception of the leader by the followers are central factors. Following the paradigm of social construction, in those perception processes leadership is created. The decision about effective or failed leadership cannot be judged objectively, it lays very much in the perception of the subject. This formulation already shows that the predictability of effective, successful leadership within this paradigm of social construction is much lower than in the paradigm of the effective leader. More variables than only the personality traits are taken into account in this new paradigm: the perception process, contextual factors, characteristics of the observer, characteristics of the leader and uncertainty about the purpose of leadership. All these variables affect the effectiveness of leadership.

The paradigm of social construction thus offers opportunities for leadership besides the person of the leader, but leadership also becomes more complex and uncertain. The context of social construction makes leadership possible, but at the same time, this context sometimes problematizes leadership. If social construction is taken seriously, leadership itself is a form of sense-making. Leadership does not exist outside our perception or construction, leadership is a form of perception and interpretation.

This fits with the modern network culture, reinforced by digitization and the dominance of social media. Personal preferences and affinity are leading for the network. The commitment is provisional, and exchangeable. Leadership in uncertain context like this focuses on inspiration and empowerment. People need to be empowered in their choices, while their personal choices have become leading motives.

These constructionist concepts of leadership have consequences for religious leadership as well. John Eliastam (2018) describes this process of sense-making as "discursive leadership," underscoring the social, linguistic, and cultural aspects of leadership. This theoretical perspective brings Eliastam to investigate the role of narratives in leadership. He shows that the leadership discourse provides for narratives helping people to connect different experiences. These narratives offer conditions to make sense of people's lifes and situations. Narratives are the told stories and myths within an organization. Leadership occurs when people recognize themselves in the narrative values and ideas that are put forward to solve problems or to achieve goals. In this perspective, leadership itself becomes a social activity of reality construction and meaningfulness. From this paradigm, Eliastam reveals opportunities for religious leadership that provide new narratives replacing existing dominant stories, opening the way for development and freedom. By the way, Eliastam connects this opportunity to the evolutionary principle of survival stating that a multiplicity of connected narratives creates a need for new sensemaking processes in order to assimilate the various stories. According to him, this need is rooted in the human need to survive or adapt to changing environments.

6   Personal Leadership

We have seen so far that there is a need for strong leadership in all kinds of societal domains. This call is in itself somewhat strange or paradoxical, since the contemporary theories and models of leadership move towards a reciprocity between leader and followers, rather than to strong focus of predictive personality traits of a successful leader.

This paradox can be dealt with in two ways. In the first place, it turns out that the research into the personality traits and the characteristics of effective leaders is a continuous line, despite the development of social constructivist views on leadership. The Center for Creative Leadership research (Van Velsor et al. 2010) forms a clear example of this ongoing line of research. In the second place, the inclusion of spirituality in leadership seems to offer an opening for this field of tension. After all, meaning and inspiration can be derived from spirituality, without being handed over to the so-called "strong leaders." There appear to be various inputs for spirituality in the leadership debate. Spirituality offers clear building blocks for a leadership concept that is focused on openness, growth and attention. The connection of leadership and spirituality can also take place by paying attention to what is happening in contemporary religious communities in terms of leadership. Within these communities, one can find a development towards professionalisation—a strong requirement in the modern complex context-, as well as developments in religious leadership, focusing on the translation of traditional religious answers to existential questions for contemporary people. Examples of these "translations" are modern rituals, symbolic actions, story telling and art.

What else do we need now if we want to make a fruitful connection between leadership and spirituality in the complex context of a VUCA world? The VUCA world is volatile, uncertain, complex and ambiguous. This means a perception of constant change, of complexity and chaos, of social constructions that are mainly uncertain and can disintegrate just like that. In this VUCA world there is a great need for spirituality. However, that spirituality must be flexible and personal, which is not always the case when spirituality is derived from traditional forms of religion.

The concept that potentially connects these different movements and needs is learning. In all these different processes, learning plays a central role; discernment and wisdom require an attitude of learning. For me, learning is part of a form of leadership known as personal leadership (van Saane 2015, 2017). Personal leadership can be defined as knowing yourself, having grip on yourself, on your personal environment, on your life as a whole. Personal leadership is thus connected to a form of learning, especially to forms of engaged or integrated learning. Personal leadership connects society, thinking about leadership and spirituality.

7 Personal Leadership: An Unknown Country

Personal leadership seems to be a promising concept to fill the gap between leadership and spirituality within the complex context of the VUCA world. Nevertheless, this statement needs further research.

I want to mention a number of aspects of personal leadership that require further research and further operationalization. The first aspect of personal leadership is transformative learning. In society, circumstances are constantly and rapidly changing. These changes require a capacity for ongoing adaptation. Learning is a process of differentiation of meanings. This means the core of learning is a process of change and transformation. This can be about small and everyday things, but also about comprehensive aspects of life. If providing for new visions is accompanied by a process of self-reflection and self-examination, space is created for exploring new options of the construction of meaning to life. Exploring new possibilities can lead to the genesis of a new frame of reference (Mezirow 2012, p. 82). A frame of reference is a meaning perspective, the structure of assumptions and expectations through which we filter our impressions. If one's own values, convictions and presuppositions are examined through processes of critical reflection and rational discussion, frames of reference can be changed and meaning perspectives can be transformed.

What is needed for this? Mezirow (2012) shows that hospitality and openness are important, so that people feel invited to participate. There must be reciprocal receptiveness to new ideas and perspectives, with the willingness to question assumptions (Graham 2012). Transformations cost effort and time, changes evoke resistance. A light tone of reflection and a sufficient degree of self-critical humor are facilitating (Mezirow 2006).

The second aspect of personal leadership includes a learning strategy known as self-directedness in learning (Mezirow 2012; Gijbels et al. 2014). This learning strategy means that one can take responsibility for the own learning process. Key concepts in self-directed learning are self-regulation and self-control. This requires some resilience, because after all, one has to be able to receive feedback, and accommodate or adjust the learning process based upon the critical feedback. The self-directed learning style includes a proactive attitude, constantly being adaptive to the environment and being aware of changes in perspective and context. Self-directed learning does not stop with the person himself. It is precisely from self-awareness that responsibility can be taken for itself and for the greater whole. Knowledge of itself then immediately is accompanied by consciousness of the other person, with openness, meaning and a broadened horizon. This leads to recognition of the individuality of the other. You underestimate the other person if the individuality of the other person is not recognized. This starts with the own individuality: self-knowledge, self-confidence and self-esteem (Tennen and Afflect 1993). This includes a balance between identification and separation (Ruijters et al. 2015; Baumeister 2011), between cooperation and empathy in the interaction.

For me, self-directedness in learning belongs to personal leadership because this is inextricably linked to an adult life attitude, which leaves room for responsive and sensitive leadership, for resilience. By learning to accept oneself, by establishing good relationships with others, by getting the best out of yourself, by giving meaning to your life and by maintaining a certain autonomy, regardless of the context, you can use the full potential, on an individual and social level (Ruijters et al. 2015; Ryff and Singer 2013; Ryff 2014).

The third and last aspect of personal leadership can be described as wisdom. Wise people are people who are careful with automatic answers because they realize that every reaction is relative and dependent on the context (Ruijters et al. 2015). Wisdom has to do with ambiguity and ambivalence. Wisdom is the integration of knowledge and experience, in a way that not only benefits you but also others (Ruijters et al. 2015; Sternberg 1990). Sternberg defines wisdom as "the application of tacit as well as explicit knowledge as mediated by values toward the achievement of a common good through a balance among intrapersonal, interpersonal, and extrapersonal interests, over the short and long terms, to achieve a balance among adaptation to existing environments, shaping of existing environments, and selection of new environments" (Sternberg 2001; via Ruijters et al. 2015, p. 439). That is the core of personal leadership: being able to see both the own interests and the interests of others in a specific context. Sternberg has made his life's work of developing a model on wisdom. He (Sternberg 2010) calls his model the Wisdom, Intelligence and Creativity Synthesized Model. With this model he wants to contribute to a better world, breaking the circle of self-interest, violence and destruction. However, he himself already distinguishes (Sternberg 2004) five biases leading tot underdevelopment of wisdom: unrealistic optimism, self-centeredness, a sense of omniscience, a sense of omnipotence and invulnerability. Wisdom will therefore always remain an endeavor, but an endeavor that helps to distinguish and discern in our contemporary complex society.

Bibliography

Barentsen J (2011) Emerging leadership in the Pauline mission: a social identity perspective on local leadership development in Corinth and Ephesus, vol 168. Wipf & Stock, Eugene

Bass BM (1996) A new paradigm of leadership: an inquiry into transformational leadership. Army Research Institute for the Behavioral and Social Sciences, Alexandria

Bass BM, Steidlmeier P (1999) Ethics, character, and authentic transformational leadership. Leadersh Q 10:181–217

Baumeister R (2011) Self and identity: a brief overview of what they are, what they do, and how they work. Ann N Y Acad Sci 1234:48–55

Brouwer R (1995) Pastor tussen macht en onmacht: Een studie naar de professionalisering van het hervormde predikantschap. Boekencentrum, Zoetermeer

Brown ME, Trevino LK (2006) Ethical leadership: a review and future directions. Leadersh Q 17 (6):595–616

Burns JM (1978) Leadership. Harper & Row, New York

Day DV, Antonakis J (eds) (2012) The nature of leadership. Sage, Los Angeles/London

Eliastam J (2018) Discursive leadership and the other. In: Brouwer R (ed) The future of lived religious leadership, the Amsterdam studies in theology and religion, vol 7. VU University Press, Amsterdam, pp 26–47

Evers W, Tomic W (2003) Burnout among Dutch reformed pastors. J Psychol Theol 31(4):329–338

Fry LW (2003) Towards a theory of spiritual leadership. Leadersh Q 14(6):693–727

Gijbels D, Donche V, Richardson JTE, Vermunt JD (2014) Learning patterns in higher education: dimensions and research perspectives. Routledge, London/New York

Graham S (2012) Christian hospitality and pastoral practices in a multifaith society: an ATS project, 2010-2012. Theol Educ 47(1):1–10

Greenleaf RK (1977) Servant leadership: a journey into the nature of legitimate power and greatness. Paulist Press, Mahwah

Haslam SA, Reicher SD, Platow MJ (eds) (2011) The new psychology of leadership: identity, influence, and power. Psychology Press, New York

Hersey P, Blanchard KH (1977) The management of organizational behavior. Prentice Hall, Englewood Cliffs

McAdams DP, Bryant FB (1987) Intimacy motivation and subjective mental health in a nationwide sample. J Personal 55:395–414

Mezirow J (2006) An overview of tranformative learning. In: Sutherland P, Crowther J (eds) Lifelong learning: concepts and contexts. Routledge, New York, pp 24–38

Mezirow J (2012) Learning to think like an adult: core concepts of transformation theory. In: Taylor EW, Cranton P (eds) The handbook of transformative learning: theory, research, and practice. Jossey-Bass, San Francisco, pp 73–96

Mintzberg H (1973) The nature of managerial work. Harper & Row, New York

Nauss A (1996) Assessing ministerial effectiveness: a review of measures and their use. Res Sci Study Relig 7:221–251

Post P, Nugteren A, Zondag H (2002) Rituelen na rampen: Verkenning van een opkomend repertoire. Gooi en Sticht, Kampen

Quinn RE, Faerman S, Thompson MP, McGrath M, Clair LS (2007) Becoming a master manager: a competing values approach. Wiley, New York

Quinn RE, Faerman S, Thompson MP, McGrath M, Clair LS (2011) Handboek managementvaardigheden. Academic Service, Den Haag

Roothaan A (2007) Spiritualiteit begrijpen: een filosofische inleiding. Boom, Amsterdam

Ruijters MCP et al (2015) Je binnenste buiten: over professionele identiteit in organisaties. Vakmedianet, Deventer

Ryff CD (2014) Psychological well-being revisited: advances in the science and practice of eudaimonia. Psychother Psychosom 83(1):10–28

Ryff CD, Singer BH (2013) Know thyself and become what you are: a eudaimonic approach to psychological well-being. In: Della Fave A (ed) The exploration of happiness. Springer, Dordrecht, pp 97–116

Shaw P (2002) Changing conversations in organizations: a complexity approach to change. Routledge, London/New York

Sternberg RJ (1990) The theory of succesful intelligence. Rev Gen Psychol 3(4):292–316

Sternberg RJ (2001) Why schools should teach for wisdom: the balance theory of wisdom in educational settings. Educ Psychol 36(4):227–245

Sternberg RJ (2004) Why smart people can be so foolish. Eur Psychol 9(3):145–150

Sternberg RJ (2010) WICS: a new model for school psychology. Sch Psychol Int 31(6):599–616

Tennen H, Afflect G (1993) The puzzles of self-esteem: a clinical perpective. In: Baumeister RF (ed) Self-esteem: the puzzle of low self-esteem. Plenum, New York, pp 241–262

van den Berg S (2016) Handel in goed nieuws: de pionierende HBO-theoloog. In: Erwich R, Praamsma JM (eds) Grensgangers: pendelen tussen geloof en cultuur. Kok, Kampen, pp 89–103

van der Woud A (2015) De nieuwe mens: de culturele revolutie in Nederland rond 1900. Prometheus/Bert Bakker, Amsterdam

van Saane JW (2010) Religie is zo gek nog niet: een introductie in de godsdienstpsychologie. Ten Have, Kampen

van Saane JW (2012) Geloofwaardig leiderschap. Boekencentrum, Zoetermeer

van Saane JW (2014) Spirituality and the psychology of leadership credibility: an analysis from the psychology of religion. In: Barentsen J, Nullens P (eds) Leadership, spirituality and innovation, Christian perspectives on leadership and social ethics 1. Peeters, Leuven, pp 41–56

van Saane JW (2015) Geloofwaardig onderwijs: van kennis naar persoonlijk leiderschap. Inaugural adress, Vrije Universiteit Amsterdam, Amsterdam

van Saane JW (2017) From cognitive science to personal leadership: the role of religion and personal life orientation in curriculum development processes within the domain of religious studies. In: Aune K, Stevenson J (ed) Religion and higher education in Europe and North America. Routledge, London/New York, pp 181–190

van Saane JW (2018) Back to the root: paradoxes in the development of leadership theories. In: Brouwer R (ed) The future of lived religious leadership: amsterdam studies in theology and religion, vol 7. VU University Press, Amsterdam, pp 208–217

Van Velsor E, McCauley CD, Ruderman MN (eds) (2010) The center for creative leadership handbook of leadership development. Jossey-Bass, San Fransico

van Vugt M, Ahuja A (2010) Naturally selected: the evolutionary science of leadership. Harper Business, New York

Verstraeten J (2003) Leiderschap met hart en ziel: Spiritualiteit als weg naar oorspronkelijkheid. Lannoor, Tielt

Yukl G (2010) Leadership in organizations. Pearson, Upple Saddle River

Yukl G, Mahsud R (2010) Why flexible and adaptive leadership is essential. Consult Psychol J, Pract Res 62(2):81–93

Joke van Saane (1968) is professor in Psychology of Religion and holds the chair of Education Theology and Religious Studies at the Faculty of Theology of the Vrije Universiteit Amsterdam, the Netherlands. The key topics of research and publications are religious experiences and conversion, faith healing, calvinism and fundamentalism, and leadership. Her book on leadership (2012) states that the credibility of leadership can be increased in different ways. Within religious contexts leadership flourishes if there is a match between the professional leader and the group. In secular contexts leadership benefits from spiritual insights, leading to value and morality based leadership.

Leading Organisations in Turbulent Times: Towards a Different Mental Model

Barney Jordaan

Abstract Organisations that are able to adapt quickly to changing circumstances in their operating environment have a competitive advantage. This level of "agility" involves more than simply developing new strategies and organisational structures to enable the rapid gathering of relevant information and equally rapid response times. Agility also—if not primarily—requires an ability on the part of people in the organisation to collaborate effectively to improve their decision-making abilities both as far as speed and quality of outcome are concerned. Collaboration involves more than the mere acquisition of a particular skills set, e.g., to listen and communicate effectively, or procedural adeptness. Creating a collaborative working environment requires a climate of trust within the organisation and a mindset that is focused on working with, rather than against others to achieve common organisational goals and objectives. Given the human propensity to compete and the so-called trust deficit prevalent in organisations, trustworthiness on the part of leaders and an ability to instil a culture of collaboration are required. However, a number of human and organisational obstacles would need to be overcome to achieve this.

1 Introduction

The contemporary business environment is characterised by increasing levels of complexity, turbulence and uncertainty. For organisations to survive and thrive in this environment, they need to become more "agile" or adaptive (Rigby et al. 2016). This is not merely a matter of developing an appropriate strategy and organisational structure, but also of leadership (Doz and Kosonen 2008). Whatever label one attaches to it, at the core of the kind of leadership that is needed to navigate this

B. Jordaan (✉)
Management Practice, Vlerick Business School, Ghent, Belgium

University of Stellenbosch Business School, Cape Town, South Africa
e-mail: barney.jordaan@vlerick.com

© The Author(s) 2019
J. (Kobus) Kok, S. C. van den Heuvel (eds.), *Leading in a VUCA World*,
Contributions to Management Science, https://doi.org/10.1007/978-3-319-98884-9_4

turbulence lies the leader's ability to instil a pre-dominant culture of collaboration both inside the organisation and between the organisation and its key stakeholders (Lash 2012).[1]

Because of our hard-wired tendency towards competition (Nicholson 2003), collaboration appears to run counter to our intuitive responses when we are faced with crises, uncertainty or threats. Moving from competition to collaboration is therefore not merely a matter of acquiring a new skills set or process expertise—important as those are—but primarily a matter of fundamentally changing mental models or mindsets.[2]

For collaboration to work optimally, a change in mindset towards a preference for collaboration is not sufficient: organisational trust[3] is a key requirement as it is associated with enhanced collaboration and improved information sharing and problem-solving (Lewicki and Tomlinson 2003). As indicated later, establishing and maintaining organisational trust—and therefore collaboration—is entirely dependent on the trustworthiness of the organisation's leadership.[4]

In this contribution, after briefly discussing the need for a change from a competitive to a primarily collaborative organisational culture and the role that trust plays in promoting collaboration, I turn to some of the obstacles and challenges that might stand in the way of achieving a leadership mindset and style that promotes a culture of collaboration. While the focus here is on business, the relevance of the points raised might extend beyond the business world as well.

2 The Current Business Reality: A "VUCA" World

The general rule seems to be that the level of consciousness of an organization cannot exceed the level of consciousness of its leader (Laloux 2014).[5]

---

[1]The choice of "pre-dominant" is deliberate: collaboration is not always possible or appropriate. For a nuanced treatment of the benefits and limits of collaboration, see Hansen (2009) *Collaboration: How Leaders Avoid the Traps, Build Common Ground, and Reap Big Results.* Boston: HBR Press.

[2]Mental models determine the strategic approach one takes to deal with problems or make decisions. This, in turn, drives the tactics and behaviour one employs in pursuit of a solution and, ultimately, determines the outcomes achieved. Van Boven and Thompson (2003). "A Look into the Mind of the Negotiator: Mental Models in Negotiation". *Group Processes & Intergroup Relations.* 6(4): 387–404.

[3]For a discussion of the different levels and dimensions of trust, see Fulmer and Gelfand (2012). "At what level (and in whom) we trust: trust across multiple organizational levels." *Journal of Management.* 38(4): 1167–1230.

[4]See, on the antecedents of organisational trust, Fulmer and Gelfand (2012). "At what level (and in whom) we trust: trust across multiple organizational levels." *Journal of Management.* 38(4): 1167–1230; Lewicki and Wiethoff (2000). "Trust, trust development, and trust repair" in Coleman et al. (eds., 2014). *The Handbook of Conflict Resolution: Theory and Practice.* San Francisco: Jossey-Bass.

[5]As quoted at http://www.reinventingorganizations.com/uploads/2/1/9/8/21988088/140305_laloux_reinventing_organizations.pdf

A corporate culture and leadership model that promote formalisation of policies and procedures, specialisation and hierarchical decision-making were well suited to the demands of a manufacturing economy. It allowed executives to understand the (fairly predictable) business environment and make decisions based on information that was not necessarily important to lower level employees, to whom clearly delineated functions within the organisation were assigned.

Today, however, businesses operate in an environment characterised by turbulence, uncertainty and rapid technological, social and political change unlike anything we have experienced before and in which the old models are becoming obsolete (Bennett and Lemoine 2014). This new environment is often referred to as a "VUCA"[6] environment, a term first applied to military strategy after the end of the Cold War but that has become a trendy managerial acronym for Volatility, Uncertainty, Complexity, and Ambiguity. The result is flux, instability, paralysis (due to information overload), doubt, dualities, distrust and increased levels of unresolved conflict. The VUCA environment affects not only business but all levels of society and its institutions. In this environment, "traditional" leadership styles fail to deliver the innovation and entrepreneurship that is required to remain competitive.[7]

3 The Antidote: "Agile" Leadership

The greatest danger in times of turbulence is not the turbulence. It is to act with yesterday's logic.[8]

The antidote to the turbulence is leadership characterised by agility (or "adaptiveness," the ability to make rapid adaptations in response to changing circumstances), creativity, improved decision-making ability through collaboration and trustworthiness (Johansen 2012).[9]

---

[6]The term "VUCA" originated with the United States Army War College to describe conditions resulting from the end of the Cold War. The VUCA concept has since been adopted throughout businesses and organisations in many industries and sectors to guide leadership and strategy planning.

[7]A lot has been written on this topic. See, e.g., Sankman (2013). *Nice Companies Finish First Why Cut-Throat Management Is Out and Collaboration Is In*. Palgrave London: St Martin's Press; Grant (2013). *Give and Take: A Revolutionary Approach to Success*. New York: Viking Press; Hansen (2009). *How Leaders Avoid the Traps, Build Common Ground, and Reap Big Results*. Boston: Harvard Business Review Press; Morgan (2012). The Collaborative Organization: A Strategic Guide to Solving Your Internal Business Challenges Using Emerging Social and Collaborative Tools. New York: Mc GrawHill. See also Hamel (2001). First, let's fire all the managers. HBR (available at https://hbr.org/2011/12/first-lets-fire-all-the-managers (last accessed 26 March 2017).

[8]Attributed to Peter Drucker (http://www.azquotes.com/quote/521436, last accessed 28 April 2017).

[9]This is reminiscent of what has been described as "Situational Leadership" in accordance with the model first developed by Hersey and Blanchard would probably be appropriate. See Hersey and Blanchard (1977). *Management of Organizational Behavior: Utilizing Human Resources*. New Jersey/Prentice Hall. See also Goleman (2000). "Leadership that gets results." *HBR*, March–April

Such leaders, it has been noted, are not driven by ego and a desire for control, but tend to possess a blend of humility, confidence and assertiveness (Botelho et al. 2017). Their humility means that they don't believe they have all the answers: in their decision-making they consciously seek information, suggestions and views from relevant others in the organisation, irrespective of their hierarchical position. Their confidence and assertiveness means they are not only inclusive but are also able to arrive at decisions and implement them. It is the ability to take charge, engage the wisdom and insights of others and then to make fast decisions on the basis of the inputs received.[10] They also focus strongly on employee development and providing those they lead with positivity and a future orientation (Gallup 2017). While they give everyone a "voice," not everyone has a "vote." A collaborative culture, in other words, does not imply that organisations must succumb to potentially debilitating consensus-driven decision-making (Botelho et al. 2017).

Yet organisations face a mismatch: while today's organisations require leaders who are trustworthy, respectful and inclusive, who can subordinate their own ego and agenda and give up power and resources for the greater organisational good, many organisations are still run by operational leaders who are competent at what they do yet have a mindset or mental model that dictates that to be effective, they need hierarchical power and direct control over a specific set of resources which they can deploy to achieve results (Botelho et al. 2017).

Organisations that are structured and operate in this manner inhibit the kind of "agile" leadership required to meet the challenges of the current environment (Lash 2012).[11] As a 2017 Gallup *Global Workplace Report* demonstrates, one key consequence of this is employee disengagement: by denying employees the opportunity to gravitate towards roles and responsibilities that play to their inherent abilities, a culture of command and control tends to stifle employee motivation and entrepreneurship.[12]

While a change in this competitive mental model is key to developing the kind of agile leadership organisations need today, this is not an easy task, largely because of how we are seemingly "hard-wired."

---

issue, 78–90. In essence, situational leadership posits that there is no single "best" style of leadership. Effective leadership is task-relevant, and the most successful leaders are those who adapt their leadership style to the ability and willingness of the individual or group they are attempting to lead or influence. Effective leadership varies, not only with the person or group that is being influenced, but it also depends on the task, job or function that needs to be accomplished.

[10]Interview with Prof John Latham, Monfort Institute on "The collaborative leader," published 10/01/2010, available at https://www.youtube.com/watch?v=QowFJswk_ZA (last accessed 3 February 2018).

[11]See also Yukl and Mahsud (2010). "Why flexible and adaptive leadership is essential." *Consulting Psychology Journal: Practice and Research*, 62(2): 81–93.

[12]The report suggests that, globally, the level of engagement is possibly as low as 15%.

4 A Bridge Too Far?

The challenge today, as Nicholson surmises (Nicholson 2003), is how to reconcile the demands of the information age with, what he refers to as "stone age minds"? It has been said that as a species, we are not programmed to compromise. We have an innate aggression that programmes us to win—and in winning we want to see others lose (Randolph 2010).

In his reflections on this "win-lose mindset" that still characterises leadership in many organisations, Finkelstein (2003) identified what he refers to as the "seven habits of unsuccessful leaders."[13] These include their belief that they have all the answers; the fact that they ruthlessly eliminate anyone who isn't completely behind them; their under-estimation of the obstacles their organisations face; and their stubborn reliance on what worked for them in the past. After recalling a number of major corporate failures presided over by such leaders, he only half-jokingly states (Finkelstein 2003, p. 73)

> What's remarkable is that the individuals who possess the personal qualities that make this magnitude of destruction possible usually possess other, genuinely admirable qualities. It makes sense: Hardly anyone gets a chance to destroy so much value without demonstrating the potential for creating it. Most of the great destroyers of value are people of unusual intelligence and talent who display personal magnetism. ... What's the secret of their destructive powers? I found that spectacularly unsuccessful people had seven characteristics in common. Nearly all of the leaders who preside over major business failures exhibit four or five of these habits. The truly gifted ones exhibit all seven. But here's what's really remarkable: Each of these seven habits represents a quality that is widely admired in the business world. Business not only tolerates the qualities that make these leaders spectacularly unsuccessful, it celebrates them.

One of our biggest distinctions as a species, however, is our unique capacity to make counter-evolutionary choices (Diamond 1997). This includes the ability to adapt our mental models or mindset[14] and in consequence of that also adapt our strategies and behaviours when, e.g., negotiating change, making decisions, or dealing with differences.[15]

Yet even with the right mindset, perhaps the biggest obstacle leaders will face in their quest to instil a collaborative culture is to gain and maintain the trust of those they lead.

---

[13] A play on Steven Covey's popular 1989 book, *The 7 Habits of Highly Effective People*. New York: Free Press.

[14] The general attitudes and the way they typically think about things—Collins Dictionary available at https://www.collinsdictionary.com/dictionary/english/mindset (last accessed 13 February 2017).

[15] Mindsets or mental models affect what we do and how we do it: Pfeffer (2005) "Changing mental models: HR's most important task." *Human Resource Management* 123–128; Van Boven and Thompson (2003). "A Look into the Mind of the Negotiator: Mental Models in Negotiation." *Group Processes & Intergroup Relations*. 6(4) 387–404.

5 Gaining Trust and Instilling a Collaborative Culture in Organisations

> Although research has identified many determinants of cooperation, virtually all scholars have agreed that one especially immediate antecedent is trust (Smith et al. 1995).

Trust is associated with enhanced collaboration, information sharing and problem-solving (Lewicki and Tomlinson 2003; Hurley 2006).

5.1 What Is "Trust"?

The phenomenon of trust has been extensively explored by scholars from a variety of disciplines across the social sciences, including economics, workplace relations, social psychology and political science.

Trust has been defined in various ways. Mayer et al. (1995) define it as "the willingness of a party (the "trustor") to be vulnerable to the actions of another party based on the expectation that the other will perform a particular action important to the trustor, irrespective of the ability to monitor or control that other party."[16]

The ability to build trust has become a key organisational competence, particularly as more and more responsibilities are devolved to teams and individuals in the pursuit of greater organisational agility (Lewicki et al. 1998).[17] Peterson and Kaplan (2016) refers to it as the main leadership competency needed today, primarily because it affects every other competency leaders need to have. The weight of evidence also suggests that trust in people outside one's own family or social group is strongly positively related to economic growth (World Development Report 2015).

Trust is essential for organisations to function properly (Hardin 2002). Deutsch (1962) refers to trust as the prerequisite for collaboration within an organisation.[18] Trusting relationships also enhance the quality of an employee's work life: when

---

[16]Many other definitions of trust exist. See, generally, Fulmer and Gelfand. "At What Level (and in Whom) We Trust: Trust Across Multiple Organizational Levels." *Journal of Management* 38 (4):1167–1230. Lewicki and Tomlinson (2003). "Trust and trust building" (available at http://www.beyondintractability.org/essay/trust-building) define trust as "a generalized expectancy that other people can be relied on." However, most definitions recognise the core ingredients of interpersonal trust, i.e., benevolence, integrity and competence. Some also add reliability.

[17]See also Kim and Mauborgne (2003). "Fair process: managing in the knowledge economy." *Harvard Business Review*, 127–136 who state: "When employees don't trust managers to make good decisions or to behave with integrity, their motivation is seriously compromised. Their distrust and its attendant lack of engagement is a huge, unrecognized problem in most organizations."

[18]But see Mayer et al. (1995) "An integrative model of organizational trust." *Academy of Management Review*. 20(3) 709–734 at 712: 'Although trust can frequently lead to cooperative behavior, trust is not a necessary condition for cooperation to occur, because cooperation does not necessarily put a party at risk." In other words, cooperation may also stem from other motives, e.g., fear of punishment.

trust is relatively high, employees are more committed to the organisation and their work (Hardin 2002).[19]

5.2   The Trust Deficit

Hurley (2006, p. 55) found that roughly half of all managers don't trust their leaders:

> That's what I found when I recently surveyed 450 executives of 30 companies from around the world. Results from a Golin Harris survey of Americans back in 2002 were similarly bleak: 69% of respondents agreed with the statement 'I just don't know who to trust anymore'. In that same year the University of Chicago surveyed 800 Americans and discovered that more than four out of five had 'only some' or 'hardly any' confidence in the people running major corporations. Granted, trusting corporate leaders in the abstract is different from trusting your own CEO, and some companies and executives are almost universally considered trustworthy; but the general trend is troubling.

Enron, the bank crisis of a almost decade ago, Volkswagen's VW emissions fiasco and other recent corporate scandals underscore just how costly and damaging a breach of trust can be.

There is a saying—apparently of Dutch origin—that goes: "Trust arrives on foot but leaves on horseback." Damaged or broken trust can leave a permanent scar not only on a company's reputation but on employees' levels of motivation and performance as well (Lewicki and Tomlinson 2003; Lewicki et al. 1998). Factors that have been found to cause a breakdown in trust include disrespectful behaviours, poor communication, broken promises, ineffective leadership, not taking responsibility for mistakes, and incongruence, or inconsistency between word and deed (Lewicki et al. 2016).

Can broken trust be repaired? Recent research indicates that this is possible, although it is not as straightforward as building trust in the first place (Lewicki et al. 2016). At the very least, the victim must be prepared to reconcile. The victim has to

---

[19]Zak (2017). "The Neuroscience of Trust," *HBR*, January–February reports on the results of a US survey conducted to determine levels of trust in a number of organisations, using certain indicators: "The effect of trust on self-reported work performance was powerful. Respondents whose companies were in the top quartile indicated they had 106% more energy and were 76% more engaged at work than respondents whose firms were in the bottom quartile. They also reported being 50% more productive—which is consistent with our objective measures of productivity from studies we have done with employees at work. Trust had a major impact on employee loyalty as well: Compared with employees at low-trust companies, 50% more of those working at high-trust organizations planned to stay with their employer over the next year, and 88% more said they would recommend their company to family and friends as a place to work. My team also found that those working in high-trust companies enjoyed their jobs 60% more, were 70% more aligned with their companies' purpose, and felt 66% closer to their colleagues. And a high-trust culture improves how people treat one another and themselves. Compared with employees at low-trust organizations, the high-trust folks had 11% more empathy for their workmates, depersonalized them 41% less often, and experienced 40% less burnout from their work. They felt a greater sense of accomplishment, as well—41% more."

be given reason to believe that the violator will make efforts at righting the wrongs and tale steps to minimise future violations (Lewicki and Tomlinson 2003). In the absence of this, the victim has no incentive to attempt reconciliation and restore trust.

The lessons for leaders should be obvious: while the task of establishing trust is in itself a difficult challenge, changing a culture of distrust caused by past violations will require a very conscious and sustained effort to win back the confidence of employees.

5.3   Trustworthiness: The Basis of Trust

Our trust in others is grounded in our evaluation of that person's trustworthiness, that is: their abilities, integrity and benevolence (Hardin 2002).[20] *Ability* refers to an assessment of the other's knowledge, skill, or competency. We need some sense that the other is able to perform in a manner that meets our expectations (Lewicki and Tomlinson 2003). *Integrity* is the degree to which we perceive that the other person adheres to principles and norms that are acceptable to us. *Benevolence* is our assessment that the other person is concerned enough about our welfare to either advance our interests, or at least not impede them.

Ability and integrity are likely to be most influential early in a relationship, as information on one's benevolence needs more time to emerge. The effect of benevolence will increase as the relationship between the parties grows closer (Lewicki and Tomlinson 2003). As perceived trustworthiness increases, trust will also increase (Hardin 2002).

5.4   Building Trust

Trust building is a two-way process. It requires mutual commitment and effort. To build their own trustworthiness, however, leaders therefore should perform competently (certainly functionally but ideally also in terms of so-called "soft skills"); be consistent and predictable; and show concern for others (empathy).

A key vehicle for establishing trustworthiness is what has been referred to as "procedural justice," or what Purcell (2012) refers to as "voice."[21] Purcell (2012), for

---

[20]Peterson with Kaplan (2016). *The 10 laws of trust.* New York: Amacom mention character, competence and authority as the key components. See further Mayer et al. (1995) "An inegrative model of organizational trust." *Academy of Management Review.* 20(3): 709–734.

[21]See also Lewicki and Tomlinson (2003). "Trust and trust building" available at https://www.beyondintractability.org/essay/trust_building (last accessed 4 February 2018) and Lash (2012). "The Collaboration Imperative." *Ivey Business Journal,* January/February issue, available at http://iveybusinessjournal.com/publication/the-collaboration-imperative/ (last accessed 2 February 2018).

example, observed how giving employees voice is intimately connected to the generation of trust in the work environment.

Kim and Mauborgne (2003, p. 8) confirm the vital role that voice—or procedural justice—plays in the trust-building process:

> The psychology of fair process, or procedural justice, is quite different. Fair process builds trust and commitment, trust and commitment produce voluntary co-operation, and voluntary cooperation drives performance, leading people to go beyond the call of duty by sharing their knowledge and applying their creativity. In all the management contexts we've studied, whatever the task, we have consistently observed this dynamic at work.

If people are not encouraged to contribute their ideas, e.g., because of a lack of trust or fear of negative consequences if and when they do, they will remain silent and thus contribute to decision-making on the basis of incomplete data. On the other hand, allowing an unfettered exchange of insights and ideas can help leaders build a comprehensive understanding of the business environment and generate appropriate adaptations and innovative solutions to challenges that arise (Kenney 2010).

5.5 Collaboration

Collaboration involves people working together to create something that no individual can create and do single-handedly. It is about positively and actively wanting and acting in unity with others to achieve a common goal (McDermott and Hal 2016).

In a collaborative environment, the leader's role is to set the vision and guide people to interact in ways that tap into, and leverage, individual strengths to create collective outcomes. Leadership is focused on guiding and facilitating outcomes—rather than directing them—and safeguarding the collaborative process. It is more about leading the process, not the people. It is about making connections between the right people, bridging diverse cultures and getting members used to sharing ideas, resources and power across hierarchies and silos (Reeves and Deimler 2011).

Collaboration works best when the roles of individual team members are clearly defined and well understood and they are then given space to do a significant portion of their work independently. Without such clarity, team members are likely to waste too much energy negotiating roles or protecting turf, rather than focus on the task at hand (Gratton and Erickson 2007).

5.6 Why Instil a Culture of Collaboration?

Collaboration has a number of advantages for organisations:

- If they are part of the process of decision-making, members of a collaborative group are more likely to be willing to buy into and take responsibility for implementing the group's action plan (Kim and Mauborgne 2003).
- Because it is an open process that encourages discussion and dialogue, collaboration builds trust among those involved in the process (Kim and Mauborgne 2003).
- Collaboration can help to "de-silo" organisational thinking and behaviour by open dialogue between different parts of the organisation across functional domains (Reeves and Deimler 2011).
- People possess information that can only be accessed with their consent and active cooperation (Kim and Mauborgne 2003). Collaboration provides access to such information and ideas and thus improves the quality of decision-making: solutions arrived at are likely to be better than those developed in a vacuum, or by only a small number of people (Kuhl et al. 2005).
- A collaborative culture leads to a different way of dealing with people-related problems, including internal conflicts (Reeves and Deimler 2011).

For all its advantages, there are potential disadvantages that go with collaborative leadership as well (Lash 2012): it can be frustrating, slow and time consuming. There is a danger of "collaborative overload" if left unguided (Cross et al. 2016). There's also no guarantee that it will work with a particular group.

Trying to instil a collaborative culture might also face tough resistance: many people in organisations would prefer a leader to tell them exactly what they need to do. Being asked to share leadership might cause resentment and leave them feeling uncertain (Cross et al. 2016).

Finally, collaboration demands that leaders subordinate their egos: they are not the boss and may have to forego any credit if the group is successful (Lash 2012).

5.7 Profile of a "Collaborative" Leader[22]

> If you bring the appropriate people together in constructive ways with good information, they will create authentic visions and strategies for addressing the shared concerns of the organization (sic) or community (Chrislip and Larson 1994, p. 89)

"Collaborative leaders" are not necessarily found in the top hierarchy of organisations. They may be external consultants, non-executive board members or team leaders (Reeves and Deimler 2011).

---

[22]The term is not used here to describe a new type of leadership but rather the characteristics of leaders who are able to instil a collaborative culture.

They are trusted and respected by the groups and individuals they have to deal with because they have a solid reputation for trustworthiness, i.e., they have competence, consistency and integrity. "Collaborative leaders" tend to have good facilitation skills and have a tolerance for and understanding of how to manage conflict. They are good listeners yet are also assertive and persuasive (Reeves and Deimler 2011).

"Collaborative leaders" are able to create the conditions and processes that would maximise synergies between people. The emphasis is less on producing a solution to a known problem and more on developing new ways to reframe situations and develop unanticipated combinations of actions (McDermott and Hal 2016).

The key to instilling a sustainable culture of trust and collaboration lies in adopting an appropriate mental model (Hill and Levenhagen 1995; Lewis et al. 2014).

6 Changing Mindsets

We don't see things as they are; we see them as we are (Nin 1993).

The frames our minds create define—and confine—what we perceive to be possible. Every problem, every dilemma, every dead end we find ourselves facing in life, only appears unsolvable inside a particular frame or point of view (Zander and Zander 2000).

6.1 Mental Models[23]

Senge (1990)[24] defines it as "deeply ingrained assumptions, generalizations, or even pictures and images that influence how we understand the world and how we take action." For Van Boven and Thompson (2003, p. 388) mental models are:

---

[23]There is an ongoing debate over where in the brain mental models are located, i.e. in the long or short-term memory. There are also different types of mental models, i.e., individual, team and shared mental models: "A shared mental model is the mental model constructed and shared when individuals interact together in a team setting, it represents the shared cognition among groups of individuals. A team model is the collective task and team relevant knowledge that team members bring to a situation. The team's collective and dynamic understanding that they bring to a specific situation is referred to as a team situation model." See Jones et al. (2011). "Mental models: an interdisciplinary synthesis of theory and methods." Ecology & Society 16(1): 46. Available at http://www.ccologyandsociety.org/vol16/iss1/art46/ (last accessed 28 April 2017).

[24]Senge also defines learning organisations as (1990, p. 3) "…organizations where people continually expand their capacity to create the results they truly desire, where new and expansive patterns of thinking are nurtured, where collective aspiration is set free, and where people are continually learning to see the whole together."

cognitive representations of the causal relationships within a system that allow people to understand, predict, and solve problems within that system. Mental models are based on people's experiences and expectations. They can guide behaviour in different situations, organise thoughts about a problem, and influence the interpretation of information.

Mental models affect our thinking and help us make sense of our world (Van Boven and Thompson 2003, p. 388).[25] They are simplified internal representations of reality that allows us to interact with the world. They enable thought and action, but also constrain them. They form the basis of reasoning, decision making, and behaviour. Without mental models of the world, decision-making would be difficult, if not impossible (World Development Report 2015). Without shared mental models, it would be impossible in many cases for people to solve collective action problems, create institutions, feel a sense of belonging and solidarity, or even understand one another (World Development Report 2015).

6.2 Changing Mindsets

Everything can be taken from a man but one thing: the last of the human freedoms—to choose one's attitude in any given set of circumstances, to choose one's own way (Frankl 1959, p. 86).

We have the power to choose the assumptions we make. Each choice has consequences for how we feel and what we do, the decisions we make, and how we act in the situations we confront in seeking to make organisations more effective and successful (Pfeffer 2005).

Mental models affect where we direct our attention and what information we rely on (Van Boven and Thompson 2003). If they are out of sync with reality they may substantially limit the type and amount of information decision makers use, greatly affecting decision outcomes. This is because we may ignore information that violates our current assumptions and automatically fill in missing information based on what our mental models suggest is likely to be true. Mental models enable thought and action, yet also constrain them. Mental models have to be highly dynamic to adapt to continually changing circumstances and to evolve over time through learning (Van Boven and Thompson 2003), yet abandoning established mental models and adopting different ones can be very difficult.[26] As Koestler (1972, p. 235) states:

---

[25]See also "Thinking with mental models" (2015) World Development Report, World Bank available at http://pubdocs.worldbank.org/en/504271482349886430/Chapter-3.pdf (last accessed 18 February 2017).

[26]The authors of the World Bank report, above, provide this example of the power of mental models and the difficulty of changing them:

"The power and persistence of mental models are strikingly captured by a story Nelson Mandela told of a time when he flew from Sudan to Ethiopia. He started to worry when he noticed that the pilot was black:

Of all forms of mental activity, the most difficult to induce . . . is the art of handling the same bundle of data as before, by placing them in a new system of relations with one another by giving them a different framework, all of which virtually means putting on a different kind of thinking-cap for the moment. It is easy to teach anybody a new fact . . . but it needs light from heaven above to enable a teacher to break the old framework in which the student is accustomed to seeing.

Policy interventions may be able to trigger a change in mental models, but may also have the opposite effect. It has been found, for example, that only under certain circumstances will affirmative action policies lead to a positive change in attitudes: "If negative stereotypes shape perceptions strongly enough, interaction may simply reinforce the negative stereotypes, undermining the hoped-for effects of the policy" (World Development Report 2015).

The formation of a mental model in a person's mind is the result of both biology, i.e., an ability inherent to the human mind, and learning (Jones et al. 2011). The discipline starts with self-reflection, learning to discover our own internal pictures of the world, and then to bring them to the surface and scrutinise them rigorously. It also includes the ability to carry on what Senge (1990) calls "learningful conversations" where people expose their own thinking effectively and make that thinking open to the influence of others.

Results from a 2015 survey conducted by McKinsey & Company found that the most effective initiatives to change mindsets and behaviours are: role modelling; fostering understanding and conviction; reinforcing changes through formal mechanisms; and developing talent and skills.

The process of how initiatives are designed is critical too: involving input from a range of company stakeholders is more likely to lead to successful transformations:

People must be exposed to their implicit mental models and examine them before we can change them. Changing what people do is easier than changing what they think since mindsets and assumptions are often deeply embedded beyond conscious thought. Yet changing the way people think about situations is, in fact, the most powerful and useful way to ultimately change behaviour and thereby affect organisational results (Pfeffer 2005, p. 125)

6.3 Embedding a New Mindset

Developing a new collaborative mental model alone is not enough, however. Institutions and mental models are closely related and sometimes a change in a

---

'We put down briefly in Khartoum, where we changed to an Ethiopian Airways flight to Addis. Here I experienced a rather strange sensation. As I was boarding the plane I saw that the pilot was black. I had never seen a black pilot before, and the instant I did I had to quell my panic. How could a black man fly an airplane?'"

See also Reger et al. (1994). "Creating earthquakes to change organizational mindsets," Academy of Management Executive 8(4): 31–43.

mental model also requires institutional change. Barker (1989) suggests that when adopting a new paradigm, all aspects of the system must change in accordance with the new paradigm. Paradigm shifting, therefore, does not become fully operable until all parts of the system are changed and aligned with the new paradigm.

Furthermore, if leaders and their organisations are to develop a different mental model to facilitate a collaborative, high trust environment, it will be necessary for people to go beyond merely learning new skills: it requires the development of new orientations, a change in corporate culture, vision and values. Moving the organisation in the right direction also entails working to transcend the sorts of internal politics and game playing that dominate traditional organisations. It means fostering openness and seeking to distribute business responsibly far more widely while retaining coordination and control (Quinn 2004).

7 Conclusion

When we commit to a vision to do something that has never been done before, there is no way to know how to get there. We simply have to build the bridge as we walk on it (Quinn 2004).

For businesses to survive and thrive in the so-called "VUCA" world, an organisational culture that fosters trust and collaboration is called for. At corporate level this will open up new paths to growth, while allowing for more autonomy for and engagement of individuals. But collaboration is more than just a matter of process or skills. For it to be sustainable, it has to be supported by a fundamental change in the traditional, competitive mental models so often found among leaders and inside organisations. This, in return, requires that issues of trust, culture and values within organisations are also addressed.

Sustained change needs a shift in mindset away from competing to survive to collaborating to win; from silo mentalities to openness; from making decisions in small, elite circles to allowing employees a meaningful "voice" in decision that affect them, including the creation of an environment that encourages their inputs and critique, from seeing conflict as bad to embracing it as a potential resource; from behaviours that destroy trust or prevent its development, to the active pursuit of behaviours that develop trust.

Bibliography

Archer D, Cameron A (2009) Collaborative leadership: building relationships, handling conflict and sharing control. Routledge, New York

Barker J (1989) Discovering the future: the business of paradigms. Infinity Limited Incorporated, St. Paul

Bennett N, Lemoine GJ (2014) What VUCA really means for you. HBR, Available https://hbr.org/2014/01/what-vuca-really-means-for-you. Accessed Feb 2017

Botelho EL, Powell RK, Kincaid S, Wang D (2017) What sets successful CEOs apart. HBR, May–June issue, 70–77

Chrislip D, Larson CE (1994) Collaborative leadership: how citizens and civic leaders can make a difference. Jossey-Bass, Boston

Cross R, Rebele R, Grant A (2016) Collaborative overload. HBR, January–February issue

Deutsch M (1962) Cooperation and trust: some theoretical notes. In: Marshall RJ (ed) Nebraska symposium on motivation. University of Nebraska Press, Lincoln, pp 275–319

Diamond J (1997) Why is sex fun? The evolution of human sexuality. Basic Books, New York

Doz Y, Kosonen M (2008) The dynamics of strategic agility: Nokia's rollercoaster experience. Calif Manag Rev 50(3):95–118

Finkelstein S (2003) Why smart executives fail. Penguin, London

Fisher R, Ury W, Patton B (2012) Getting to yes: negotiating an agreement without giving in. Random House Business Books, London

Forrester JW (1971) Counterintuitive behavior of social systems. Technol Forecast Soc Chang 3:1–22

Frankl V (1959) Man's search for meaning. Beacon Press, Boston

Fulmer CA, Gelfand MJ (2012) At what level (and in whom) we trust: trust across multiple organizational levels. J Manag 38(4):1167–1230

Gallup (2017) State of the global workplace report. Available http://www.gallup.com/services/178517/state-global-workplace.aspx. Accessed 3 Feb 2018

Goleman D (2000) Leadership that gets results. HBR, March–April issue, 78–90

Grant A (2013) Give and take: a revolutionary approach to success. Viking Press, New York

Gratton L, Erickson TJ (2007) Eight ways to build collaborative teams. HBR, Available https://hbr.org/2007/11/eight-ways-to-build-collaborative-teams. Accessed March 2016

Hamel G (2001) First, let's fire all the managers. HBR, Available https://hbr.org/2011/12/first-lets-fire-all-the-managers. Accessed March 2017

Hansen M (2009) How leaders avoid the traps, build common ground, and reap big results. Harvard Business Review Press, Boston

Hardin R (2002) Trust and trustworthiness. Russel Sage Foundation, New York

Hersey P, Blanchard KH (1977) Management of organizational behavior: utilizing human resources. Prentice Hall, New Jersey

Hill RC, Levenhagen M (1995) Metaphors and mental models: sensemaking and sensegiving in innovative and entrepreneurial activities. J Manag 21(6):1057–1074

Hurley RF (2006) The decision to trust. HBR, September, 55–62

Ibarra H, Hansen MT (2011) Are you a collaborative leader? HBR, Available https://hbr.org/2011/07/are-you-a-collaborative-leader. Accessed April 2017

Johansen B (2012) Leaders make the future: ten new leadership skills for an uncertain world. Berret-Koehler, San Francisco

Jones NA, Ross H, Lynam T, Perez P, Leitch A (2011) Mental models: an interdisciplinary synthesis of theory and methods. Ecol Soc 16(1):46. Available http://www.ecologyandsociety.org/vol16/iss1/art46/. Accessed 28 April 2017

Kenney S (2010) Creating adaptive organizations, American management association. Available http://www.amanet.org/training/articles/creating-adaptive-organizations.aspx. Accessed Aug 2017

Kim WC, Mauborgne R (2003) Fair process: managing in the knowledge economy. Harv Bus Rev, January issue, 127–136

Koestler A (1972) The roots of coincidence. Vintage Books, New York

Kuhl S, Schnelle T, Tillmann F-J (2005) Lateral leadership: an organizational approach to change. J Chang Manag 5(2):177–189

Laloux F (2014) Reinventing organizations. Nelson Parker, Brussels

Lash R (2012) The collaboration imperative. Ivey Bus J, January/February. Available http://iveybusinessjournal.com/publication/the-collaboration-imperative/. Accessed Feb 2017

Lewicki RJ, Tomlinson EC (2003) Trust and trust building. Available http://www.beyondintractability.org/essay/trust-building. Accessed Feb 2017

Lewicki RJ, Wiethoff C (2000) Trust, trust development, and trust repair. In: Coleman P, Deutsch M, Marcus EC (eds) (2014) The handbook of conflict resolution: theory and practice. Jossey-Bass, San Francisco

Lewicki RJ, McAllister DJ, Bies RJ (1998) Trust and distrust: new relationships and realities. Acad Manag Rev 23:438–458

Lewicki R, Elgoibar P, Euwema M (2016) The tree of trust: building and repairing trust in organizations. In: Elgoibar P, Euwema M, Munduate L (eds) Building trust and constructive conflict management in organizations. Springer, Switzerland

Lewis MW, Andriopoulos C, Smith WK (2014) Paradoxical leadership to enable strategic agility. Calif Manag Rev 56(3):58–77

Mayer RC, Davis JH, Schoorman FD (1995) An inegrative model of organizational trust. Acad Manag Rev 20(3):709–734

McDermott I, Hal CM (2016) The collaborative leader. Crown House Publishing, London

McKinsey & Company (2015) The science of organisational transformations. Available http://www.mckinsey.com/business-functions/organization/our-insights/the-science-of-organizational-transformations. Accessed 18 Feb 2018

Morgan J (2012) The collaborative organization: a strategic guide to solving your internal business challenges using emerging social and collaborative tools. McGraw-Hill, New York

Nicholson N (2003) Managing the human animal. Texere Publishing, Florence

Nin A (1993) Seduction of the minotaur. Penguin Books, London

Paul J. Zak (2017) The Neuroscience of Trust, HBR, January–February.

Peterson J, Kaplan DA (2016) The 10 laws of trust. Amacom, New York, p XII

Pfeffer J (2005) Changing mental models: HR's most important task. Hum Resour Manag:123–128

Purcell J (2012) ACAS future of workplace relations. Discussion paper series. Available http://www.acas.org.uk/media/pdf/g/7/Voice_and_Participation_in_the_Modern_Workplace_challenges_and_prospects.pdf. Accessed Feb 2017

Quinn RE (2004) Building the bridge as you walk on it: a guide for leading change. Jossey-Bass, San Francisco

Randolph P (2010) Compulsory mediation? Blog piece. Available at https://www.newlawjournal.co.uk/content/litigation-v-mediation. Accessed 13 Feb 2018

Reed M (2001) Organization, trust and control: a realist analysis. Organ Stud:201–228

Reeves M, Deimler M (2011) Adaptability: the new competitive advantage. Harv Bus Rev:1–15

Rigby DK, Sutherland J, Takeuchi H (2016) Embracing agile. HBR, Available https://hbr.org/2016/05/embracing-agile. Accessed March 2017

Sankman P (2013) Nice companies finish first: why cut-throat management is out and collaboration is in. St Martin's Press, New York

Senge P (1990) The fifth discipline: the art and practice of the learning organization. Doubleday, New York

Smith KG, Carroll SJ, Ashford SJ (1995) Intra- and interorganizational cooperation: toward a research agenda. Acad Manag J 38(1):7–23

Van Boven L, Thompson L (2003) A look into the mind of the negotiator: mental models in negotiation. Group Process Intergroup Relat 6(4):387–404

World Development Report (2015) Thinking with mental models. Available http://pubdocs.worldbank.org/en/504271482349886430/Chapter-3.pdf. Accessed 18 Feb 2017

Yukl G, Mahsud R (2010) Why flexible and adaptive leadership is essential. Consult Psychol J: Pract Res 62(2):81–93
Zander RS, Zander B (2000) The art of possibility. Harvard Business School Press, Boston

Barney Jordaan holds a doctorate in law from Stellenbosch University, South Africa. He is currently professor of management practice (negotiation and dispute resolution) at Vlerick Business School, Belgium. Jordaan is also an Extraordinary Professor at the University of Stellenbosch Business School. Prior to moving to Belgium in 2014 he held a number of academic appointments in South Africa. These included 14 years as professor of law at Stellenbosch University and thereafter as professor of negotiation and conflict management at the University of Stellenbosch Business School and the Graduate School of Business, University of Cape Town. In conjunction with his academic involvement, Barney also practised as human rights lawyer in South Africa during the apartheid era before co-founding a consulting firm in 1998 which advises corporate clients on conflict management strategies, negotiation and related matters. He has been involved in the mediation field since 1989 as practising mediator, trainer and coach. He is an internationally certified as mediator with, amongst others, the Centre for Effective Dispute Resolution (CEDR, UK) and the International Mediation Institute in The Hague.

Spirituality and Leadership in a South African Context

Anoosha Makka

Abstract This chapter discusses spirituality and leadership in a South African context. Leadership theories that are situated in the spiritual paradigm such as authentic, servant, spiritual and transformational leadership are considered in this chapter. It is argued that leadership practices and styles in South Africa are heavily influenced by British and American approaches. The notion of *"ubuntu,"* which is a central component of Afrocentric leadership is thus largely ignored in literature on the topic. This chapter draws attention to the influence of Western approaches on leadership in South African organisations with particular reference to the Afrocentric notion of *ubuntu*. It is recommended that further research be undertaken on *ubuntu* leadership in the South African context and beyond. Another recommendation is that research should be undertaken on blending Afrocentric and Eurocentric leadership styles in order to identify how this combined leadership approach can be implemented in South Africa.

1 Introduction

With the rise in unethical behaviour and recent business scandals around the world, many organisations are now focused on hiring leaders who understand the workplace and lead "with their heart and soul" (Siddiqi et al. 2017, p. 63). Leadership is not easy during difficult times, and with the current complexities confronting organisations globally, it is imperative that there be a new type of leadership (George 2003), a leadership that is genuine (Avolio and Gardner 2005, p. 316).

Kakabadse et al. (2002) assert that spirituality is a dimension of leadership that has long been overlooked. Yukl (2005) notes that there is no generally accepted definition of spiritual leadership. Spirituality is defined by Stamp (1991, p. 80) as "an awareness within individuals of a sense of connectedness that exists between inner

A. Makka (✉)
Johannesburg Business School, University of Johannesburg (Rand Afrikaans University), Johannesburg, South Africa
e-mail: amakka@uj.ac.za

© The Author(s) 2019   77
J. (Kobus) Kok, S. C. van den Heuvel (eds.), *Leading in a VUCA World*,
Contributions to Management Science, https://doi.org/10.1007/978-3-319-98884-9_5

selves and the world." Kouzes and Pozner (1987, p. 30) indicate that "leadership is the art of mobilizing others to want to struggle for shared aspirations." According to Reave (2005) spiritual leadership occurs when individuals in leadership positions demonstrate values such as trustworthiness, integrity, truthfulness and humility. He points to the sound connection between spiritual values and successful leadership, noting that spiritual leadership is "demonstrated through behaviour, whether in individual reflective practice or in the ethical, compassionate and respectful treatment of others" (Reave 2005, p. 663).

The effectiveness of classical leadership theory, which focuses chiefly on the roles, responsibilities, traits and skills of leaders rather than the consequences of their actions, has been widely questioned (Duthely 2017). Pruzan and Pruzan-Mikkelsen (2007) believe that the leaders who will be successful in the twenty-first century will be those who demonstrate a spiritual dimension.

Galperin and Alamuri (2017) point to the scarcity of research on African leadership. Punnett (2017), Nkomo (2011), Lutz (2009) and Fry (2008) note that the majority of literature on leadership has been written from a Western perspective and lacks insight into the characteristics of effective leadership in an African context. Galperin and Alamuri (2017, p. 39) indicate that research which examines "Western-based management theories" in Africa makes scant reference to the local context and local cultural matters. Leadership practices and styles in South Africa are heavily influenced by British and American approaches (van den Heuvel 2006). The notion of "*ubuntu*," which is a central component of Afrocentric leadership (Yawson 2017), is thus largely ignored in literature on the topic.

The aim of this chapter is to discuss spirituality and leadership in South Africa. This chapter examines the influence of Western approaches on leadership in South African organisations with particular reference to the Afrocentric notion of *ubuntu*. The rest of the chapter is organised as follows: Sect. 2 discusses leadership in South Africa, Sect. 3 examines *ubuntu* leadership, Sect. 4 looks at four leadership theories in the spiritual paradigm, namely, authentic, servant, spiritual and transformational leadership, while Sect. 5 concludes the chapter.

2   Leadership in South Africa

Africa is portrayed by many authors as being under-developed, poverty stricken, overtaken by corruption, characterised by unsuccessful corporate and government sectors and ineffective political leadership (Kiruhi 2017). Adei, who specialises in African leadership claims that leadership plays a vital role in the transformation of countries (Kiruhi 2017). Rothberg (2003) contends that Africa's socio-economic, political and governance challenges can be attributed to bad leadership.

In 1994 South Africa became a democracy and Nelson Mandela was elected as the first democratic president. The country has a rich diversity of people. According to Statistics South Africa (2017) the population stands at 56.52 million and consists of 80.8% Africans, Coloureds make up 8.8%, Whites make up 8% and Indian/Asians 2.5%. However, even after 24 years of democracy, black Africans are underrepresented in management and leadership positions while white males continue to be overrepresented (Booysen 2001).

The Employment Equity Report for 2016–2017 indicates that in South Africa, 50.8% of top management positions are held by white males (mainly in the corporate sector) and 10.9% by white females. In comparison, only 9.2% of top management positions are held by African males and 2.8% by African females (Department of Labour 2017). This disparity in the South African workforce means that South African organisations are characterised by a Western leadership style (Lutz 2009), with corporate culture being dominated by an Anglo-Saxon approach (Dube 2016). Despite this, South African businesses have seen a steady increase in "an Afrocentric approach to management" (Booysen 2001, p. 37), embodied by the concept of *ubuntu*.

In South Africa, business leaders were traditionally required to lead "Eurocentric, autocratic and hierarchical conglomerates which were based on Western value systems but in the post-apartheid era, they find themselves leading a multicultural workforce that is more collectivist and less competitive" (Shrivastava et al. 2014, p. 49). Due to this diversity of cultures in South Africa, effective leadership is particularly challenging. The dichotomy between Afrocentrism and Eurocentrism thus poses a crucial challenge for managers and leaders (Booysen 2001).

In a study conducted by Booysen (2001) on the management and leadership styles of black (Afrocentric) and white (Eurocentric) managers in the South African corporate sector, it was found that:

- Black and white managers both avoid uncertainty or risk. However, white managers score highly on uncertainty avoidance and demonstrate "more worry about the future" while black managers show an "average uncertainty avoidance" score with a "greater readiness to live for the day" (Booysen 2001, p. 55);
- White managers are highly individualistic, display characteristics of "autocratic dictators" and consider that "organisations are not expected to look after employees." In contrast, black managers are highly collectivistic and inclusive and seek consensus before making decisions (which may be perceived as being indecisive). They believe that "employees expect organisations to look after them and can become alienated if organisations dissatisfy them" (Booysen 2001, p. 56);
- White managers are highly assertive and are "direct and aggressive" whereas black managers are "less direct and more face-saving" (Booysen 2001, p. 55);
- White managers are strongly future-oriented and "due dates, schedules and promptness are important." Black managers have a low future orientation and "relationships are more important than time" (Booysen 2001, p. 55);
- White managers have a low human orientation and demonstrate "unfair and selfish behaviour." Black managers have a high human orientation and display "respect and concern for all employees" (Booysen 2001, p. 56);
- White managers have a high performance orientation and "tradition, convention, saving face and social reciprocation are not so important." Black managers, on the other hand, score above average in performance orientation and "tradition, convention, saving face and social reciprocation are emphasised" (Booysen 2001, p. 56).

The history of the workplace in South Africa has traditionally focused on production, with less emphasis placed on human relations between top management and their employees (Msila 2015). Leadership has predominantly been transactional, with leaders seeking to ensure that contractual obligations are fulfilled. This has often resulted in employees being treated as less than human beings (Msila 2015). Galbraith (1977) notes that transactional leadership emphasises control through compliance with rules.

Unsurprisingly, labour relations in South Africa are often strained and characterised by violence (International Monetary Fund 2013) while its labour laws are inflexible (World Economic Forum 2017). An extreme example of this occurred on 16 August 2012 when the Marikana massacre took place and 34 striking platinum miners were killed by the South African police (Alexander 2013). Msila (2015) points out that an *ubuntu leadership* approach can be followed in order to improve human relations between leaders and followers without sacrificing production.

Unethical leadership practices in the public and corporate sectors in South Africa are widespread. Multinational enterprises such as KPMG, SAP and McKinsey have been implicated in scandals regarding unethical business practices involving the Gupta family in South Africa.[1] The biggest corporate scandal in South Africa in recent years involved Steinhoff International, a prominent South African retailing company, which committed accounting fraud and is currently being investigated in South Africa and Europe.[2]

Corruption in South Africa's public sector is rife. For instance, the country's score on the Corruption Perceptions Index 2015 was 44; in 2016, the score was 45 while in 2017 it dropped to 43[3] (Transparency International 2017). A score that is close to 0 implies that corruption is very high while the closer a score is to 100, the greater the freedom from corruption (Transparency International 2015). Former South African president, Jacob Zuma, was recalled by the ruling African National Congress party on 13 February 2018 for his implication in numerous corruption cases relating to state capture[4] with the Gupta family as well as 18 criminal charges for 783 instances of fraud and corruption.[5] South Africa's state-owned enterprises such as Eskom (electricity), the Passenger Rail Agency of South Africa, South African Airways, the South African Broadcasting Corporation and Transnet (transportation and infrastructure) are on the brink of collapse due to poor leadership, corruption, fraud and financial mismanagement.[6] South Africa's

---

[1]For more information, see Pilling (2017) KPMG Urged To Act Over South Africa Gupta Scandal.

[2]For more information, see Lungisa (2017) The Steinhoff Debacle—The biggest fraud in SA history.

[3]For more information, see Transparency International (2017) Corruption Perceptions Index 2017.

[4]For more information on state capture, see Bhorat et al. (2017) Betrayal of the Promise: How South Africa is Being Stolen.

[5]For more information, see Umraw (2018) All The Damage Jacob Zuma Has Wrought Over His Tenure.

[6]For more information, see eNCA (2017) All SA's State-Owned Enterprises Captured: Deputy President.

new president, Cyril Ramaphosa, has sworn to eradicate corruption, fraud, state capture and mismanagement from the public sector.[7] This prevalence of corruption in the country's public sector is seen as occurring due to a departure from *ubuntu* leadership (Yawson 2017).

3 Ubuntu Leadership

Msila (2015) states that numerous African authors have called for the implementation of *ubuntu* leadership on the African continent. *Ubuntu* is a concept stemming from Bantu languages and means "humanness" (Ngunjiri 2010, p. 763). It has further been defined as meaning "I am because we are" (Swanepoel et al. 2009, p. 360). *Ubuntu* is not simply a particular type of management; it is a "humanistic philosophy—an African humanism, which focuses on people and provides some guidelines for leadership style and management practices" (Booysen 2001, p. 38).

Msila (2015) explains that the concept of *ubuntu*, which is strongly linked to African spirituality, has been in existence for many years and predates colonisation. *Ubuntu* implies care, respect, tolerance, compassion, communality, protecting others, living selflessly and is linked to "servant" leadership (Lutz 2009; Msila 2015). Swanepoel et al. (2009) state that *ubuntu* is a leadership style which emphasises a collectivist rather than an individualist approach. Msila (2015) stresses, however, that *ubuntu* is far from fostering mediocrity by limiting competition in organisations. Instead, it promotes competition within the context of collective values and excellence (Msila 2015).

At the heart of *ubuntu* is concern for the individual, the idea of "servanthood," the interests of the team and achieving prosperity for all (Booysen 2001). Ntuli (as cited in Msila 2015) argues that many African leaders have lost their moral compass because they have failed to practice *ubuntu* leadership, embracing instead the values of greed and self-interest. Woermann and Engelbrecht (2017) state that the main purpose of a business that implements *ubuntu* principles is not profit maximisation but the promotion of harmonious relationships with stakeholders, especially with employees. Mangaliso and Damane (2001) regret that *ubuntu* has not been adequately implemented in workplaces in South Africa and indicate that its benefits to organisations have not been properly understood.

Yawson (2017) points out that there are some firms in South Africa which are successfully incorporating *ubuntu* into their business models. Examples cited include South African Airways, Eskom, MTN, CIDA City Campus, Tea Estates in Eastern Highlands and First National Bank (Yawson 2017). However, as Eskom and South African Airways are on the brink of financial collapse, it would be interesting to find out to what extent *ubuntu* has been implemented in those organisations.

---

[7]For more information, see Mokone (2018) Ramaphosa Focuses On The Economy: Announces SOE Clean-Up.

Nelson Mandela has been praised for incorporating the principles of *ubuntu* into his leadership style (Rodny-Gumede and Chasi 2017). At Nelson Mandela's memorial, former American president, Barack Obama, stated that Mandela had demonstrated the values of *ubuntu* through his recognition of the value of all people (Rodny-Gumede and Chasi 2017). Malunga (2009, p. 2) specifies that *ubuntu* is made up of five people-centred principles:

- *"Sharing and collective ownership of opportunities"*—this means that people are encouraged to work together in organisations and communities (Malunga 2009). It emphasises a worker-centred approach as opposed to solely focusing on the leader (Msila 2015);
- *"Responsibilities and challenges"*—in many organisations there is conflict because leaders and followers blame one another when things go wrong, thereby relinquishing their responsibilities. *Ubuntu* promotes taking collective responsibility which is important for the success of an organisation (Malunga 2009);
- *"Importance of people and relationships over things"*—*ubuntu* supports "servant" leadership. This notion implies that true African leaders serve their followers; thus they put their followers' interests first, before their own interests (Msila 2015). Followers are more motivated to contribute to an organisation if they feel that they are valued (Mangaliso and Damane 2001);
- *"Participatory leadership"*—although African leadership is widely regarded as being autocratic, *ubuntu* leadership is based on participation, with leaders gaining the trust and respect of followers through accountable and selfless behaviour (Malunga 2009);
- *"Decision-making, loyalty and reconciliation as a goal of conflict management"*—this refers to collective decision-making promoted by leaders (Msila 2015). *Ubuntu* encourages discernment when making decisions, which should be achieved through consensus and inclusivity. Although this may be perceived as delaying action in organisations, it secures both leaders' and followers' long-term commitment to a goal (Mangaliso and Damane 2001).

Ubuntu African philosophy can make an important theoretical contribution to the ethics in management "because it correctly understands that we are truly human only in community with other persons" (Lutz 2009, p. 314). Galperin and Alamuri (2017) confirm the value of *ubuntu* and suggest that it can be included in leadership practices outside the African continent.

There are several criticisms of *ubuntu*. Woermann and Engelbrecht (2017) caution that implementing *ubuntu* can be problematic. West (2014) and Yawson (2017) argue that to date, there is scant empirical evidence regarding the effectiveness of *ubuntu*. Advocates of *ubuntu* have been accused of commodifying the concept and using it to stereotype individuals (Yawson 2017). West (2014) contends that it is merely an assumption that African people practise and uphold *ubuntu* values. Matolino and Kwindingwi (2013, p. 202) argue that *ubuntu* is an "Africanist agenda" which is being propagated by the African elite. They claim it has largely failed to serve the collective and there are very few individuals who actually practise it.

4 Leadership Theories

4.1 Introduction

Authentic, servant, spiritual and transformational leadership theories are situated within the spiritual paradigm and differ from classical leadership theories. These theories share similarities insofar as they emphasise personal value, transparency and service to others, taking personal responsibility, self-awareness and personal development (Kakabadse et al. 2002). Nkomo (2011) points out that Nelson Mandela is associated with both servant leadership and transformational leadership. On the other hand, Thabo Mbeki, who succeeded Nelson Mandela as president, was perceived as an inflexible leader, as portrayed in the book *Bad Leadership* by Barbara Kellerman (Nkomo 2011).

4.2 Authentic Leadership

In 2003 Luthans and Avolio (2003) and Avolio et al. (2004) developed authentic leadership theory. Luthans and Avolio (2003, p. 243) claim that authentic leadership is derived from "positive psychological capacities and a highly developed organizational context." This leads to increased "self-awareness and self-regulated positive behaviours" by leaders and followers and promotes personal development. Authentic leaders are those individuals who are characterised by self-acceptance, being true to who they are (Klenke 2007) and "owning" their personal experiences (Avolio and Gardner 2005).

Authentic leadership has gained prominence due to its emphasis on leaders who are transparent and have a strong ethical dimension (Dhiman 2017). Authentic leaders are described as "those who are deeply aware of how they think and behave and are perceived by others as being aware of their own and others' values/moral perspectives, knowledge and strengths" (Avolio et al. 2004, p. 4). George (2003) argues that business journalists, the media and Hollywood have placed strongly ego-driven leaders on a pedestal and celebrate such personalities. However, it is precisely this type of leader who is at the centre of the leadership crisis in the world (George 2003).

Authentic leadership is seen as being closely associated with transformational leadership (Dhiman 2017) and servant leadership. Authentic leaders have a strong inclination to serve others (George 2003). In addition to qualities of the mind, authentic leaders have "qualities of the heart" such as compassion for others and passion for what they do (George 2003). Authentic leaders are regarded as positive examples and models by those who follow them because they behave with integrity, are deeply committed to ethical values and promote a conducive organisational climate (Klenke 2007). When making decisions, authentic leaders are able to clearly discern right from wrong as they are guided by their core values (George 2003).

Avolio and Gardner (2005) acknowledge that there is a lack of consensus about how to measure the effectiveness of authentic leadership. Fry and Whittington (2005) warn against the negative consequences of leaders practising authentic leadership when they are driven by self-interest and consequently behave true to who they are.

4.3   Servant Leadership

In 1970 Robert Greenleaf, a retired American management executive, put forward the idea of servant leadership, which he believed was lacking in organisations (Greenleaf and Spears 1998). Greenleaf maintained that leadership should prioritise serving others (this includes an organisation's workers and customers as well as the broader community) instead of simply serving one's own personal needs (Greenleaf 1970).

Servant leaders are motivated by their personal belief that they are servants first and leaders second (Sendjaya and Pekerti 2010). Such leaders thus serve their "followers and the organization" (Winston and Fields 2015, p. 415). Servant leadership does not favour any particular supervision style. Instead, it stems from a personal conviction to serve others when there is a need (Sendjaya and Pekerti 2010). Strong personal values are at the core of servant leaders (Russell 2001) and define their moral thinking, leadership approach and ethical behaviour. These qualities appeal to followers and draw them to such leaders (Liden et al. 2014). Sendjaya and Pekerti (2010) add that servant leadership reflects moral accountability and the ability to discern right from wrong.

Liden et al. (2014) state that due to their respect and admiration for servant leaders, followers imitate their leaders' behaviour. Such leaders are regarded as role models who guide their followers in determining acceptable and unacceptable behaviour (Jaramillo et al. 2015). According to van Dierendonck (2011), servant leaders enable, inspire and develop their followers; they demonstrate humility, they are authentic and have a strong moral compass. Such leaders display empathy in providing direction to their followers and have a stewardship (focus on service to others instead of self-interest). Servant leaders thus prioritise their employees' wants and well-being ahead of organisational goals and interests (Jaramillo et al. 2015).

Larry Spears from the Greenleaf Center introduced the ten qualities of a servant leader: being a good listener, empathizing with other people, the ability to heal oneself and others by developing good relationships, self-awareness, being able to persuade others instead of coercing them into doing something, conceptual thinking abilities, having foresight and intuition, stewardship, committed to advancing followers and a willingness to building community (Spears 2010). Servant leadership thus encourages a serving culture in organisations characterised by a common understanding that others' needs should be put first before one's own needs (Liden et al. 2014). The success of servant leadership is therefore largely dependent on the personal values of individuals (Russell 2001).

There is no commonly accepted definition or a specific theory of servant leadership (van Dierendonck 2011). Winston and Fields (2015) note that there are 28 different dimensions that describe servant leadership and there is very little guidance as to applying such principles in practice. It is also not made explicit whether all 28 dimensions are of equal importance (Winston and Fields 2015).

4.4 Spiritual Leadership

Spiritual leadership theory was developed in 2003 by Fry. It refers to "the values, attitudes and behaviours that one must adopt in intrinsically motivating oneself and others so that both have a sense of spiritual survival through calling and membership—i.e. they experience meaning in their lives, have a sense of making a difference, and feel understood and appreciated" (Fry et al. 2005, p. 836). Reave (2005) adds that spiritual leaders believe in fair play, show respect for others' values, are concerned about others, are good listeners, recognise contributions made by others and are reflective and introspective. Benefiel (2005) argues that one of the major shortcomings in organisations today is that they lack a spiritual foundation.

In leadership, character is important (Bass and Steidlmeier 1999). Spiritual leaders are often referred to as moral leaders (Kakabadse et al. 2002). Moral leaders refuse to co-operate or work in an environment where their core values are compromised (Kakabadse et al. 2002). A spiritual leader's personal values, beliefs, actions and vision influence the behaviour and moral code in an organisation (Banerji and Krishnan 2000). Duthely (2017) argues that spiritual leadership can thus contribute to promoting positive practices and ethical behaviour in the workplace. Fairholm (1996) explains that spiritual leaders do not manipulate their followers into achieving desired goals; instead they energise and transform them. He goes on to say that unlike other leadership models which emphasise self-interest, personal power, materialism and prestige, spiritual leadership is a departure from values characterised by self-interest.

Spiritual leadership theory is well researched in comparison to other leadership approaches and includes explicit guidance on the higher order needs and cultural and organisational qualities of both spiritual leaders and followers. However, Benefiel (2005) notes that although many leadership scholars have a sound knowledge of leadership theory, they have a limited understanding of the literature of spirituality. Krishnakumar et al. (2015) caution against the negative aspects of workplace spirituality whereby leaders develop a cult-like following and manipulate their followers.

4.5 Transformational Leadership

In 1978 James MacGregor Burns, a leadership expert, historian and political scientist, wrote a book entitled *Leadership*. This work explores both transformational leadership and transactional leadership. Transactional leadership, he argues, refers to leaders whose relationship with their followers is based on barter and agreements. Bass and Steidlmeier (1999) note that transactional leadership is founded on self-interest where followers are either rewarded or penalised depending on their performance (Bass and Avolio 1994). Transformational leadership, on the other hand, extends beyond transactional leadership (Bass and Avolio 1994).

Burn's work on transformational leadership was further developed by Bernard Bass in 1985 in his book entitled *Leadership and Performance Beyond Expectations*. Bass argues that values are at the core of transformational leadership (Bass and Steidlmeier 1999) and transformational leaders encourage their followers to focus on the collective needs rather than on their own self-interest (Bass 1990). Yukl (1999) adds that the respect, trust, admiration and loyalty engendered by transformational leaders motivates their followers to deliver more than is usually required.

Bass (1990) identified four characteristics of a transformational leader, namely, personal charisma, the capacity to inspire and motivate followers, encourages problem solving and is personally attentive to employees. Idealised influence is associated with charismatic leaders who are powerful, influential and trusted by their followers (Bass 1990). However, charisma can equally have a negative connotation when leaders become self-absorbed, egotistical, manipulative and distrustful (Parry and Proctor-Thomson 2002). Bass and Steidlmeier (1999) believe that transformational leaders lead by example and their followers copy their behaviour (Bass and Steidlmeier 1999). Sinek (2017) in *Leaders Eat Last: Why Some Teams Pull Together and Others Don't*, emphasises that leaders recognise the value of their employees, put the interests of their employees first and lead their employees into an unfamiliar situation.

Burns (1978, p. 20) asserts that transformational leadership motivates and uplifts followers and is "moral [insofar as] it raises the level of human conduct and ethical aspirations of both the leader and the led." Leaders become transformational when they are guided by a moral compass (Bass and Steidlmeier 1999) and encourage that which is "right, good, important and beautiful" (Bass 1998, p. 171). Parry and Proctor-Thomson (2002) emphasise that although there is a conceptual relationship in literature between transformational leadership and ethics, justice and integrity, there is scant empirical evidence in this regard.

Yukl (1999) points out that there are many positives regarding transformational leadership. Studies conducted by Lowe, Kroeck and Sivasubramaniam in 1996 and Bass in 1998 provide evidence that transformational leadership is positively correlated with motivation, performance and follower satisfaction (Yukl 1999). Jamaludin et al. (2011) add that transformational leadership results in higher levels of productivity, staff morale and job satisfaction. It is also strengthens commitment to the organisation and promotes good citizenship behaviour.

The weakness of transformational theory, however, is that it can lead to followers over-identifying with transformational leaders and becoming too dependent on them (Yukl 1999). Bass and Steidlmeier (1999, p. 208) also caution that "pseudo-transformational leadership" may result in the abuse of power (especially in politics) as it lacks the checks and balances associated with genuine transactional leadership.

5 Conclusion

This chapter explored leadership in the South African context with specific reference to the Afrocentric leadership style known as *ubuntu*. Four leadership theories in the spiritual paradigm were presented, namely, authentic, servant, spiritual and transformational leadership.

In light of the limited information available on *ubuntu* leadership in the South African context and beyond, it is recommended that further research be undertaken in this regard. Research should also be undertaken on blending Afrocentric and Eurocentric leadership styles in order to identify how this combined leadership approach can be implemented in South Africa.[8]

References

Alexander P (2013) Marikana, turning point in South African history. Rev Afr Polit Econ 40 (1):605–619

Avolio BJ, Gardner WL (2005) Authentic leadership development: getting to the root of positive forms of leadership. Leadersh Q 16:315–338

Avolio BJ, Luthans F, Walumba FO (2004) Authentic leadership: theory building for veritable sustained performance. Gallup Leadership Institute, Nebraska

Banerji P, Krishnan VR (2000) Ethical preferences of transformational leaders: an empirical investigation. Leadersh Org Dev J 21(8):405–413

Bass BM (1985) Leadership and performance beyond expectations. Free Press, New York

Bass BM (1990) From transactional to transformational leadership: learning to share the vision. Organ Dyn 18(3):19–31

Bass BM (1998) Transformational leadership: industrial, military and educational impact. Erlbaum, Mahwah

Bass BM, Avolio BJ (eds) (1994) Improving organizational effectiveness through transformational leadership. Sage, Thousand Oaks

Bass BM, Steidlmeier P (1999) Ethics, character and authentic transformational leadership behaviour. Leadersh Q 10(2):181–217

Benefiel M (2005) The second half of the journey: spiritual leadership for organizational transformation. Leadersh Q 16:723–747

Bhorat H, Buthelezi M, Chipkin I, Duma S, Mondi L, Peter C, Qobo M, Swilling M, Friedenstein H (2017) Betrayal of the promise: how South Africa is being stolen. Available http://pari.org.za/wp-content/uploads/2017/05/Betrayal-of-the-Promise-25052017.pdf. Accessed 23 Feb 2018

Booysen L (2001) The duality in South African leadership: Afrocentric or Eurocentric. S Afr J Labour Relat 25(3–4):36–64

Burns JM (1978) Leadership. Harper & Row, New York

Department of Labour (2017) 17th commission for employment equity annual report 2016–2017. www.labour.gov.za/...reports/Commission%20for%20Employment%20Equity%20Re. Accessed 23 Feb 2018

Dhiman S (2017) Leadership and spirituality. In: Marques J, Dhiman S (eds) Leadership today: practices for personal and professional performance, 1st edn. Springer, Switzerland, pp 139–160

---

[8]The author would like to express gratitude to Mrs Camilla Smolicz for language editing and proofreading this chapter.

Dube ZL (2016) The king report on corporate governance in South Africa: an Ubuntu African philosophy analysis. In: Howell KE, Sorour MK (eds) Corporate governance in Africa: assessing implementation and ethical perspectives, 1st edn. Palgrave, London, pp 199–222

Duthely LM (2017) Individual flourishing and spiritual leadership: an approach to ethical leadership. J Leadersh Stud 11(2):66–68

eNCA (2017) All SA's state-owned enterprises captured: deputy president. Available https://www.enca.com/south-africa/watch-all-sas-state-owned-enterprises-captured-deputy-president. Accessed 23 Feb 2018

Fairholm GW (1996) Spiritual leadership: fulfilling whole-self needs at work. Leadersh Org Dev J 19(4):187–193

Fry L (2003) Toward a theory of spiritual leadership. Leadersh Q 14:693–727

Fry L (2008) Spiritual leadership: state-of-the-art and future directions for theory, research and practice. In: Biberman J, Tishman L (eds) Spirituality in business: theory, practice and future directions, 1st edn. Palgrave, New York, pp 106–124

Fry L, Whittington JL (2005) Spiritual leadership as a paradigm for organisation transformation and development. Paper presented at the 65th Annual Meeting of the Academy of Management, Honolulu, Hawaii. 5–10 Aug 2005

Fry L, Vitucci S, Cedillo M (2005) Spiritual leadership and army transformation: theory, measurement and establishing a baseline. Leadersh Q 16(5):835–862

Galbraith JR (1977) Organisation design. Addison-Wesley, Massachusetts

Galperin BL, Alamuri SC (2017) Leadership style and qualities in Africa: a literature review. In: Lituchy TR, Galperin BL, Punnett BJ (eds) LEAD: leadership effectiveness in Africa and the African diaspora, 1st edn. Palgrave, New York, pp 33–43

George B (2003) Authentic leadership: rediscovering the secrets of creating lasting value. Jossey-Bass, San Francisco

Greenleaf RK (1970) The servant as leader. Greenleaf Center for Servant Leadership, Atlanta

Greenleaf RK, Spears LC (1998) The power of servant leadership. Berrett-Koehler, San Francisco

International Monetary Fund (2013) South Africa: 2013 article IV consultation. IMF country report no. 13/303. Available www.imf.org/external/pubs/ft/scr/2013/cr13303.pdf. Accessed 14 Nov 2017

Jamaludin Z, Rahman NMN, Makhbul ZM, Idris F (2011) Do transactional, transformational and spiritual leadership styles distinct? A conceptual insight. J Glob Bus Econ 2(1):73–85

Jaramillo F, Nande B, Varela J (2015) Servant leadership and ethics: a dyadic examination of supervisor behaviours and salesperson perceptions. J Pers Sell Sales Manag 35(2):108–124

Kakabadse NK, Kouzmin A, Kakabadse A (2002) Spirituality and leadership praxis. J Manag Psychol 17(3):165–182

Kiruhi TM (2017) Accelerating Africa's renaissance using contextual holistic leadership development. In: Patterson K, Winston B (eds) Leading an African renaissance: opportunities and challenges, 1st edn. Springer, Basel, pp 115–132

Klenke K (2007) Authentic leadership: a self, leader and spiritual identity perspective. Int J Leadersh Stud 3(1):68–97

Kouzes JM, Pozner BZ (1987) The leadership challenge. Jossey-Bass, San Francisco

Krishnakumar S, Houghton JD, Neck CP, Ellison CN (2015) The "good" and the "bad" of spiritual leadership. J Manag Spiritual Relig 12(1):17–37

Liden RC, Wayne SJ, Liao C, Meuser JD (2014) Servant leadership and serving culture: influence on individual and unit performance. Acad Manag J 57(5):1434–1452

Lungisa A (2017) The Steinhoff debacle – the biggest fraud in SA history. Available https://www.dailymaverick.co.za/opinionista/2017-12-13-the-steinhoff-debacle-the-biggest-fraud-in-sa-history/#.Wo-agVpubIU. Accessed 23 Feb 2018

Luthans F, Avolio BJ (2003) Authentic leadership: a positive developmental approach. In: Cameron KS, Dutton JE, Quinn RE (eds) Positive organizational scholarship: foundations of a new discipline, 1st edn. Berrett-Koehler, San Francisco, pp 241–258

Lutz DW (2009) African *Ubuntu* philosophy and global management. J Bus Ethics 84:313–328

Malunga C (2009) Understanding organizational leadership through Ubuntu. Adonis and Abbey, London

Mangaliso MP, Damane MB (2001) Building competitive advantage from "Ubuntu": management lessons from South Africa. Acad Manag Exec 15(3):23–34

Matolino B, Kwindingwi W (2013) The end of Ubuntu. S Afr J Philos 32(2):197–205

Mokone T (2018) Ramaphosa focuses on the economy: announces SOE clean-up. Available https:// www.timeslive.co.za/politics/2018-02-16-ramaphosa-focuses-on-the-economy-announces-soe-clean-up/. Accessed 23 Feb 2018

Msila V (2015) Ubuntu: shaping the current workplace with (African) wisdom. Knowres, Randburg

Ngunjiri FW (2010) Lessons in spiritual leadership from Kenyan women. J Educ Adm 48(6):755–768

Nkomo SM (2011) A post-colonial and anti-colonial reading of 'African' leadership and management in organization studies: tensions, contradictions and possibilities. Organization 18(3):365–386

Parry KW, Proctor-Thomson SB (2002) Perceived integrity of transformational leaders in organisational settings. J Bus Ethics 35(2):75–96

Pilling D (2017) KPMG urged to act over South Africa Gupta scandal. Available https://www.ft.com/ content/c525699e-a6a5-11e7-ab55-27219df83c99. Accessed 23 Feb 2018

Pruzan P, Pruzan-Mikkelsen K (2007) Leading with wisdom: spiritual-based leadership in business. Greenleaf, Sheffield

Punnett BJ (2017) Africa: open for business. In: Lituchy TR, Galperin BL, Punnett BJ (eds) LEAD: leadership effectiveness in Africa and the African diaspora, 1st edn. Palgrave, New York, pp 1–18

Reave L (2005) Spiritual values and practices related to leadership effectiveness. Leadersh Q 16 (5):655–687

Rodny-Gumede Y, Chasi C (2017) Ubuntu values individuals: an analysis of eulogies of Mandela. J Lit Stud 33(4):106–123

Rothberg RI (2003) The roots of Africa's leadership deficit. Compas J Leadersh 1(1):28–32

Russell RF (2001) The role of values in servant leadership. Leadersh Org Dev J 22(2):76–84

Sendjaya S, Pekerti A (2010) Servant leadership as antecedent of trust in organizations. Leadersh Org Dev J 31(7):643–663

Shrivastava S, Selvarajah C, Meyer D, Dorasamy N (2014) Exploring excellence in leadership perceptions amongst South African managers. Hum Resour Dev Int 17(1):47–66

Siddiqi LA, Chick H, Dibben M (2017) Spirituality and its role in responsible leadership and decision-making. Res Ethical Issues Org 17:63–71

Sinek S (2017) Leaders eat last: why some teams pull together and others don't. Penguin, New York

Spears L (2010) Character and servant leadership: ten characteristics of effective, caring leaders. J Virtues Leadersh 1(1):25–30

Stamp K (1991) Spirituality and environmental education. Aust J Environ Educ 7(1):79–86

Statistics South Africa (2017) Mid-year population estimates of South Africa 2017. Available www.statssa.gov.za/publications/P0302/P03022017.pdf. Accessed 23 Feb 2018

Swanepoel BJ, Erasmus BJ, Schenk HW (2009) South African human resource management. Juta, Cape Town

Transparency International (2015) Corruptions perceptions index 2015. Available https://www.transparency.org/cpi2015. Accessed 23 Feb 2018

Transparency International (2017) Corruptions perceptions index 2017. Available https://www.transparency.org/news/feature/corruption_perceptions_index_2017#table. Accessed 23 Feb 2018

Umraw A (2018) All the damage Jacob Zuma has wrought over his tenure. Available http://www. huffingtonpost.co.za/2018/02/14/all-the-damage-jacob-zuma-has-wrought-over-his-tenure_a_ 23356393/. Accessed 23 Feb 2018

van den Heuvel H (2006) Prophecies and protests: signifiers of Afrocentric management discourse. In: van den Heuvel H, Mangaliso M, van de Bunt L (eds) Prophesies and protests, Ubuntu in global management, 1st edn. Rozenburg & Unisa Press, Amsterdam/Pretoria, pp 1–21

van Dierendonck D (2011) Servant leadership: a review and synthesis. J Manag 37(4):1228–1261

West A (2014) Ubuntu and business ethics: problems, perspectives and prospects. J Bus Ethics 121 (1):47–61

Winston B, Fields D (2015) Seeking and measuring the essential behaviours of servant leadership. Leadersh Org Dev J 36(4):413–434

Woermann M, Engelbrecht S (2017) The Ubuntu challenge to business: from stakeholders to relationholders. J Bus Ethics: 1–18. EJournals *EBSCOhost*. Accessed 23 Feb 2018

World Economic Forum (2017) Global competitiveness report 2017–2018. Available http://www3. weforum.org/docs/GCR2017-2018/05FullReport/TheGlobalCompetitivenessReport2017%E2% 80%932018.pdf. Accessed 23 Feb 2018

Yawson RM (2017) Leadership development in South Africa. In: Ardichvili A, Dirani K (eds) Leadership development in emerging market economies, 1st edn. Palgrave, New York, pp 93–109

Yukl GA (1999) An evaluation of conceptual weaknesses in transformational and charismatic leadership theories. Leadersh Q 10(2):285–305

Yukl GA (2005) Leadership in organisations. Prentice-Hall, Upper Saddle River

Anoosha Makka is a Senior Lecturer in Business Management at the University of Johannesburg, South Africa. She has earned one bachelor and two masters degrees (an MBA in International Business from Leeds University Business School, UK and the other an MRes in Educational Research at the University of London, UK). Anoosha has earned her Ph.D. in Business Management from the University of Johannesburg, South Africa. Her areas of interests are: spirituality and management, spirituality and leadership, CSR and multinational enterprises and mindfulness and business strategy. She currently lectures Strategy and International Management in the Honours and Masters programme at the University of Johannesburg. Prior to joining academia, Anoosha worked for 10 years in the corporate sector and 5 years in the public sector in South Africa.

Still Points: Simplicity in Complex Companies

Calvyn C. du Toit and Christo Lombaard

Abstract Building on a previous contribution on "negative capability" (Lombaard, Leadership as spirituality *en route*: "negative capability" for leadership in diversity, Increasing diversity: loss of control or adaptive identity construction? 103–114; 2017) as a non-directive but actively searching and highly influential (Chia and Holt, Strategy without design: the silent efficacy of indirect action, Cambridge University Press, 2009) style of leadership, this paper investigates aspects of the concept of simplicity and its relation to leadership. As management literature has recognised of late, simplicity as a spiritual orientation to life has deep historical roots and various dimensions. One predictable response to simplicity as orientation points to societies invariable complexity. Hence organisations, companies, and almost all human social systems defy attempts at effortless, simplistic illumination. However, niche building within complex systems allow leaders and managers influence. Such influence either aligns interdependent parts of a complex system or distorts the illusions of cheap harmony within it. Here, in these niches, insights and practices of simplicity cultivated in various spirituality traditions may fruitfully be employed. Such insights and practices might steer groups and entities, always awash in entropy, towards coherence, constrained (i.e., strategically guided) action and consistence. Thus, neither social system's complexity nor their entropy are denied or disingenuously reinterpreted. Rather, they are acknowledged and valued as key operational kernels giving structural stability, strategic progress and conceptual clarity to the whole. In this manner, simplicity contributes not only to the resilience organisations and companies but also to sense-making amongst people involved, namely as a dimension of experiencing fulfilment in life. Examples are provided, and spheres of applicability indicated.

C. C. du Toit (✉)
University of South Africa, Pretoria, South Africa

Department of Dogmatics and Christian Ethics, University of Pretoria, Pretoria, South Africa

C. Lombaard (✉)
University of South Africa, Pretoria, South Africa

© The Author(s) 2019
J. (Kobus) Kok, S. C. van den Heuvel (eds.), *Leading in a VUCA World*,
Contributions to Management Science, https://doi.org/10.1007/978-3-319-98884-9_6

1   The Human Yearning for Simplicity

Complexity has become a contemporary buzzword; one which illuminates something new but also has ancient roots. Its ancient roots open the possibility of drawing
from the past to assist us in the present.

The observation of complexity as an *intense involvedness* characterising our lives,
private and professional, is valid for many people. This complexity could be taken as
a problem, in the sense that we may wish to live in an age in which we have a more
secure sense, a more solid grasp of our social world. However, as the South African
philosopher Danie Goosen (2007) argues, in a notably optimistic tone, the sheer
abundance that life offers us, is precisely one of the characteristics of our modern age.
The interwoven tapestry (a concept here borrowed from Boersma 2011) of our
existence is such that it provides a rich resource for constant wider referentiality,
and does so in almost every dimension of human life. This includes, positively, the
ability of seeking deep personal, social and transcendent significance within one's
work life. In quite a surprising way, Marxist philosophy and Calvinist theology come
very close to one another on the aspect of the significance of work: in work, one finds
fulfilment—not only as duty, but also for meaningful existence.

The above-mentioned transcendent aspects refer, here, also to the complementary
interaction of other fields which had in earlier decades and centuries been deemed
either at odds with one another or fully incompatible. This includes fields such as
theology and the natural sciences. Van Huyssteen (2006), for instance, argues on
evolutionary grounds that religion had always been inherent to the advancement if
our species: without religion, *homo sapiens* would have had less chance of survival.
Religion, like technology and language and other aspects related to being human,
constitutes part of the resources our species could draw on, in order to survive and
thrive.

In the previous century, which may be termed the post-modernist decades, meaning was regarded as an almost impossible feature of humanity's language of life. Mere
traces of significance may have remained, it was argued, but even then such sense was
always beyond our reach (Derrida 1976). In our current, unfolding cultural era of
post-secularism (Lombaard et al. 2018), however, it has been realised that meaning
can indeed be sensed, namely *experienced*. Such experience does not have be viewed
as a-contextual or anti-intellectual (Biernot and Lombaard 2017, pp. 1–12); still, the
meaningfulness reflex of our times lies for more and more people in what they *sense*
as valid or *feel* to be meaningful. What people reflexively *undergo*, what makes them
feel existentially at home, is accepted as compatible with their sense of being and of
wellbeing, without further questioning or validation required.

This age of interrelatedness, also, finds expression in a growing body of writings
on management and spirituality, to which this contribution adds. For instance, in
"'Visionaries . . . psychiatric wards are full of them': religious terms in management
literature," Kessler (2017, pp. 1–9) recently reviewed this trend, to which also one of
the present authors (Lombaard 2017, pp. 103–114) contributed, with "Leadership as
spirituality *en route*: 'negative capability' for leadership in diversity." In many other

instances, some of which are referred to by these two recent studies, concepts from spirituality are drawn on in order to think through aspects of management in particular contexts.

The growth in this management interest in spirituality is telling, not only of our current age of interrelatedness, but also of the sense of meaning yearned for by many people, also in their professional lives. Spirituality is namely often associated with a kind of clarity of mind, a sense of purpose and groundedness, combined with an awareness of emotional rest or lucidity—orientations which unite many aspects of being human under an overarching (consciousness of) wholeness and wholesomeness (wellbeing).

Without diminishing the magnitude of this totality, or whole-person orientation, one may still discern core constitutive elements. Kernels are thus acknowledged: niches in which all, or much, of this totality is concentrated. These kernels carry extraordinary power of influence, for guiding from there the rest of the network which is humanity and institutions, interconnected. This foundational orientation on such kernels may be termed *simplicity*.

Such simplicity should not to be confused with religious fundamentalism, where a kind of "oneness" is found in a single truth which is sourced from a single source (a holy book or perhaps a revelation) to be forced onto everything and everybody, "for their own good" (a term from the Inquisition, often unknowingly appropriated in less-than-democratic moments). That constitutes false simplicity, because it supresses complexity by means of an overarching, "heavy" truth. In an expression attributed variously to several philosophers and theologians: we should fear those who know only one book well. Rather, here, more organisational-architecturally than philosophical-theologically, the most important operational hinges which afford structural integrity, strategic progress, and conceptual clarity to the whole are acknowledged for their essential value. Without these hinges, the doors of process do not just open or close. Importantly, the nature of complexity is neither denied nor disingenuously reinterpreted, as seems to be the case in some pop literature on the matter. The central cores and their hinge functions are, rather, acknowledged for the disproportionally high value that they, in fact, do contribute. Thus understood, *this attribute of simplicity* adds not only to the resilience of organisations and companies, but also improves sense-making among the people involved, namely as a dimension of experiencing fulfilment in life.

Neither should the spiritual impulse, here, be equated with a yearning to escape from reality into a secluded sphere, cut off from the rest of life. Where such an understanding is ascribed to, the metaphor of the monastery in mediaeval times is often employed, and falsely so. Monasteries had namely been communities only minimally separated from other societal spheres, but their strength and success lay precisely therein that they were institutions also established with an explicit orientation to serving their immediate community. Similarly, the current turn to spirituality (an expression from e.g. Kourie 2006, pp. 19–38) in many aspects of society involves precisely a turn *to* the world (that is, to *this* world, rather than to only the inner world or the above world). For precisely this reason, it is not surprising that even an atheist could formulate his spiritual intentions as "to believe in spiritualities that open onto the world, onto other people, onto everything ... to inhabit the universe" (Comte-Sponville 2007, p. 197).

With these two possible misconceptions prevented, our concrete "age of complexity" moreover does not only refer three-dimensionally to the events and structures of society we encounter. Perhaps as the single most noticeable characteristic of our time, the fourth dimension, that of time, comes into play ever more strongly: because of economic, technological and cultural-personal drives, all things go faster—as argued influentially by Rosa in *Social acceleration: a new theory of modernity* (2013). In corporate life, this is seen as dramatically as anywhere else: the quicker things go, paradoxically, the less time there is—to cope, to reflect, to be. To adapt somewhat the ancient philosophical conundrum: speed as an *unstoppable force* is not met by any *unmovable wall*—be the latter workers' rights and/or wellbeing, the limitations of present states of (financial, technical, geographical, etc.) affairs, or laws (as recent corporate scandals have again shown). The quickening of everything seems like the lessening of humanity—an attenuation of being human.

In the busy-ness of business, work's multidimensionality often defies clear grasp, opening the gates, also, to the other kind of corporate scandal, the managerial, in which executive oversight just does not seem possible anymore. This is the void into which rogue stock traders, for instance, drift. The central beams or the key foundation points on which the construction of the business reality rests, have become unknown—often to most employees, at times to all, including management. This runs fully parallel to the phenomenon in spirituality which is, as stated above, associated with "clarity of mind, a sense of purpose and groundedness." On the absence of a *still point* which balances essential aspects of being human, follows disorientation, loss of contact with reality, and ultimately disintegration.

The *still point* is a term from TS Eliot (1943; *Four Quartets: Burnt Norton, II*)—a point where important things (the above-human, the three usual dimensions, and then the dimension of time) converge. Such convergence, not as a passive rest-point, but as an essential point of activity (the latter indicated by the italics added below), carries pivotal weight:

> At the still point of the turning world. Neither flesh nor fleshless;
> Neither from nor towards; at the still point, there the dance is,
> But neither arrest nor movement. And do not call it fixity,
> Where past and future are gathered. Neither movement from nor towards,
> Neither ascent nor decline. *Except for the point, the still point,*
> *There would be no dance, and there is only the dance.*

The influence of the still point as concept runs widely within spirituality literature (e.g. Colacurcio 2015; Martin 2012; Beaudoin 2006; Harpur 2000). Echoing Psalm 46:10 and the dual Greek time concepts of *chronos* (times-as-flow) and *kairos* (time-as-event; Whitstable 2007, p. 23), the idea of a central point or a few such central points that have at once centrifugal and centripetal importance, is a fruitful and enriching analogy to the concept that will be discussed next with relation to Complexity Theory: key niches in complex organisations.

2   The Niche: Key Points in Complex Companies

The managerial-doctrinal lie of full efficiency, drawn from Fordism, implemented without care, and attenuating meaningful work, dominates to a substantial extent to this day. Even if organisations accept, or plan for, wasted time as inevitable, the dream of machine-like corporate productivity continues. Machines, however, ironically also *require* "down time" for maintenance purposes. No matter how hard an efficiency leader may try to limit wasted time, wasted time, nonetheless, persists. Quashed somewhere, it reconfigures in another place. The so-called "effective leader" would, in this line of thinking, pounce on such new wastes and refocus employees; such leadership becomes reactive vigilance rather than reflective guidance. *Chronos* tyrannises *kairos* at every corner where work tries turning the alchemic trick of wrangling efficient work from meaningful work.

Of these, the three metaphoric horsemen of chronic efficiency—speed, information and communication—are the main culprits which spread leaders thin. As speed increases, a useful knotting of information and communication becomes complicated and a scattered fool's errand. Enter, then, the already mentioned contemporary leadership synthesis: complexity and spirituality. Complexity is, however, itself a fuzzy concept, requiring a brief parsing (Loubser 2014, p. 1).

2.1   General Complexity Theory

Seldom, when drawing on complexity theory, do authors frame the complexity they have in mind. Often, this masks deep epistemic commitments; it is therefore important that we play an open hand from the start. With complexity, here, is meant General Complexity and not Restricted Complexity. Restricted Complexity designates some systems as complex and others as complicated, while General Complexity sees all systems as complex at certain levels (Morin 2007, p. 10). Restricted Complexity and General Complexity include various additional internal complications and categorisations not relevant here. For our part, we will keep to General Complexity, with this exception: we borrow from Restricted Complexity the difference between *complicatedness* and *complexity*. Drawing on this distinction we can illuminate how classical models of business are different from newer ones prevalent in information and service industries. *Complexity* suggests that social systems, such as human organisations, differ from complicated mechanistic assemblages, such as aeroplanes, in three important ways. First, the primary attribute of complex systems is *connections*, while *information* mark complicated systems (Cilliers 1998). For instance: although a mobile phone is very complicated, one can often troubleshoot a technical defect of a device with relative certainty; however, tracing a mobile phone maker's loss of market share is much more difficult and much less predictable—it is *complex*. An analysis of the latter must consider the *connections* between multiple factors, and even then, no single answer may crystallise.

The second difference between complicated and complex systems, following from the first, is *memory management*. Stagnant storage, as in a computer hard drive, marks complicatedness, whereas complexity's memory remains *dynamic*, akin to a brain. Like a brain, memory stored through connections give the memory of complexity its vibrancy. Repetition is the key to complexity's retention; "use it or lose it" remains the hallmark of complex recollection (Cilliers 2016). Another quality of complex systems follows from this: a particular *slowness* marks complex systems (Cilliers 2016).

Now, calcified memory means complicated systems can tunnel through their environment with rapidity, with little regard or sensitivity to that environment. Complex systems, however, always remain entangled within their surroundings. Such an entanglement means complex systems remain semi-permeable, even though they may identifiably be outlined. Evaluative processes then become necessary, considering the semi-permeability of complex systems. Memory provides such an outlining discernment. Slow integration of environmental changes through memory procedures gives complex system adaptability, while also making them longer-lasting though pliable. Complicated machines like cars, for example, on the other hand ignore large parts of their environment up until the point at which they break down.

As e Cunha and Rego (2010, pp. 85–86) point out, many an organisation wants leaders to live in the gingerbread house of complexity, but they are at the same time encouraged to eat it with simplicity. Simplicity and complexity, however, are not the strangers one might assume. For instance, "fractals"[1] are complex patterns born from simplicity folding in on itself (Wheatley 2011, p. 273). The seeming paradox, then, is that simplicity and complexity can be partners. However, leaders often confuse complicatedness with complexity. Leadership in such circumstances becomes a question of information volume and speed: a *complicated* problem, and not one of connection—hence a *complexity* problem. As markets drift from an industrial economy to knowledge or service based economies, a leadership cohort that can manage the *volume and complexity* of such information-rich environments, are key (Uhl-Bien et al. 2007, p. 299). Information, here, designates more than the overt and networked data-sea; it also covers the multifaceted intercultural and interdisciplinary meshes stirring underneath the social surface.

Such profound and occluded connections, then, are opportune only if leaders are comfortable with a short-term time expenditure for the sake of long-term creativity, stability and gain. Allowing for short-term wastage does, however, mean cultivating discipline. In brief, for *chronos* to transmute into lasting *kairos*, time and attentiveness, both as marks of ancient spiritualities, are required. Restraint from quick-turnaround strategies is of great importance as leaders find multiple organisational tools at their disposal designed simply to reduce wasted time. Email, online

---

[1]Fractals are complex mathematical sets created by repeating a simple formula. The Mandelbrot set where the function does not diverge when iterated from, is one example of such a set. Every time the function is reiterated, complexity increases, until one arrives at a mindboggling amount of complexity, all through reiterating simplicity (Mandelbrot 2004, pp. 9–26).

collaborative platforms, and infograms are only a few of the tools available to the contemporary managerial reductionist who focusses on efficiency alone. Although such instruments may carry the accurate label of "productivity suites," in an ironic twist, their productivity sometimes undermine effectivity.[2] We will return to this point below to provide some examples.

To summarise: complexity means that the primary task of leadership is no longer to manage information, but rather to link the cluttered multiplicity. Of course, productivity tools are also helpful when searching for notable connections in the brute information haze. Their principal value, however, are as utilities for *administrative leadership*, which manage the bureaucracies and ruling regimes which large organisations bring (Uhl-Bien et al. 2007, p. 307; Uhl-Bien and Marion 2009, pp. 631–650). *Administrative leadership however* manages a different set of complexities than *adaptive leadership*, which focuses on the implementation and inculcation of organisational culture.[3] One area adaptive leadership guides, perhaps without explicitly realising it, is the waste which complexity brings.

Indeed, leaders in any organisation should pause to reconsider "waste management." Systems wading into the stormy waters of complexity produce superfluous communication, which in turn may leave the human actors confused and unfocused. Here, again, this contribution wants to marry complexity, simplicity and spirituality. We do this by considering time wastage, simplicity and the negative capabilities[4] key to *adaptive leadership*. In the conclusion, we describe what *adaptive leadership* can learn from spirituality.

2.2   Niches Within Complex Companies

An often-overlooked part of a complex system is the waste produced. As complexity in systems increase, so waste inevitably increases as well. Were we to forget this important part of complexity, we quickly fall into the trap of pretending that no waste exists. Leaders, then, only manage positive outcomes and are prone to forget about

---

[2]To accede for a moment to the predilection of philosopher *Slavoj Žižek* for using examples from human ablutions in order to illustrate a point: toilets may be ever increasingly *productive* in saving water, up to the point where they are no longer *effective* in clearing away waste. Being ever more productive does not equate to being ever more effective.

[3]Here lie echoes of the two types of thinking identified by Martin Heidegger (1998), summarised recently by le Roux (2016) as follows (italics added): "*rekende denke* en *nadenke. Rekende denke* fokus op beplanning, ordening, sistematisering, regulering, administrasie en organisasie. Alhoewel dié soort denke onontbeerlik is, is dit nie egte of eintlike denke nie. Alles draai egter om *nadenke*, diepdenke, kontemplasie oor ons wêreld en menswees."

[4]"Negative capability" of leaders (cf. Lombaard 2017, pp. 103–114) is, briefly defined, "the capacity to contain one's fear and anxiety when faced with a challenging situation and not respond with a knee-jerk reaction. Rather than 'doing nothing' negative capability is the capacity to wait, observe and enquire into a situation as it unfolds in order to discover an optimal way forward" (Ladkin 2015, p. 214, see also pp. 195–196).

negative management. The best leaders, however, manage waste through discernment as complexity increases (Simpson et al. 2002; on the *modus operandi* of discernment, cf. Waaijman 2013, pp. 13–24; applied to organisational context, cf. Bouckaert 2017, pp. 15–25).

What is meant by waste? As complexity increases, so too do connections increase. Increased communication, however, does not produce the utopia some would suggest (Angelopulo 2014). More links mean greater complexity, but it also means the possibility of needless communication, miscommunication and (where complexity is mistaken for complicatedness) the fear of communication. Waste management does not mean cutting out all possible wastefulness, for as stated above, there will always be some waste in a complex system. If cut off at one junction, it will reconfigure somewhere else. Leaders with deeply reflective capacities ("negative capability," cf. Lombaard 2017, pp. 103–114) seek to understand how to manage such structured, incidental and angst-driven waste.

As businesses increase in complexity, needless communication is equally inevitable. A quick glance at most people's email inbox will confirm how menial administrative tasks can distract one from one's core business. No job advertisements, however, contain the requirement that one answers hundreds if not thousands emails each week, with many of these messages being superfluous. Large corporate meetings offer another example. Such gatherings tend to find yet another PowerPoint masterpiece that should convince all of the poetry of a prosaic detail, which is somehow key to everyone's function in the organisation. Such meetings often inspire participants to take out their own smaller screens . . . ironically, probably to catch up on the just mentioned emails.

Often it is in unstructured work periods, such as the coffee breaks between possibly mediocre speakers, that the really thought-provoking connections are made. Companies like Google, for example, "manages" such creative waste by demanding employees "waste" 10% of their time on creative projects. From Sweden hails a whole culture of such "waste management" called Fika[5]—the now widely adopted extended coffee breaks during a work day. In other words, effective leadership in such instances manages "waste" by making it mandatory, ritualising and simplifying it—a simplification which takes place precisely through ritualisation.

Such a simplification of waste within complexity creates space for niches to grow. Niches, in this instance, are understood as pockets within the dominant system that foster novel ideas (Westley et al. 2011, p. 767). Such niches are, however, also managed. Managers are essential to niches, but their leadership style cannot be

---

[5]"The word *fika* (from *ka-fi*) coffee backwards is a vague concept. It means taking a coffee break, but has other meanings as well. When a boss says, "let's *fika*"—it could be to discuss work, give advice, ask advice, give caution, talk promotion, or just gossip. This is not gossip in the negative sense of slander and malice, but constructive, "coffee-break gossip": exploring ideas, debating rumours and conjecture, considering different views, and finding out about what's going on... What for many is a hidden code in Swedish decision-making processes, is quite apparent in Swedish corporate décor—the coffee break area is the central hub to the Swedish organisation" (Alexander 2010, pp. 38–39).

traditional: they do not lead through express instructions or orders. Such leaders require "negative capabilities": an orientation of listening and facilitation, rather than of being forcefully directive (our traditional associations with a "strong leader"). In other words, a niche leader would not say, "you must" or "you cannot," but instead encourages with something akin to "you can." In a sense, what a niche leader is doing, is through this proclamation of "you can" releasing participants to rearrange the business culture—what would be called in complexity theory its memory. Furthermore, with the liberative "you can," the manager also implicitly makes a covenant to protect niche participants from what could be a negative dominant regime or remnants thereof.

Although in zen-like thinking small things, such as a butterfly, are understood potentially to have a larger effect than a volcano erupting, such change happens from locality to locality within a corporation, and not all at once. The possibility of such larger events from a small occurrence, or the reverse, cannot be guaranteed—which brings us again to memory in complexity systems. Although some niches may namely not be taken up in dominant regimes, they remain useful as contributors to the superfluity of a system; a necessary by-product of meaningful interaction.

We now turn to another type of "time drag" created by complexity. Wasteful niches cannot always be structured. Complex systems draw on connections rather than on calcified hierarchies. Even if one structures superfluous communication in complex systems through niches, emergence means wasteful residues persist. As with structured waste, incidental waste can equally lead to creative solutions. Unlike structured waste, however, resistance is built into incidental waste, and thus requires a different set of (also negative) capabilities of a leader.

Incidental waste requires what Schreiber and Carley (2008, pp. 291–331) call *contextual* and *process* leadership. In brief, contextual leadership realises that knowledge and expertise do not reside in a single person, but are distributed over the whole network. Process leadership remains sensitive to where meaningful connections coalesce, fostering them. Schreiber and Carley, however, add a descriptive modelling of context and process. Such an analysis not only divulges their Restricted Complexity assumptions, but also works against their comment about the quick-paced change and the complexity of organisations today, which produce as pointed out above, incidental waste.

The management of incidental waste through *contextual* and *process* leadership should be seen as parallel to negative capabilities. Analysis and modelling may serve as training ground for contextual and process sensitivities, but no emergent moment waits for an analysis to be complete. Incidental waste, as the name suggests, occurs haphazardly. Thus, context analysis and process facilitation require more than analysis; it entails embodied awareness.

Simpson et al. (2002, pp. 1211–1218) of how *context* and *process* as embodied negative capabilities turn incidental waste into a creative and educational process:

Nicholas is sent to negotiate a deal with Russian and Chinese counterparts for a certain multinational company. As the orchestrator of the deal, Nicholas must deliver swift results. Soon, however, he faces resistance from his compeers. At first,

Nicholas struggles to understand why various parties resist what seems to him to be reasonable demands.

Nicholas's mistake, which he is slow to realise, is his single focus—get the deal done. When working with other cultures, age-groups, or companies, one soon learns, like Nicholas, that one cannot steamroll decisions without collateral damage or encountering cooperative refusal.

Adaptive leadership, here, would mean drawing on the negative capabilities of allowing and acknowledging resistances, namely as a cooperative learning experience. In other words, if Nicholas overpowers his peers with the minutiae of the deal, without acknowledging the resistances and differences represented, he not only misses an educational moment, but he also reduces the resilience of future cooperative calibration.

We have now covered how leadership can leverage structured and incidental waste for learning and creativity. There remains, however, one more category of potential waste that a complex system can produce. The third type of waste in complex systems trains others into its own ways. Thus, whereas structured waste through niches protect the creativity of its members from dominant regimes, and incidental waste require an inculcation of reflective values, *textured waste* trains other human actors, which in companies means employees, to live within complexity.

The difference pointed out earlier between complex systems and complicated systems becomes important here. Social systems such as businesses are complex, and treating them as only complicated is reductive, in many ways. With complicatedness, operational units stand in a mono-modal relationship. In other words, each component is functional to another component. In contrast to this, however, complex interactions are multi-modal: one interaction has multiple effects throughout the system.

Thus, leaders who collapse complexity in mere complicatedness are short-sighted. Often such leaders see employees as means instead of as ends in themselves. The workers must, thus, be tapped for all their worth, and no mistakes on their part are allowed. Quite naturally, such a rigid approach soon spirals into error-shaming. Such a system may appear, at least in the short term, to produce less waste. The long-term price, however, does not justify the short-term thriftiness. The complicated system may seem more "toned," but it also breaks far easier than a complex system. A short-lived complicated view of a team would accordingly make everyone puppets of the leader. Such draconic leadership encourages grovelling instead of appreciation, reluctance instead of willingness, and insipidness instead of ingenuity—the seeds herein of longer-term effects are clear to be seen.

The three described kinds of waste may be employed to guide leaders beyond over-psychologised business babble. Caution against such cheap, short-termed "solutions" is a must for managers who draw on a humanity endeared with traits related to our spirituality. An important difference remains between spiritualties that feign wholeness or existential meaning, and a complexity-model-focused locale of spirituality with integrity. A manipulative use of spirituality directs its canons at the employee. As more integral spirituality and view of humanity transmutes demands like "Work harder!" and "Be loyal to the company!" into questions like "What makes your work meaningful?" and "How can you draw on your inner strengths within difficult projects?," wholeness and wholesomeness are, thus, non-forced and well-facilitated.

In contrast to control sublimated as care, a complex way of approaching spirituality requires not more from the employees, but from managers. Overseers may thus orient themselves to understand the conditions under which a deeper humanity is fostered, risking the valuable possibility of "waste."

3   Whyte Noise

British philosopher-poet David Whyte—no stranger in the world of business, as demonstrated by his 2002 volume *The heart aroused: poetry and the preservation of the soul in the new workplace* (an updated version of his 1994 *The Heart Aroused: Poetry and the Preservation of the Soul in Corporate America*)—illustrated in one of his poems how what may seem intangible or unfathomable, in reality has high concrete impact. In his 1996 poetry collection titled *The House of Belonging* is found:

Working Together
We shape our self
to fit this world
and by the world
are shaped again.
The visible
and the invisible
working together
in common cause,
to produce
the miraculous.
I am thinking of the way
the intangible air
passed at speed
round a shaped wing
easily
holds our weight.
So may we, in this life
trust
to those elements
we have yet to see
or imagine,
and look for the true
shape of our own self,
by forming it well
to the great
intangibles about us.

In this poem, the interactive reciprocity between the concrete and the ethereal, the individual and the group, agency and determinism, what is at hand and what is elusive are balanced, and not only aesthetically. The word *balance* is central here: with each of the elements of these four seeming pairs of opposites, foundationally, the one cannot exist without the other. The elements may seem like opposites, but they are more like two sides of the same coin. Thus we find *interactive reciprocity*— not only as symbiotic concepts, but as a way of living and working: aspects that seem clear and aspects that seem less tangible form a network of understanding which constitutes life.

The same holds true for the key niches within complex organisations discussed above. For the most part, those associated with a business (and the larger the business, the more this is the case) know neither of key niches that impact on them nor how they fulfil for others that role. Not because key niches are in any sense ethereal; their concreteness speak clearly from the huge (potential for) influence they hold. Like "white noise" in shared modular office environments, employees may not be conscious of how niches work, how it affects them or how they contribute to them, but its enabling effect within the workspace is concrete.

One question remains: how to convey to supervisors who are used to traditionally-styled leadership approaches the orientation for adaptive leadership, for structuring waste and for such alternate, more fruitful and more humanly-meaningful leadership roles? For some decades now, religious organisations have tended to borrow "best practices" from corporate governance theories, with questionable results. Perhaps, in today's *complex* environment, organisations would consider the reverse, namely how corporate leadership may benefit from more humane, more spiritually-inclined practices of facilitation. The above thoughts hope to act as a primer for such a future discussion.

Bibliography

Alexander J (2010) How swedes manage. Intermedia Publications, Ingarö
Angelopulo G (2014) Connectivity. Communicatio 40(3):209–222
Beaudoin J (2006) Return to still point: transcending the modern separate self. Trafford Publishing, Victoria
Biernot D, Lombaard C (2017) Religious experience in the current theological discussion and in the church pew. HTS Theol Stud 73(3):1–12
Boersma H (2011) Heavenly participation: the weaving of a sacramental tapestry. William B Eerdmans, Grand Rapids
Bouckaert L (2017) Spiritual discernment as a method of judgment. In: Nandram S, Bindlish P (eds) Managing VUCA through integrative self-management: how to cope with volatility, uncertainty, complexity and ambiguity in organizational behavior. Springer, Halfweg, pp 15–25
Chia R, Holt R (2009) Strategy without design: the silent efficacy of indirect action. Cambridge University Press, Cambridge
Cilliers P (1998) Complexity and postmodernism. Routledge, New York
Cilliers P (2016) Complexity and philosophy: on the importance of a certain slowness. In: Critical complexity. De Gruyter, Boston, pp 211–222

Colacurcio R (2015) Applied spirituality: seeing through the illusion of our separateness, vol 1. Xlibris, Bloomington

Comte-Sponville A (2007) The little book of atheist spirituality. Viking Press, New York

Derrida J (1976) Of grammatology. Johns Hopkins University Press, Baltimore

e Cunha MP, Rego A (2010) Complexity, simplicity, simplexity. Eur Manag J 28(2):85–94

Eliot TS (1943) Four quartets. Harcourt, New York

Goosen D (2007) Die Nihilisme: Notas oor ons Tyd. Praag, Pretoria

Harpur T (2000) Finding the still point: a spiritual response to stress. Northstone Publishing, Kelowna

Heidegger M (1998) Zijn en tijd. Nijmegen, SUN

Kessler V (2017) "Visionaries … psychiatric wards are full of them": religious terms in management literature. Verbum et Ecclesia 38/2:1–9

Kourie C (2006) The 'turn' to spirituality. In: de Villiers P, Kourie C, Lombaard C (eds) The spirit that moves: orientation and issues in spirituality. Acta Theologia Supplementum 8. University of the Free State Press, Bloemfontein, pp 19–38

Ladkin D (2015) Mastering the ethical dimension of organizations: a self-reflective guide to developing ethical astuteness. Edward Elgar Publishing, Cheltenham

Le Roux J (2016) Hoe pas Teologie en Universiteit bymekaar? http://teo.co.za/hoe-pas-teologie-en-universiteit-bymekaar-jurie-le-roux. Accessed 27 Nov 2016

Lombaard C (2017) Leadership as spirituality *en route*: "negative capability" for leadership in diversity. In: Barentsen J, van den Heuvel SC, Kessler V (eds) Increasing diversity: loss of control or adaptive identity construction? Peeters, Leuven, pp 103–114

Lombaard C, Benson IT, Otto E (2018) Faith, Society and the post-secular. Private and Public Religion in Law and Theology. Australian lecture tour presentation at the Notre Dame School of Law, Sydney; the Australian Catholic University, Brisbane; Pilgrim Theological College, Centre for Research in Religion and Social Policy, University of Divinity, Melbourne; and in Adelaide, the School of Ministry, Theology and Culture, Tabor College and the Adelaide Law School of the University of Adelaide, 2018. HTS Theol Stud (forthcoming)

Loubser GM (2014) Engaging Complexity. Verbum et Ecclesia 35(1):1–7. https://doi.org/10.4102/ve.v35i1.1316

Mandelbrot BB (2004) Introduction to papers on quadratic dynamics: a progression from seeing to discovering. In: Fractals and chaos. Springer, New York, pp 9–26

Martin R (2012) Still point: loss, longing and our search for god. Ave Maria Press, Notre Dame

Morin E (2007) Restricted complexity, general complexity. In: Gershenson C, Aerts D, Edmonds B (eds) Worldviews, science and us. World Scientific, Hackensack

Rosa H (2013) Social acceleration: a new theory of modernity. Columbia University Press, New York

Schreiber C, Carley KM (2008) Networked leadership: leading for learning and adaptivity. In: Uhl-Bien M, Marion R (eds) Complexity leadership: conceptual foundations, vol 1. Information Age Publishing, Charlotte, pp 291–331

Simpson PF, French R, Harvey CE (2002) Leadership and negative capability. Hum Relat 55 (10):1209–1226

Uhl-Bien M, Marion R (2009) Complexity leadership in bureaucratic forms of organizing: a meso model. Leadersh Q 20(4):631–650

Uhl-Bien M, Marion R, McKelvey B (2007) Complexity leadership theory: shifting leadership from the industrial age to the knowledge era. Leadersh Q 18(4):298–318

Van Huyssteen W (2006) Alone in the world? Human uniqueness in science and theology. William B. Eerdmans, Grand Rapids

Waaijman K (2013) Discernment – the compass on the high sea of spirituality. Acta Theol 17:13–24

Westley F et al (2011) Tipping toward sustainability: emerging pathways of transformation. AMBIO 40(7):762–780

Wheatley M (2011) Leadership and the new science: discovering order in a chaotic world. Berret-Koehler, San Francisco

Whitstable M (2007) The Eucharistic vision and the spirituality of St Francis of assisi. Gracewing, Leominster
Whyte D (1994) The heart aroused: poetry and the preservation of the soul in corporate America. Doubleday, New York
Whyte D (1996) The house of belonging. Many Rivers Press, Langley
Whyte D (2002) The heart aroused: poetry and the preservation of the soul in the new workplace (rev. ed.). Spiro Press, London

Calvyn C. du Toit is a Ph.D.-candidate in Christian Spirituality at the University of South Africa, and a Research Associate in the Department of Dogmatics and Christian Ethics at the University of Pretoria. His interests include: how Christian Spirituality intersects with cities and technologies, places where religious and philosophical metaphysics intersect, and how complexity studies might assist in building awareness of memory as key to emerging ethics. His most recent publications, in collaboration with Gys Loubser, focus on liturgy as one contemplative space for the ethical integration of technology, and myth as a technic of knowing with a specific focus on Big History.

Christo Lombaard is Research Professor of Christian Spirituality at the University of South Africa, in Pretoria. His research specialisms include Biblical Spirituality, Post-Secularism, Spirituality Theory and Applied Spirituality. He holds two doctorates: a Ph.D. in Communications (North-West University, Potchefstroom, specialising in Religious Communications) and a DD in Theology (University of Pretoria, specialising in Old Testament Studies). He is a South African National Research Foundation rated researcher, and a regular contributor to conferences across the globe. His most accessible publication is *The Old Testament and Christian Spirituality* (Atlanta, Georgia: Society of Biblical Literature, 2012), which was awarded the 2013 Krister Stendahl medal for Bible scholarship by the Graduate Theological Foundation, USA. This volume may be downloaded at http://ivbs.sbl-site.org/uploads/SBL%20book%20%28final%20edit%29.pdf.

How to Integrate Spirituality, Emotions and Rationality in (Group) Decision-Making

Volker Kessler

Abstract This chapter presents a model on decision-making published by Ignatius of Loyola, which integrates spirituality, emotions and rationality. The three different modes are analyzed. Some parallels to modern management advice are shown. The model is then especially applied to group-decision making, which was already done by Ignatius and his "companions of Jesus." I then use the Six Thinking Hats method developed by Edward de Bono, which I adapt in order to integrate the Ignatian model of decision-making.

1 Introduction

According to Luhmann's theory, "organizations can be designated as decision machines" (Nassehi 2005, p. 85). The German sociologist Niklas Luhmann distinguished three types of decision premises within organizations: (1) decision programs, (2) communication structures, and (3) persons (Luhmann 2011, pp. 222–255). In this chapter we deal with the third type, decisions made by persons.

Ignatius of Loyola (1491–1556), the founder of the Jesuits, reflected in his *Spiritual Exercises*, on "decision making." He grew up in the beginning of the Modern Era, during which time more options became available, thus offering opportunities for decisions. Ignatius discovered three modes "in which a sound and good choice may be made" (*Sp.Ex.* 175–177).[1] Here "good choice" is meant

---

[1]Since the Spiritual Exercises are numbered, the format "*Sp.Ex.* No" is commonly used for reference. Re the paragraphs *Sp.Ex.* 175–188, I follow Gallagher's translation, which is based on the Spanish original (Gallagher 2009, pp. 141–144). In the other cases I use the translation given by Louis J. Puhl (Ignatius 1951) spex.ignatianspirituality.com, accessed 12 Dec 2016.

V. Kessler (✉)
Akademie für christliche Führungskräfte, Gummersbach, Germany

GBFE, Oerlinghausen, Germany

Department of Philosophy, Practical and Systematic Theology, University of South Africa, Pretoria, South Africa

© The Author(s) 2019
J. (Kobus) Kok, S. C. van den Heuvel (eds.), *Leading in a VUCA World*,
Contributions to Management Science, https://doi.org/10.1007/978-3-319-98884-9_7

spiritually: what does God want me to do? The first mode in discerning God's will is "immediate intuition," where God moves so clearly "that a devout soul will follow without hesitation." The second mode refers to the emotions, and the third mode to the rationalization of the process.

Ignatius' model is worth studying for several reasons: First, it is a model for spiritual decision-making; it integrates spiritual intuition, emotions and rationality in a coherent and structured way. Secondly, Ignatius' preference for relying on feeling more than on thinking challenges the modern Western preference for thinking (cf. O'Sullivan 1990; Moberg and Calkins 2001, p. 263). Thirdly, in his explanatory notes on the third mode, Ignatius gives some practical advice that can be regarded as a forerunner to modern management techniques of decision-making. Fourthly, "the deliberation of the first fathers," which led to the founding of the Jesuit order, is a model of good practice for group decision-making.

This chapter will investigate the three modes and discuss possible applications. It will also point out similarities) between some of Ignatius' advice and modern management techniques. Finally, I will suggest a way to integrate Ignatius' model into group decision-making.

The focus of this chapter is on the three different modes of decision-making (*Sp.Ex.* 169–189) and their possible applications. This chapter does not deal with spiritual discernment as such, because this is the topic of another chapter.[2]

2   The Three Modes

2.1   The Context

Ignatius, born as Iñigo López de Loyolas, started his spiritual journey in 1521. During his journey he was confronted with existential decisions, such as whether or not to become a priest. All the while, Ignatius was taking notes, recording insights and "movements" of his soul. He began to distribute this spiritual record because he thought it could help others as well (Knauer 2015, p. 11). The greater part of his originally Spanish text was done by 1541. With papal approval, a Latin translation was published in 1548. The Spiritual Exercises have in time become fundamental to the Society of Jesus and far beyond. Even Protestants practice the Spiritual Exercises,[3] despite their battles with the Jesuits since the Reformation. The Spiritual Exercises have also been received outside of theology. For example, Fortemps and Slowinski (2002, p. 109) in their mathematical paper refer to Ignatius' method of decision-making.

---

[2]See the chapter by Patrick Nullens, "From Spirituality to Responsible Leadership: Ignatian Discernment and Theory-U," pp. 185–207.

[3]For example (Kusch 2017, p. 122ff).

A number of books have been written on the Spiritual Exercises, and there are diverse interpretations of this work, the first of which already appeared in the sixteenth century, after the death of Ignatius (Sampaio Costa 2003, p. 75). Modern prominent interpreters are the German Jesuit Karl Rahner and the American Jesuit Jules Toner (1974, 1991) with his monumental work on the Spiritual Exercises.[4] I especially make use of the following publications: the American theologians Christina Astorga (2005) and Timothy M. Gallagher (2009), the Brazilian Jesuit Alfredo Sampaio Costa (2003), the German Jesuits Stefan Kiechle (2008) and Peter Knauer (2015), and the Irish Jesuit Michael J. O'Sullivan (1990).

The Spiritual Exercises have a natural rhythm. Ignatius divided these exercises into four "weeks." This does not necessarily mean calendar weeks but refers rather to phases or movements felt within a person (*Sp.Ex.* 4). The modes of decision-making are part of the second week, which starts with an introduction to making a choice of a way of life (*Sp.Ex.* 169). Two fundamental prerequisites are named there:

1. One has a choice between two alternatives which are both good in themselves (or at least not negative) (*Sp.Ex.* 170)
2. One has a free choice between these two alternatives (*Sp.Ex.* 171–173)

These prerequisites deal with the ethical issue. If one alternative is ethically good and the other one is ethically bad, then there is no need for a further decision-making process. It is evident that the ethically sound one should be chosen. If one introduces the three modes to an audience without mentioning this fundamental prerequisite, it might lead to an application of the Ignatian process, which would not please Ignatius at all.[5] People might say: "Well, I know that this decision violates God's commandments, but I had a good feeling doing it and therefore it must be right."

The second prerequisite is necessary because, according to Ignatius, "there are things that fall under an unchangeable choice, such as the priesthood, marriage, etc" (*Sp.Ex.* 171). "With regard to an unchangeable choice, once it has been made, for instance, by marriage or the priesthood, since it cannot be undone, no further choice is possible," even "if the choice has not been made as it should have been" (*Sp.Ex.* 172). Nowadays, mainstream Protestant theology would regard neither priesthood nor marriage are "unchangeable." Still, there are choices which are unchangeable. One may for instance decide whether one would like to have children or not, but as soon as one has become a father or mother one cannot simply undo this decision. Some choices in life lead to responsibilities one cannot escape. Parents therefore do not have a real choice "between proper care of their children or additional voluntary activities, no matter how good" (Gallagher 2009, p. 17).

These two prerequisites must be fulfilled in order to apply the following three modes of decision-making (*Sp.Ex.* 175–178):

---

[4]See, for instance, the review of both in Astorga (2005, p. 89ff), the review of Rahner's interpretation in Waaijman (2002, p. 485, 497f), and the review of Toner's book in Africa (Mugabe 2005, p. 130).

[5]Unfortunately, Gallagher (2009, p. 141) starts with *Sp.Ex.* 175 and not with *Sp.Ex.* 170.

175	*Three times in which a sound and good choice may be made.*
	The first time is when God our Lord so moves and attracts the will that, without doubting or being able to doubt, the devout soul follows what is shown to it, as St. Paul and St. Matthew did in following Christ our Lord.
176	*The second time* is when sufficient clarity and understanding is received through experience of consolations and desolations, and through experience of discernment of different spirits.
177	*The third time* is one of tranquility. ... I said a "tranquil time," that is, when the soul is not agitated by different spirits, and uses its natural powers freely and tranquilly.
178	If the choice is not made in the first or second time, two ways of making a choice in the third time are given below.

These two ways within the third mode are by (a) weighing the pros and cons of the various options (*Sp.Ex.* 178–183) or by (b) considering the end, what one would like to have chosen if one were facing death and the day of judgment (*Sp.Ex.* 184–189); more on this in Sect. 3.

2.2   Analyzing the Three Modes

Ignatius locates rational reasoning in the third step, which only becomes relevant if neither of the first two steps has led to a decision (*Sp.Ex.* 178). Thus the rational option appears as a last resort (Kiechle 2008, p. 29). In my longstanding participation in church board meetings, I have observed that today usually the opposite order is practiced: one starts with rational discourse (mode 3). If and only if this does not work out, one tries to incorporate intuition and emotions, "the gut feelings."

Gallagher (2009, p. viii) uses the following headings for the three modes[6] of decision-making:

First mode: Clarity beyond doubting
Second mode: An attraction of the heart
Third mode: A preponderance of reasons

The first mode seems to be the most attractive one because "when God gives this gift, no further discussion is necessary" (Gallagher 2009, p. 82) and there is no need to proceed to the other modes (p. 151). However, even in the Bible records, the first mode is not the typical one.[7] There were situations where the person involved knew

---

[6]In the *Spiritual Exercises* Ignatius used the word "time," but in his *Autograph Directory* he used two words, "time" (tiempo) and "mode" (modo). Gallagher (2009, p. 69ff) opts for the word "mode" and so does Kiechle (2008, p. 27ff).

[7]There are many different opinions on the frequency of the first mode. Some take the extreme view that it is quite rare; others say it is exceptional but not too rare; others say it happens quite frequently, is ordinary. The Ignatian texts say nothing to answer this question (Astorga 2005, p. 79). Based on the Bible records of spiritual experiences, I would argue that it does happen now and then, but not as often as mode 2 or mode 3.

immediately what to do; for example, the calling of Matthew is reported in one verse (Mt 9:9): Jesus said to him "Follow me," and Matthew rose and followed him. In many other situations in the Old and the New Testament, though, the believers did not know what to do and asked for guidance from God.

At a first glance, one is tempted to label the three modes as:

1. *Immediate intuition;*
2. *Emotional process;*
3. *Rational reasoning.*

Then Ignatius' advice in *Sp.Ex.* 175–177 could be presented as an algorithm:

Start with step 1, spiritual intuition;
If there is no clear spiritual intuition, go to step 2, listen to your emotions;
If the emotions are not clear, go to step 3, use your mind.

However, we have to be cautious about the connotations of the terms "intuition," "emotion" and "rational." When, for instance, I mentioned the three modes to a German business consultant, his spontaneous reply was: "This is well known in marketing. We make our decision by heart (emotions), and then we use our head to rationalize this decision." Although there is some truth to his reply, this message is different from what Ignatius had in mind. The emotions listed by Ignatius are *spiritual* emotions, i.e. emotions initiated either by the Spirit of God or perhaps by a deceitful spirit (according to the warnings in the New Testament, e.g. 1 Tim. 4:1). Furthermore, Ignatius had a *process* in mind, with its own possible ups and downs. Thus, these sorts of emotions are to be distinguished from the so-called "affect heuristic" (Kahneman 2011) or from the spontaneous consumerist emotion we might have when we see a new car or a new smart phone for the first time.

In his *Spiritual Diary* Ignatius described a process he himself underwent (Gallagher 2009, pp. 83–85). The decision to be made was: should he and his companions live in radical poverty? In the first six days, Ignatius felt more inclined to this option; this inclination he interpreted as "spiritual consolations." Later, more troubling experiences entered the process. Mode 2 does not happen in a moment; it requires at least a few days and may in some cases last several months or even years (p. 92).

It is actually the second mode that requires and involves *discernment of spirits* "for only in this time do we find feelings to be discerned" (Astorga 2005, p. 73). The distinction between consolation and desolation, and openness to both, are crucial to the right application of the second mode. Ignatius understood consolations as "feelings of peace and/or other positive emotions which draw one toward God" (O'Sullivan 1990, p. 5).

Differences between the modes The following is a comparison of the different modes in order to highlight the specific characteristics of each mode.[8]

First, in mode 1 one has absolute clarity; one is not even able to doubt (*Sp.Ex.* 175). Conversely, doubt is typical of mode 2 and mode 3.[9]

Secondly, mode 2 is a process that unfolds gradually, sometimes over several months, whereas in mode 1 it happens suddenly.

Thirdly, in mode 1 the person is totally passive while receiving God's gift of clarity. In modes 2 and 3 the person has to be active, either observing his/her emotions over a long period or by weighing pros and cons. "The second and third modes are made available for human effort and striving in decision-making; the first mode is a pure gift from the freedom of God's love" (Astorga 2005, p. 98).

Fourthly, one's emotional state differs from mode to mode. In mode 1 the person experiences "certitude and deep peace." Gallagher (2009, p. 72) reports the experience of Malia, who considered becoming a nun: "There was a sense of great peace and joy and direction. In fact, it was the only time she had experienced such certitude." In mode 2, (strong) emotions can arise, consolations and desolations. Mode 3 requires a calm heart ("tranquil," *Sp.Ex.* 177), being "indifferent" toward the two alternatives (*Sp.Ex.* 179). "The third mode is bereft of consolation and desolation, indicating that a different kind of discourse is used to make it distinct from the second and first" (Astorga 2005, p. 87). Gallagher (2009, p. 106) therefore recommends: "If the heart is not calm—is not in a 'tranquil time'—the third mode of discernment should not be attempted."

In spite of the apparently different focuses of modes 2 and 3 it should be noted that mode 2 cannot be reduced to pure affections, nor can mode 3 be reduced to pure rationality. "It is necessary to get beyond a false contrast between a second 'time', arising from affectivity, and a third that is more rational. In different ways, heart and head are present in both these 'times'" (Sampaio Costa 2003, p. 87). Mode 2 requires *observing* and *evaluating* the emotions. "Such tasks require substantial amounts of

---

[8]Some Ignatian experts deny any real distinction between the modes. Rahner, for instance, regards the three modes as constituting one identical kind of choice. Astorga (2005, p. 89) summarizes his position: "All Ignatian discernment of God's will, in his view, is ultimately a second-mode discernment, with the first mode an extraordinary phenomenon whose practical importance is secondary. The third mode is a deficient modality ... the less perfect mode of the second." According to Rahner the third mode is contained in the second mode.

Rahner's interpretation is criticized by Toner (1991) who argues that "Ignatius presented each mode as fully distinct from each other and that each is able to function autonomously as adequate in itself" (Astorga 2005, p. 91). Sampaio Costa (2003) gives further evidence for this position by investigating the Jesuit documents of the sixteenth century. Sampaio especially follows the directory written by Polanco, Ignatius' former secretary, which he regards as "one of the most balanced and illuminating documents we possess illustrating Ignatius' thought" (p. 77). From his investigation Sampaio concludes: "It is important to be able to distinguish what is characteristic of each of the 'times', and to understand their fundamental rationales" (p. 87). I follow this interpretation and will therefore list some differences between the modes.

[9]It is disputed in the Jesuit tradition whether mode 2 or mode 3 will lead to greater certainty (Sampaio Costa 2003, p. 86).

Table 1 Similarities and differences between the three modes

	Mode 1	Mode 2	Mode 3
Time period	One moment	At least several days	At least several hours
Activity of the person	Passive, receiving	Active, observing emotions	Active, weighing pros & cons
Human reasoning?	No	Affective reasoning	Discursive reasoning
Heart activity	100% certitude, deep peace	Strong emotions	Must be tranquil
Doubts	No doubting possible	Doubts throughout the process	No 100% clarity
Spiritual?	Yes	Yes	Yes

cognitive processing and rational judgment" (O'Sullivan 1990, p. 38). Astorga (2005, p. 98) uses the terms "affective reasoning," "judgment of the heart" for the second mode and "discursive reasoning," "operations of the brain" for the third mode.

Modes 2 and 3—sequential or parallel? The advice in *Sp.Ex.* 176 and 177 reads as if they were to be done sequentially, i.e. mode 3 is only be used if mode 2 does not lead to a decision. Thus the third mode appears as something like a last resort. "You only go to the third 'time' if the second has not brought sufficient light" (Sampaio Costa 2003, p. 85). However, as pointed out by Gallagher (2009, p. 156f), Ignatius himself employed mode 2 and mode 3 in parallel when he had to decide about radical poverty for his society. Thus, although Ignatius presents mode 3 more as a last resort, in practice both modes can be done in parallel. This procedure is also suggested by Kiechle on the basis of his and other people's experiences. Both modes should complement and confirm each other.[10]

All modes are spiritual The distinctions between the modes could give the impression that only the first mode is a truly spiritual one. On the contrary, Ignatius was convinced that God would speak through the consolations and desolations in mode 2 and that God would guide the person's will in mode 3 (*Sp.Ex.* 180). The decisive criterion when evaluating the different options in mode 3 remains a spiritual one: which option will "be more for the glory and praise of God our Lord and the salvation of my soul" (*Sp.Ex.* 179)? This is called the Magis principle, i.e., the greater glory principle (Toner 1991, p. 173; Astorga 2005, p. 87). Moreover, both ways of deliberating in the third mode close with bringing the election before God so that He may confirm the choice (*Sp.Ex.* 183, 188). Thus the whole decision-making process, including all three modes, can be regarded as a "spirituality of choice" (Byron 2008, p. 59) (Table 1).

---

[10]"Die Erfahrung jedoch zeigt, dass das Entscheiden meist in einer Verbindung aus zweiter und dritter Weise des Wählens zustande kommt. Man prüft Gefühlsregungen *und* Argumente. ... Beide Ebenen sollten sich ergänzen, ineinander fließen und sich gegenseitig *bestätigen*." (Kiechle 2008, p. 29).

No priority Since all modes are spiritual, one should not consider any mode to be better than any other. The wording in *Sp.Ex.* 178 might create the impression that Ignatius saw the third mode as deficient compared to the other two. Thus it is interesting to note that some of the first-generation followers in the sixteenth century saw the third mode as the safest one (Sampaio Costa 2003, p. 86).[11] An investigation of the different Ignatian texts on this topic leads Sampaio to the conclusion: "Ignatius had confidence that all three 'times' could lead to a good and healthy Election, and that consequently we were in no position to decide which way was better or safer" (p. 86). As a practical application, Sampaio teaches: "It is not for us to decide which 'time' of Election is be used: we need to accept with humility the 'time' that God chooses to give us" (p. 88).

3 Forerunner of Modern Management Advice

Some suggestions within the two ways of making a choice in mode 3 sound like a herald of modern management advice. For instance, Fortemps and Slowinski (2002, p. 109) explicitly refer to the first way of mode 3. I will point out five more similarities.[12]

First, Ignatius taught that "the first point is to place before myself the thing about which I wish to make a choice" (*Sp.Ex.* 178). Fredmund Malik, one of the most influential management thinkers in German-speaking countries, lists seven steps for a decision-making process (Malik 2006, p. 211). His first step is almost identical to Ignatius' first point: "the precise determination of the problem." One might argue that this first step is just common sense, but Malik (p. 203) explicitly warns against the illusion of assuming that the problem is clearly defined. Ignatius and Malik agree that the first step in a decision-making process must be the identification of the problem.

Secondly, in *Sp.Ex.* 181 it is suggested that one should list the advantages or benefits and the disadvantages or dangers if one accepts an opportunity, and then should list the advantages and disadvantages if one does not accept this opportunity. By looking at these lists one should notice to "which alternative reason inclines more" (*Sp.Ex.* 182). In a modern manner of representation this leads to the following 2×2-matrix, which could be a typical flipchart presentation in a modern group meeting (Table 2).

The scientists Figuiera et al. (2005, p. xii) appreciate Ignatius' "approach of explicitly taking into account the pros and cons of a plurality of points of view." They regard his method as an early example of Multiple Criteria Decision Analysis.

---

[11]Probably this shift occurred because of the fear of the Inquisition which suppressed any trace of illuminism (Sampaio Costa 2003, pp. 76, 78).

[12]O'Sullivan (1990, pp. 28–34) lists some parallels to modern psychological models of decision making.

Table 2 Illustration of *Sp.Ex.* 181

	Accept the opportunity	Reject the opportunity
Advantages	1. ... 2. ... 3. ...	1. ... 2. ... 3. ...
Disadvantages	1. ... 2. ... 3. ...	1. ... 2. ... 3. ...

Thirdly, *Sp.Ex.* 185 reads like advice from a modern book on self-management:

185   ... To look at a man whom I have never seen or known, and, desiring all perfection for him, consider what I would tell him to do and choose for the greater glory of God our Lord and the greater perfection of his soul; and doing myself the same, follow the rule that I propose.

In modern terminology, this is often called "self-coaching" (Dießner 1999), i.e. a person treats himself or herself as a person to be coached.

Fourthly, in the second way of deliberating, Ignatius suggests looking at the alternatives "as if I were at the point of death, what procedure and norm of action I would then wish to have followed in making the present choice" (*Sp.Ex.* 186). This suggestion is similar to advice from modern management books on imagining one's own funeral: what would the people say about me? (Knoblauch et al. 2007, p. 138). Some authors suggest even writing one's own funeral speech in order to find out: what do I want the people to think about me upon my death? Answering this question will give direction to one's life.

Fifthly, Ignatius distinguished between times for emotion, for reason, for pros and for cons. This is also the basic idea of the "Six Thinking Hats," which will be discussed in the next section.

4   Group Decision-Making

4.1   The Deliberation of the First Fathers

The well-known "deliberation of the first fathers"[13] offers a good example of how to apply these principles to group decision-making. In the year 1539 Ignatius and his other nine "companions of Jesus" lived in Rome to serve the Pope. The Pope then decided to send them into different parts of the world. Thus several questions were on the table: Shall we continue our companionship? If yes, shall we found a religious order? They were all searching for God's will on these questions, but they had diverse opinions (Toner 1974, p. 185). So they took 3 months to find the answers. In

---

[13]"Beratung der ersten Väter" (Waldmüller 2008, p. 13).

this process they developed new methods for consulting and decision-making within a group. During the day they would pray and think about the decision to be made. At night they would meet for consultation, during which each of them shared his thoughts and feelings about the decision (p. 187). Thus they came to the decision to continue their companionship.

> The first question now answered and a decision made, we came to another question more difficult and no less worthy of consideration and forethought. All of us had already pronounced a vow of perpetual chastity and a vow of poverty ... The question was this: would it be advantageous to pronounce a third vow, namely, of obedience to someone from among us ...? (p. 194)

But even after many days the uncertainty about this question remained. The companions then reflected on their initial method of consultation and modified it. In particular, they implemented a procedure for separating the discussions on pros and cons. On one evening they would collect all the reasons *against* a vow of obedience. "On the next day we argued for the opposite side of the question" (p. 202). The advantage of this method is that the group focuses on one aspect at a time, i.e. they are all looking at the pros and later they are all looking at the cons. This is actually the essential feature of the De Bono method, explained below.

From today's perspective the method of the first fathers was very innovative. But it only became popular after their Superior General Pedro Arrupe, in 1971, encouraged the Society of Jesus to apply this method of the first fathers. It was seen as a good method to work out the participation processes initiated in Vatican Council II.

4.2   Modern Adaptations of This Method Within the Ignation Tradition

The American Jesuit Byron (2008, pp. 64–75) has developed a method of group decision-making, which is rooted in the deliberation of the first fathers.[14] Byron stresses the importance of discernment. As a method he suggests having different times and phases. For example, he would start with laying out the relevant facts; then he would give room for people to express their emotions towards this decision (p. 65). "Before any major decision is made, the decider, in the Jesuit tradition, will want to ask how he or she feels when considering the options" (p. 73). Participants should try to evaluate the source of these feelings: is it the Spirit of God or evil spirits? Then there must be room for listening to God. "This calls for more than just a quick invocation or prayer of petition; the decision-making process has to be laced with a quest for God's will" (p. 66). Byron (p. 68) also suggests separating the discussion of positive and negative arguments, i.e. the pros and cons.

In the Swiss culture, participation and democracy are important values. The Swiss Catholic Waldmüller (2008, pp. 13–17) refers to the deliberation of the first fathers

---

[14] An adapted extract is available on the Internet Byron (n.d), "A method of group decision making."

as a good model for participatory processes: "*Gemeinsam* entscheiden" (deciding *together*). He applies it to the retreat of a church board (pp. 59–70).

4.3 Six Thinking Hats

The idea of structuring the group discussion into different times for facts, emotions, pros and cons is also part of the "Six Thinking Hats," a method published in 1985 by the Maltese author Edward de Bono (1990). As far as I know de Bono never refers to the deliberation of the early fathers as a source. Instead he refers to the Japanese meeting culture (pp. 44–46).

The basic idea of the Six Thinking Hats is that there are six modes of thinking, and at a given time the whole group is in the same thinking mode. This avoids the so-called "spaghetti thinking," when for instance one person is thinking about the benefits of an idea, a second person is considering the facts, and a third person is dealing with emotions.

The six thinking hats are distinguished as follows (pp. 31–32):

- The blue hat is concerned with organizing and controlling the thinking process.
- The white hat is concerned with objective facts and figures
- The red hat gives room for the emotions
- The green hat indicates creativity, brain-storming for new ideas.
- The yellow hat reminds us of the sun and looks at the positive aspects of a new idea.
- The dark hat reminds us of the rain and looks at the negative aspects of a new idea.

A possible structure for a group discussion could be as follows:

1. Start with the blue hat, agreeing on the target and the structure of the meeting;
2. White hat: collect the necessary facts
3. If there are strong emotions about the decision, use the red hat to elicit feelings (in a structured manner);
4. Green hat: look for new ideas and collect them;
5. Blue hat: select some ideas which are to be analyzed during this meeting;
6. Yellow hat: list the advantages of the first idea;
7. Black hat: list the disadvantages of the first idea;
8. Yellow hat: list the advantages of the second idea;
9. Black hat: list the disadvantages of the second idea (and so forth . . .);
10. Blue hat: Make a decision

Of course, many variations are possible. Sometimes one has to switch to the red hat more often; sometimes it may be necessary to go back to the white hat, because one discovers during the process that important facts are lacking.

Some ideas from the Six Thinking Hats can already be discovered in Ignatius' teaching on decision-making and in the deliberation of the first fathers: separation between emotions (red hat) and facts (white hat), separation between listing pros (yellow hat) and listing cons (black hat).

Since 2003, I have been teaching a modified de Bono method. There I use the word "mode/phase" instead of "hat," because the latter is sometimes perceived as childish. This modified method consists of eight modes. I have included a "purple mode," reserved for spiritual aspects, a time for prayer and listening to God's voice. (Furthermore, I split the blue mode into two modes, one for chairing the meeting, one for making the final decision.) This method requires time, at least 90 min, and it requires several flipcharts and pin boards to visualize the facts, the ideas, the pros and cons etc. The participants always appreciate the clarity of the process because the rationale for the final decision becomes very transparent. Many of my students then apply this method in their contexts and later write a report on it. These reports give good evidence for the usefulness of this method.

After this study on Ignatius, I would definitely stress the purple mode in order to give more room for listening to God and spiritual guidance. For example, I would apply the purple mode quite early, to provide room for spontaneous spiritual intuition (mode 1 in Ignatius' model). Perhaps God will speak so clearly to everyone in the group that doubting becomes impossible. If this is not the case, I would then use the red mode after the purple mode so that the participants can share the feelings they had during the purple mode (mode 2). Then I would go on with the more rational modes, i.e. facts (white), pros (yellow) and cons (black). After making the final decision, one could again switch to the purple mode in order to ask God for his confirmation. This would constitute the final point in the Ignatian mode 3 (*Sp.Ex.* 183, 188).

5 Conclusions

In his *Spiritual Exercises* Ignatius presented a holistic model for decision-making that integrates spirituality, intuition, emotions and reasoning. An important advantage of his method is the separation between the different modes. The "deliberation of the first fathers" provides a good model for how to apply this method in group decision-making. Their approach has some parallels to de Bono's "Six Thinking Hats." Integrating the Ignatian ideas into the Six Thinking Hats will lead to a method of group decision-making that leaves sufficient room for spirituality, emotions and reasoning. Thus, it will strengthen the nexus between leadership, spirituality and discernment within an organization.

Bibliography

Astorga C (2005) Ignatian discernment: a critical contemporary reading for Christian decision making. Horizons 32(1):72–99

Byron WJ (2008) Sharing the Ignatian spirit with friends and colleagues. Loyola, Chicago

Byron WJ (n.d.) A method of group decision making. Making Good Decisions. http://www.ignationspirituality.com. Accessed 24 Aug 2016

De Bono E (1990) Six thinking hats. Penguin, London

Figuiera J, Greco S, Ehrgott M (eds) (2005) Multiple criteria decision analysis. State of the art surveys. Springer, Boston

Fortemps P, Slowinski R (2002) A graded quadrivalent logic for preference modelling: Loyola-like approach. Fuzzy Optim Decis Making 1(1):93–111

Dießner H (1999) Praxiskurs Selbst-coaching. Junfermann, Paderborn

Gallagher TM (2009) Discerning the will of god: an Ignatian guide to Christian decision making. Crossroad, New York

Ignatius of Loyola (1951) Spiritual exercises. Translated by Louis J. Puhl, 1951. http://spex.ignatianspirituality.com. Accessed 12 Dec 2016

Kahneman D (2011) Thinking, fast and slow. Farrat, Straus and Giroux, New York

Kiechle S (2008) Sich entscheiden. Ignatianische Impulse, Echter, Würzburg

Knauer P (ed) (2015) Ignatius of Loyola Geistliche Übungen. Nach dem spanischen Autograph übersetzt von Peter Knauer. Echter Würzburg

Knoblauch J, Hüger J, Mockler M (2007) Dem Leben Richtung geben, 5th edn. Campus, Frankfurt

Kusch A (2017) Entscheiden im Hören auf Gott. Vandenhoeck & Ruprecht, Göttingen

Luhmann N (2011) Organisation und Entscheidung, 3rd edn. Verlag für Sozialwissenschaften, Wiesbaden

Malik F (2006) Führen, Leisten. Leben. Wirksames Management für eine neue Zeit. Campus, Frankfurt

Moberg DJ, Calkins M (2001) Reflection in business ethics: insights from St. Ignatius' spiritual exercises. J Bus Ethics 33(3):257–270

Mugabe M (2005) Teaching on the discernment of God's will. Reading Jules Toner's Discerning God's will, Ignatius of Loyola's teaching on Christian decision making. In: Kiti PC (ed) Dynamics of the spiritual exercises. African perspectives. Paulines Publ. Africa, Nairobi, pp 129–154

Nassehi A (2005) Organizations as decision machines: Niklas Luhmann's theory of organized social systems. Sociol Rev 53(s1):178–191

O'Sullivan MJ (1990) Trust your feelings, but use your head. Discernment and the psychology of decision making. Stud Spirituality Jesuits 22(4):1–41

Sampaio Costa A (2003) The 'Times' of Ignatian election: the wisdom of the directories. Way 42 (4):73–88

Toner JJ (1974) The deliberation that started the Jesuits. A commentary on the deliberation primorum partum. Stud Spirituality Jesuits VI(4):179–213

Toner JJ (1991) Discerning god's will: Ignatius of Loyola's teaching on Christian decision making. Institute of Jesuit Sources, St. Louis, St. Louis

Waaijman K (2002) Spirituality: forms, foundations, methods. Peeters, Leuven

Waldmüller B (2008) Gemeinsam entscheiden. Ignatianische Impulse. Echter, Würzburg

Volker Kessler   (Ph.D.; D.Th.), holds a Ph.D. in Mathematics, University of Cologne, and a D.Th. in Practical Theology, University of South Africa. For 12 years he worked for the Siemens Company, Munich, as a researcher in cryptography. Since 1998 he is director of the Akademie für christliche Führungskräfte (www.acf.de) and since 2002 he is also dean of the GBFE (www. gbfe.org). In 2012 he was appointed as professor extraordinarius at the Department of Philosophy, Practical and Systematic Theology, University of South Africa. He teaches (Christian) Leadership at different universities and also does professional trainings for business companies and NPOs worldwide. He authored many academic articles and many books, among others the bestsellers *Kritisieren ohne zu verletzen* and *Die Machtfalle*, which were re-printed several times and also translated in five other languages.

Embodied Realism as Interpretive Framework for Spirituality, Discernment and Leadership

Jack Barentsen

Abstract There appear to be two ways of knowing, the one driven by scientific evidence, the other by practice and intuition. The concept of embodiment brings these two ways together. Embodiment is now widely studied, as in the disciplines of nursing (Benner), cultural psychology (Voestermans and Verheggen), and cognitive psychology (Lakoff and Johnson). These developments point to the philosophical perspective of "embodied realism," as initially outlined by Merleau-Ponty and Dooyeweerd. Our human system of knowing is directed and limited by the way our bodies enable us to interface with the world we inhabit. It requires dialogue to transcend our individuality, without arriving at universals, as research on cognitive bias by Kahneman has demonstrated. The centrality of embodiment, then, implies that spirituality is not in opposition to material concerns, but rather that embodiment is foundational for spirituality, as evident in religious ritual practices as well as in the Christian confession of the Incarnation. Moreover, spiritual discernment takes shape, not as a disembodied practice of meditation to access the divine, but as embodied seeing, listening and feeling in a collective effort to understand God's call in the middle of one's rapidly changing world. Finally, leadership can be seen as the embodied performance of providing a safe holding environment amidst liminality in order to enable people to cope, to be transformed and to develop a new sense of personal and social identity.

J. Barentsen (✉)
Department of Practical Theology, Evangelische Theologische Faculteit, Leuven, Belgium

Institute of Leadership and Social Ethics, Evangelische Theologische Faculteit, Leuven, Belgium

Faculty of Theology, North-West University, Potchefstroom, South Africa
e-mail: jack.barentsen@etf.edu

J. (Kobus) Kok, S. C. van den Heuvel (eds.), *Leading in a VUCA World*,
Contributions to Management Science, https://doi.org/10.1007/978-3-319-98884-9_8

1   Introduction

Evidence-based strategies seem to be the answer to everything, from evidence-based
coaching, evidence-based nursing, evidence-based horsemanship, evidence-based
psychotherapy, evidence-based investing and evidence-based vitamins.[1] A particular example of this trend was when my daughter explained that after changing her
baby's diaper, she needed to take his temperature. If the temperature was below
36.5°C she should put on his cap; if it was above 37.5°C, he didn't need a cap and
probably not even socks. This lasted only 2 weeks. Such a technical approach might
provide the needed personal security; it was after all her first baby. It might also teach
her to distrust her developing motherly instincts. Or perhaps she learned to discover
her motherly instincts through this more technical approach rather than through
networking with family and friends. Such a priority of "evidence-based baby care"
probably spawned reactions in the opposite direction, namely "natural" baby care,
natural pregnancies, hypno-birthing and a veritable "baby wrap consultant" to assist
in carrying your baby more "naturally" against your body instead of in highly
mechanized baby carriages.[2] Presumably, mothers are encouraged to trust nature's
care processes, including their own intuitions about baby care, where "nature"
becomes a rather romanticized opposite of "science."

   This phenomenon juxtaposes two ways of knowledge, one through evidence-
based approaches supported by scientific research, the other through more intuitive
ways of knowing, sometimes labeled as "natural" or "spiritual." These might be
viewed as complementary, as when my daughter would be helped to develop her
motherly intuitions by first relying on evidence-based strategies, but they might also
be conceived of as competitive or in opposition, proposing that the scientific way
(like taking the temperature) is better than the intuitive or spiritual way (following
motherly instincts), or vice versa.

   The same duality can be recognized in the domain of spirituality and religion.
Theological scholarship has always devoted considerable effort to historical and
empirical research in a search for theological knowledge. Since the Enlightenment
this search has become dominated by a strictly critical and a-religious approach to
historical and empirical religious claims. For more liberal theologies, this often
meant applying a hermeneutic of suspicion to any historical or empirical aspect
before they would be counted as trustworthy evidence of theological knowledge
(Gill et al. 2013, pp. 47–50). In my field of Practical Theology, this approach has
sometimes led to purely descriptive approaches, bracketing any claims about transcendental realities (van der Ven 1998), or to forms of pastoral care that seemed to
have more in common with psychotherapy than with spiritual guidance and
"shepherding" (Graham 2002, chapter 3). Based on the understanding that

---

[1] An internet search for "evidence-based" on amazon.com yielded these and other results for recent
book titles with this phrase in the title.
[2] From http://natural-baby-care.nl/, carrying the baby in a wrap-around cloth or sling
("babydraagdoekconsulent").

transcendental phenomena cannot properly be the subject of scientific inquiry, these theological approaches have principally not counted transcendental claims and spiritual experiences as theological knowledge, leaving them to the realms of personal faith or spiritual practice.

More conservative approaches have taken a different approach to what counts as theological knowledge. This form of theological inquiry often operates from a mode of "faith seeking understanding," adopting a hermeneutic of faith. Again, in my field of Practical Theology, this has led to renewed attention to a normative engagement with faith praxis as a primary avenue of scholarly research. Browning, De Ruijter and Osmer each advocate in their own way a normative assessment of practice as part of the practical theological enterprise (Browning 1991; Ruijter 2005; Osmer 2008). More recently, some practical theologians have argued that spiritual experiences or divine encounters are an explicit concern or even a center of practical theological reflection (Root 2014; Cartledge 2015; Iyadurai 2015). These conservative approaches have been more generous in counting a wider range of evidences as theological knowledge.

The debate between the liberal and conservative approaches has changed with the onset of postliberalism in a postmodern climate (Michener 2013, 2016). Nevertheless, these approaches all use certain scientific criteria for establishing what counts as evidence for religious phenomena and theological knowledge. They may differ on the criteria, but they seek to operate as an evidence-based scholarly discipline.

However, what counts as theological knowledge in the setting of a faith community or in Christian praxis may be quite different. Religious leaders, for instance, deliberately speak and lead in such a way, that people connect their lives with God or the divine. They aim to lead believers in experiencing divine presence and recognizing God's work in and among them. In many churches, testimonies of miraculous religious experiences or dramatically transformed lives count as key evidences for God's presence and transforming work. There is usually little concern over whether these testimonies can stand the test of scholarly scrutiny and interpretation, and in some quarters such scholarly scrutiny is even rejected as potentially harmful. On a more scholarly level, some discussions of missional leadership focus on discerning the Spirit's work and joining God in serving the neighborhood (Roxburgh 2015; Vlaardingerbroek 2011). In these instances, knowledge of divine presence and activity is quite intuitive and experiential. There seems to be quite a gap between the logic and the evidences of formal, academic theology, and the evidences as experientially encountered in vital faith communities that are intuitively accepted as true.

This raises a question of discernment: "How does one discern God's presence and the Spirit's work?" It seems that there are two different sources for theological knowledge, the one scholarly, the other more intuitive. Should we privilege scientific theological knowledge, for instance in its historical-critical form, over the non-critical faith experience of believers? Or should we prioritize spiritual knowledge arising from faith praxis over against rigorous scholarly theological analysis? It does not seem sufficient to identify one area with objective fact-finding, concerned with "truth," and the other area with subjective meaning making and identity construction. In fact, both areas are concerned with facts, and both areas contribute a sense of meaning, belonging and identity for its practitioners. What is needed is a way to bring these two sources of knowledge together.

This chapter proposes that the concept of "embodiment" links these areas of knowledge to each other.[3] Moreover, the chapter will argue that "embodiment" provides a fruitful tool for deepening our understanding of spirituality, and the practices of discernment and of leadership. The research question can now be phrased as: "How can the concept of 'embodiment' link scientific and spiritual streams of knowledge together, and what does this imply for spirituality, discernment and leadership?" This question will be answered, first by an exposition of the concept of embodiment as illustrated by its reception in various disciplines. Second, the paper will present a more philosophical case for "embodied realism" as a primary way to bridge the scholarly and experiential dimensions of our knowledge. Third, the paper will analyze the implications of embodied realism for our understanding of spirituality, discernment, and leadership.

2 The Turn Towards the Body: Embodiment

The relationship between emotions and the body on the one hand, and knowledge and reasoning on the other, has been a subject of intense study over the last decades in disciplines such as sociology, cultural theory, and cognitive psychology. Gabriel Ignatow presents an overview of how disembodied theories of knowledge have been changed by what he calls "the bodily turn." Newer theories consider the body as location of symbols and meaning, so that knowledge is foundationally embodied (Ignatow 2007). Taking a closer look at these developments, I focus on embodiment in nursing, cultural psychology and then cognitive psychology.

2.1 Embodiment in Nursing

The concept of "embodiment" is perhaps easiest understood by considering briefly the discipline of nursing, which is both a highly demanding medical and technical profession, as well as a professional practice that is strongly focused on embodied intuitions and interventions. By this, I mean more than simply that nurses care for hurting bodies. Dr. Patricia Benner, herself a nurse, academic and educator, is known in her field for her study of learning and skill acquisition throughout a nurse's career (Benner 2000, 2001). Much of this learning is technical or medical skill, but a good nurse also learns to recognize early warning signs of conditions like shock or embolism and to detect slight variations in patient color and demeanor. This

---

[3]See similar arguments in Bass et al. (2016), especially in Chapter 6 on the eclipsing of embodied knowledge and Chapter 7 on recovering it within practical theology.

represents a fuzzy recognition process with varying degrees of vagueness that develops throughout a nurse's career and becomes an embodied, non-rational process of discernment that is vital for patients in their time of need. Referring to philosopher Merleau-Ponty's work on embodiment, she writes that "the sensing, skilful body allows one to negotiate and flourish in the context of the inevitable human condition of ambiguity." She continues, with reference to Dreyfus' model of skills acquisition: "Through our embodied capacities of perception we are able to notice subtle, imprecise changes, recognize family resemblances and comparisons with past whole clinical situations" (Benner 2000, p. 7).

Benner argues that medical and experiential or embodied knowledge are complementary, both necessary for developing excellence in nursing (Benner 2000, pp. 6–10). These bodies of knowledge are developed differently, the first through the study of theories and books, the second through reflective practice which develops increasingly trustworthy levels of intuition. She compares these bodies of knowledge with the Aristotelian distinction between *techne* as knowledge about production and goal accomplishment, and *phronesis*, discernment rooted in embodied and experiential knowing that requires moral agency. Moreover, she critiques the overreliance on rationalization in some forms of nursing practice with a critique of Cartesian mind/body dualism that is continued in the Kantian reason/moral agency dualism. Instead, she sides with Merleau-Ponty who views the body as mediating our access to the world (instead of through "pure reason"). Dualistic approaches that posit a rational subject "I" over against an external objective world imply a commitment to the correspondence theory of truth; instead, Benner is committed to "a socially constituted, embodied view of agency" with "socially intelligible terms and intersubjective knowledge that reflect skilful comportment and knowing" (Benner 2000, pp. 11–12). Such intuitive practices develop and improve within a community of practice that upholds particular standards of excellence (Wenger et al. 2013).

Benner's arguments are intended to correct an overreliance on formal, medical knowledge by pointing out the importance of more tacit forms of knowledge that are learned through repeated experiences. As Merleau-Ponty points out, such experiences over time become like layers of sediment in the body, so that nurses are able to respond adequately and quickly to situations that are similar to previous experiences. In other words, repeated experience allows rational medial knowledge to become part of a bodily repertoire of nursing interventions that requires only minimal reflection in order to be effective. This is not so much to argue that *techne* is gradually overshadowed by *phronesis*, since unfamiliar cases are typically discussed in interdisciplinary consultations, so that doctors and nurses alike determine (and learn) how to act in this new situation. Rather, I would interpret Benner as arguing that both forms of knowledge are necessary and integrated in how nurses interact with patients and situations *as embodied practitioners*.

This brief consideration of nursing demonstrates how various forms of knowledge converge as embodied knowledge, how they develop through experience and within community, and how they lead to intuitive assessments as part of a discernment process for providing excellent care.

2.2 Embodiment in Cultural Psychology

Benner's views that nursing practice is nurtured and developed in a community of practice move us towards the concept of embodiment in the discipline of cultural psychology. Voestermans & Verheggen, educators at Dutch universities in this discipline, argue that culture should not be treated as the cause or explanation of behavior, as if "culture" explains that certain people behave in a particular fashion. "Culture does not do anything, only people act." That is, agency should not be attributed to culture but to people (Voestermans and Verheggen 2007, pp. 18–20; English translation 2013). They ask how it is possible that we intuitively recognize particular behaviors as belonging to our culture. To explain this, they speak about the body not primarily as a collection of complex biological and biochemical processes, but as the visible and practiced body that is the carrier of social norms and meanings. Through being raised in a particular family and within intrinsic social groups, our bodies are trained, literally "in-corporated," into the life of the group. These "intrinsic social groups" consist of social groups that are held together by a mixture of rules, conventions and arrangements that together constitute the culture of the group. Furthermore, they also demonstrate how our emotions, as the primary embodied responses that set us in motion, and our feelings as an imaginative or conceptual layer between these primary responses and our environment, are trained and shaped within our cultural group (Voestermans and Verheggen 2007, pp. 65–90). Culture then, is "created" by our bodies, trained and sensitized in particular social groups, where norms are internalized and embodied in a pre-reflexive process of socialization and inculturation. This creates a community of skilled practitioners, whose bodily interactions will be intuitively recognized as fitting (or not so fitting) participation in the group's culture. Such a group cannot be joined simply by taking the multicultural integration exam that governments typically require of immigrants; however, one can grow into it, gradually developing more of the sensitivities and patterns of behavior of the host culture (Voestermans and Verheggen 2007, p. 95).

Thus, while our considerations of nursing discussed the norms and practice, i.e. the culture of a particular community of nursing practice, cultural psychology broadens the scope from professional to larger cultural groupings that share certain cultural identity markers. In both cases, it is clear that the groups being discussed are socially constructed, and that our bodies are primary and visible carriers of this social construction. Our bodies are shaped and sensitized through daily practice in a particular culture, or, we should say, in particular cultures (plural), since we may identify with varying groups depending on what is relevant in a given social context.

2.3 Embodiment in Cognitive Psychology

When we deal with nursing or culture, we can readily admit that embodiment is an important if not crucial dimension for understanding these disciplines, because it is fairly intuitive that nursing and culture are not only and perhaps not even primarily cognitive constructs that we adopt through deliberate rational processes. Yet, when we speak of "scientific knowledge" in comparison with or even in contrast to "experiential knowledge," it may appear as if "scientific knowledge" relates to the rational and universal, while "experiential knowledge" is merely local or personal, and intuitive. However, a consideration of embodiment within the discipline of cognitive psychology helps us realize that even scientific knowledge is an embodied form of knowledge.

Lakoff and Johnson, well known within theological studies for their study on metaphor (Lakoff and Johnson 1980), extend their work in their magnum opus, *Philosophy in the Flesh* (Lakoff and Johnson 1999). In an ambitious project, they aim to revise 2000 years of philosophy, since it is based on the allegedly mistaken assumption that reason is independent of our body and senses, and that there are such things as universal rational principles. Instead, they propose that: "The mind is inherently embodied. Thought is mostly unconscious. Abstract concepts are largely metaphorical" (Lakoff and Johnson 1999, p. 3). These propositions are the three major findings of cognitive science, according to Lakoff and Johnson.

Their argument begins with the recognition that our mind is embodied not merely in the trivial sense that our brains are part of our physical bodies. Rather, based on our particular sensory-motor system, our bodies have distinct ways of perceiving, moving and applying force, which are the source of spatial and causal categories in our conceptual system. Our concepts are particular neural patterns in our brain, originating in embodied experiences, that allow us to categorize our concepts and to reason about them. Human categories are typically conceptualized as prototypes with rather general or fuzzy elements, but we think of them as sharply distinct, envisioned spatially as containers. The container schema turns out to be a very basic schema of perception and reasoning. Lakoff and Johnson describe how spatial concepts depend on our capacity for vision, how the logic of causality depends on our capacity for bodily movement, and how the aspectual structure of actions and events depends on how bodily movements create a perspective of "before" and "after," generating a basic concept of time (Lakoff and Johnson 1999, pp. 18–39).

Next, in their analysis of abstract thinking, Lakoff and Johnson explain that primary metaphors are based on our bodily capacities. A few primary metaphors are (Lakoff and Johnson 1999, pp. 50–54):

- Affection is warmth
- Important is big
- Happy is up
- Intimacy is closeness
- Bad is stinky
- Difficulties are burdens, etc.[4]

Abstractions are then created by combining primary metaphors into complex metaphors, such as the "a purposeful life is a journey" metaphor (Lakoff and

---

[4]These primary metaphors are not arbitrary social constructs, but have been shown to be consistent across many different languages and cultures in the world.

Johnson 1999, p. 61ff). In the remainder of their book, they describe how time, events, causes, the mind, the self and even morality all consist of one or more complex metaphors that can be analyzed in terms of primary metaphors, that in turn are grounded in our bodily constitution and capacities. Thus, they make a case that even abstract thinking is, in its very roots, embodied thinking, in the sense that our bodies intimately and subconsciously shape our categories and direct our thinking.

They describe from the perspective of cognitive psychology what Merleau-Ponty said much earlier, that our bodies mediate our access to the world (quoted above). Lakoff and Johnson add to that perspective that our bodies also shape, empower and limit the ways in which we talk and reason about the world. That is, embodiment not only affects a particular kind of knowledge (i.e. tacit knowledge in a well trained nurse), but all our knowledge of whatever kind is essentially embodied.

3   The Case for Embodied Realism

Lakoff and Johnson stand within a philosophical tradition that seeks to overcome dualistic thinking in terms of the subject/object divide that permeates much of Western philosophical thinking. Merleau-Ponty's phenomenology of perception is a key resource for understanding this movement. Although Merleau-Ponty was a careful student of Husserl and Heidegger, he differs from them in significant ways. Husserl's phenomenology was built on the assumed distinction between the inner and the outer, between the immanent sphere of consciousness with its "ideal essences," and the transcendental sphere of external, "real" objects. Merleau-Ponty rejects this subject-object duality by focusing on the body, which is neither object in the world, nor ideal essence in our consciousness, but our way of being in and interacting with the world (Merleau-Ponty 1978, pp. xv–xvi; Carman 1999, pp. 205–207). Moreover, in contrast to Heidegger, Merleau-Ponty does not focus on the abstract nature of Being, but rather on understanding concrete human experience in all its immediacy (Thomas 2005). For instance, in discussing intentionality he describes how an infant does not watch its hand but focuses on the object it attempts to grab. The members of our body are only known in their functional value and their coordination (Merleau-Ponty 1978, p. 174). Also, a door does not appear in the world as an object with an ideal essence, but as a passageway through which to enter or exit a room, with which we engage automatically and intuitively. The door has significance, constructed through social interaction, as I inhabit the world, quite apart from my critical reflection on the "nature" or "function" of the door. It is through and with our bodies, as well as in interaction with others that we perceive and interact with the world. Our bodies give us a world (Scharen 2015, pp. 52–54).

Merleau-Ponty argues that we are, as it were, thrown into the world bodily (cf. Heidegger's "Being-in-the-world"). With our bodies we "get" a world. Our bodies participate in the world and it is through this embodied participation that the "I" constitutes itself as consciousness in relation to the world and itself. We do not *have* a body as we might have a house, but we *are* bodies (Carman 1999, pp. 218–221; Scharen 2015, pp. 54–55). Merleau-Ponty drew heavily on empirical psychology (Gestalt psychology, psychoanalysis), neuroscience, physiology and Saussurian linguistics for his phenomenology (Toadvine 2016), and offers a perspective that Lakoff and Johnson build on with their research in cognitive psychology. Although their *Metaphors We Live By* does not refer to Merleau-Ponty, they credit him for his pioneering work on "flesh" in their *Philosophy in the Flesh* (Lakoff and Johnson 1999, pp. xi, 97).

The lesser-known Dutch philosopher Herman Dooyeweerd, a contemporary of Merleau-Ponty, shares the focus on concrete human experience, which he labels as the non-theoretical attitude of naïve experience (Dooyeweerd 1999, p. 12). Although Dooyeweerd speaks of the subject-object relationship, he denies that the human subject can describe qualities to objects as if they pertain to the metaphysical realm of being. These qualities cannot be abstracted from the experience of an object within a subject-object relationship. For instance, the color red has no meaningful metaphysical conception as a quality of flowers, but is only grasped as an aspect of daily human experiences of a flower.

> The subject-object relations of naïve experience are, consequently, fundamentally different from the antithetical relations which characterized the theoretical attitude of thought. Subject and object are certainly distinguished in the non-theoretical attitude, but they are never opposed to each other. Rather, they are conceived in an unbreakable coherence. In other words, naïve experience leaves the integral structural coherence of our experiential horizon intact (Dooyeweerd 1999, p. 14).

Dooyeweerd investigates the relationship between our naïve, pretheoretical experience and the antithetical theoretical attitude. This relationship cannot be founded by further abstractions of theoretical thought, but must find its origin in "the inner nature of the human *I*" by way of critical self-reflection (Dooyeweerd 1999, pp. 15–23). This *I* can only find its source and meaning in "the central religious relation between the human ego and God, in whose image man was created," which is at the same time intimately connected to the selfhood of "our fellow-men." Dooyeweerd speaks of this religious center as the human heart, which is the integrative point of human experience and knowledge (Eikema Hommes 1982, pp. 112–121). He began work on a philosophical anthropology, including theoretical reflections about the various modal aspects of the human body, such as the physical-chemical and biotic functions and its "act-structure," but unfortunately this work was never finished, and it would take us too far afield for this chapter. Suffice to say that Dooyeweerd aimed to offer a Christian critique of theoretical thought that transcended the usual conceptions of the subject-object relationship, and identified the integrative center of human experience not as much in the human body, as Merleau-Ponty, but in the human heart with its religious orientation towards its Origin.

For readers of Kahneman, *Thinking, Fast and Slow*, it may appear strange that a prereflective attitude towards concrete human experiences is valued as the primary mode of being and knowing by these twentieth century philosophers, over against more reflective, theoretical reasoning and its strategies of knowing. In his research on cognitive bias, Kahneman and his team found that intuitive reasoning, based on impressions, feelings and fuzzy categories (stereotypes) provides solutions to puzzles in our daily human experience (Kahneman 2011). Experts may render intuitive judgments that are quite accurate, even without much rational processing, based on years of training and experience in their field, as Kahneman and his team carefully documented. However, in difficult puzzles where the answers are not immediately apparent, sometimes our intuitions hide our ignorance and mask the uncertainty in the world as they point confidently to solutions that may prove false upon further rational examination, even though we are not aware of that. The intuitive level of thinking is labeled "System 1" and is compared with "System 2" that is effortful, more deliberate, rational thinking which kicks in when we encounter new situations in which we need to learn or when we discover that our System 1 conclusion may not be adequate. Kahneman's theory seems to suggest, then, that reflective or theoretical thinking is more reliable then intuitive thinking, and should have priority—which appears to contradict the priority that both Merleau-Ponty and Dooyeweerd gave to embodied human experience and non-theoretical thinking.

This is, however, not the case. Rather, System 1 and System 2 thinking are both aspects of human experience and embodiment. First, note that Kahneman himself observes that much intuitive thinking, especially by experts in a matter related to their field of expertise, is very helpful and often on target, even if not perfect. This parallels descriptions in the first section of this paper of the intuitive and embodied judgments of well-trained and experienced nurses and reflects precisely the present argument on embodiment. Second, Kahneman acknowledges that though he deals with cognitive bias, this is not meant to imply that intuitive reasoning as a whole malfunctions—only that occasionally it is inadequate (Kahneman et al. 2011). Rather, System 2 supplements System 1 thinking when an error is detected or when rule-based reasoning is required. It is unclear precisely how System 1 and System 2 thinking are related, or how they could be mapped biologically and psychologically, but clearly System 2 receives input from System 1 thinking (Shleifer 2012).[5] That is, both systems are rooted in human experiences and in embodied knowing. Third, in a popularizing article, Kahneman et al.'s theory describe how difficult it is for corporate decision makers to detect their own System 1 biases, and that they should use their System 2 rational thinking to ask questions and uncover biases in the reasoning of their subordinates in the proposals they bring to them (Kahneman et al. 2011, pp. 50–52). This presents a communicative strategy for overcoming the limitations of our embodied knowledge. Through dialogue and interaction, multiple perspectives are brought to bear on a particular situation or proposal, resulting in the detection and correction of cognitive biases. This strategy links System 1 and System 2 thinking from a variety of actors, so that the pool of embodied knowledge is enlarged, and personal limitations are transcended. This implicitly reflects Herbert Simon's theory of bounded rationality (Simon 1972),

---

[5]Note that Lakoff and Johnson's *Philosophy in the Flesh* is an extended discussion of this psychological mapping.

which acknowledges that people rarely have all the relevant knowledge or insight at their disposal in making choices. Their rationality is bounded:

> Rational behavior in the real world is as much determined by the 'inner environment' of people's minds, both their memory contents and their processes, as by the 'outer environment' of the world on which they act, and which acts on them (Simon 2000, p. 25).

In this way, Kahneman's theory about cognitive bias and System 1/2 thinking confirms rather than contradicts the emphasis on concrete human experience and embodied knowledge that we found in Merleau-Ponty and Dooyeweerd.

We now return to Lakoff and Johnson's proposal to label their account of how reason and reality interact as "embodied realism." This view accepts the "assumption that the material world exists and ... [that] we can function successfully in it," as well as the assumption that we have direct access to the world (no mind-body gap). However, it denies that there is one and only one correct description of the world, since our knowledge is based upon the nature of our bodies and brains, and upon our particular location in the world. This is a form of relativism that is connected to the nature of our bodies and the way our bodies enable us to see, to know and to be carriers of practices and cultures. Yet, it also remains connected to the real world to which we all have direct access (Lakoff and Johnson 1999, pp. 94–96).

Our entire human knowledge system is so finely attuned to the world we live in that, even though we cannot access that reality without our cultural and physical conditioning, nevertheless we generally succeed well in functioning in this world. We not only have access to reality, but we also succeed in communicating about it with others who are similarly equipped. The various groups within which we find ourselves influence our habits, our movements (literally) and our communicative patterns, giving rise to communities of practice and, on a larger scale, to cultural groups. All of this is implied in the argument that we live in and know the world in the form of embodied realism.

Embodied realism has fascinating implications for how we think about concrete experiences in all their diversity. For "pure reason," diversity is simply the contingent part of our experience that needs to be "peeled away" to attain universal knowledge. For practical reason, however, diversity is precisely the stuff from which we discover and attain knowledge. Such embodied forms of knowledge require relationships, interaction and dialogue to share personal embodied knowledge, to make it explicit or public. This can be done informally through common manipulation of the material world, and through conversation and dialogue, or more formally through community negotiations and scientific research. Dialogue within relationships is needed to supplement our own embodied knowledge with that of others, which turns it into what Merleau-Ponty described as public, intersubjective knowledge which is open to debate and questioning (Benner 2000, p. 8). It is thus, by interacting with the specific and particular, by being confronted with diversity, that we gain a broader appreciation of certain phenomena, without necessarily ever reaching an absolute level of universal knowledge. Embodied knowledge, then, also implies a process of community formation and development, which implicates ethical qualities like patience, openness, respect and perseverance in the process of knowledge formation.

4 The Importance of the Concept of Embodiment for Spirituality, Discernment and Leadership

After describing the "turn towards the body" in various disciplines, and making a case for embodied realism, the next task is to apply this perspective to the key dimensions of this book: spirituality, discernment and leadership.

4.1 Embodiment as Foundational Mode of Spirituality

Much of theological thinking seems unaware of the embodied nature of our religious knowledge. That is not surprising, since theological scholarship often focuses on texts and the history of ideas. Moreover, there is a tendency to reduplicate the mind-body dualism by focusing religious knowledge on that which is spiritual, in contrast to the body as a material dimension of faith. However, since time immemorial, Christian beliefs and practices are inherently linked to embodiment. Sacred objects point to spiritual presence or have spiritual significance. Rituals involve the body in patterns of behavior as a way of interacting with or presencing the divine. Christians regularly celebrate how the Spirit transforms people's lives and gives gifts in ways that can be bodily experienced. Christians confess that God entered human experience in bodily fashion through the Incarnation. Finally, as followers of Christ, Christians typically picture themselves as incarnating Christ anew in their own lives and experiences. Thus, embodiment is an essential part of Christian thinking and practice, even if much of academic theology has been disembodied, perhaps even disincarnated.[6]

Yet, following the dictum that all theology is born of practice, theology is called to be empirically responsible. If theology is not in some significant sense a theology of embodied practice, it is not theology at all since it has lost sight of the primary mode for living theologically, that is, through incarnating Christ daily in our bodily existence. What is needed is a theological account of embodied spirituality as basic feature of Christian living.

Lived religion and religious embodiment have surfaced recently as important themes in the study of religion. First, sociologist of religion McGuire demonstrates that the long centuries of reformation, from 1300 to 1700, led to the historical marginalization of embodied practice. During this period, people's everyday religious practices, especially where they involved the body and the emotions, were

---

[6]See Bass et al. (2016) for an extended discussion of the historical background and current issues on embodiment.

devalued, while religion was defined more institutionally and theology more cognitively. In short, "church" became organized religion which was seen as a "creed" or "faith" (McGuire 2007, pp. 188–190).[7] Much of the modern sociology of religion betrays this institutional bias, surveying people's institutional attachments as markers of religiosity. Instead, McGuire argues, sociologists should be more sensitive to daily spiritual practices, which may or may not reflect the institutional practices that people are connected to:

> Lived religion is constituted by the practices by which people remember, share, enact, adapt, and create the 'stories' out of which they live. And it is constituted through the practices by which people turn these 'stories' into everyday action. Ordinary material existence—especially the human body—is the very stuff of these meaningful practices. Religious and spiritual practices—even interior ones, such as contemplation—involve people's bodies and emotions, as well as their minds and spirits (McGuire 2007, pp. 197–198).[8]

Second, psychologist of religion Luhrman investigated extensively how people learn to recognize God's voice. She found that newcomers in certain charismatic faith communities went through a process whereby they learned to distinguish an internal mental process as not their own, but God's. Trained in psychoanalysis, Luhrman uses the technical term "dissociation" to describe this practice, which refers to the phenomenon that individuals may dissociate themselves from some of their own mental processes as if they came from another, external source (Luhrmann 2006). Although Luhrman does not self-identify as a Christian, and makes no claim about the reality of the transcendent that her respondents claim to experience, she describes a psychological and even physiological learning process that leads some individuals to conclude that they hear the voice of God in their own mind and body. Even if this process is experienced differently in other types of faith communities, this case study shows that there is an embodied process involved in learning to know God.[9]

As a theologian, I would argue that God has created a world with human beings in such a way that they are intimately attuned to this world and to one another. It is a material and embodied world that serves as stage for humans and God to know each other and to interact.[10] Our entire human system of perceiving and knowing is attuned not only to knowing the world and the other, but also to knowing God. Moreover, God entered upon this creaturely stage to literally flesh out the bridge between the human and the divine. The gospel writers testify that it is in the life and death of Jesus of Nazareth, that is, in his embodied experience, that we observe and experience God the Father: "Have I been with you so long, and you still do not know me, Philip? Whoever has seen me has seen the Father" (John 14:9, ESV).

---

[7]For the extended argument, see her monograph, McGuire (2008).

[8]James K. Smith makes a similar argument in developing a theological anthropology in which human beings are portrayed as essentially liturgical beings (Smith 2009, 2016).

[9]See her full length study on this phenomenon in Luhrmann (2012).

[10]For a theological argument about human nature as essentially relational, based on an understanding of the Trinity, see Grenz (2001).

Knowing God, then, comes through our human capacities for knowledge, as described by the perspective of embodied realism. This implies, first, that spirituality is essentially an embodied phenomenon, like all other human forms of being and knowledge. God created an embodied system of knowing people, God and the world. Thus, knowing God does not take place without our bodies for we simply have no language and no way of being other than embodied.

Second, embodied spirituality is essentially a relational phenomenon. Our embodied, metaphorical mode of thinking, and our embodied discernment in communities of practice assume a social and ecological system in which we live. Humans cannot function otherwise. It is only in relational fashion that our embodied intuitions and knowledge become shared, open for discussion and dissent, whether this knowledge concerns the physical or the spiritual world. Knowing God and knowing the world is to participate in the material, social and spiritual world by sharing with and relating to other participants. Although we dare not minimize the impact of divine-human encounters,[11] humans need the context of a community of practice to begin to interpret the significance of these encounters and to translate them into knowledge of God.[12]

4.2 Discernment as Embodied and Extended Cognition

This conception of spirituality as an embodied and relational form of knowing God has significant consequences for processes of discernment. Usually, Christian discernment is conceived of as a process of finding the will or call of God. It involves a sense of vision, seeing "the essence of the matter," that cannot always be achieved through "reasoned discourse" and "business-as-usual meetings" (Morris and Olsen 2012, pp. 3–8). It also involves close listening for God's call and guidance, sometimes discerned through impressions and emotions. It may take some solitude, but it always needs the Christian community in an effort to determine how to act faithfully. Contemporary Christian practices of discernment stand in a tradition of two millennia and more (Morris and Olsen 2012; Liebert 2015). These aspects indicate an awareness of the embodied nature of discernment, with its attention for vision, hearing and feeling in the context of relationships, dialogue and commitment.

Moreover, discernment should be distinguished from decision-making, since it focuses on the processes of "seeing," "listening" and dialogue more than on the final result, the decision. Of course, discernment usually leads to a decision. However, rational decision-making processes, with their focus on rational techniques like a

[11]Root offers an extended argument that divine-human encounters should be moved to the center of practical theological investigation (Root 2014), and Iyadurai argues that "religious experience" should be a prime focus in studying conversion, next to psychological and sociological aspects (Iyadurai 2015).
[12]For a further theological assessment of embodied spirituality, see Murphy 2006, Brown & Strawn 2012).

SWOT analysis, seem to presuppose that a group of people deliberating an issue see through a single lens, and should find the one right solution (Berlinger and Tumblin 2004). Discernment, instead, acknowledges our embodied situatedness, which leads to multiple competing and incomplete perspectives on the issue that cannot always be resolved through rational methods. Realizing that there may be more than one "right" solution, or even that several "right" solutions might yield significantly different results, discernment helps weigh the alternatives while listening closely to intuitive and more rational assessments in the group. Thus, discernment processes may complement more rational techniques for decision-making (Kaak et al. 2013).

Thus, the current literature on discernment already demonstrates various features of embodiment. The perspective of embodied realism adds more depth. Our bodies are the interface with the world, so we think in terms of sensing, motor movements and action—this even applies to more abstract domains of theoretical thinking (Brown and Strawn 2017, p. 414). Long years of socializing in social and cultural groups shaped our habits, our movements (literally), and our communicative patterns, giving rise to communities of practice. Thus, our bodies are shaped socially and culturally, often in a prereflective attitude. Discernment, then, is the interactional and communicative process that takes place within a community of practice to reflect on these habits, actions and communication patterns, and to bring to the surface that which is relevant but hidden, in order to determine the best course of action for a particular situation.

Such a process of discernment is helpful in overcoming the limitations of our situated embodiment. Asking reflective questions about our habits and (intuitive) practices—reminiscent of Kahneman's research—surfaces both practical knowledge as well as cognitive bias. Communication enables multiple actors together to overcome the limitations of their personal embeddedness in concrete situations by becoming aware of and compensating for our biases, and by enlarging the shared pool of experiences and knowledge. The aim is not to produce universal knowledge—which is beyond our reach—but to develop a broader social consensus suitable for a particular time, place and culture.

Newer theories of extended cognition enhance our understanding of this process (Teske 2013). In this communal discernment process, a dynamic occurs that makes it difficult to decide from which person the solution originated. Cognition is not limited to what happens within one individual (embodied cognition), but can be extended across a larger collective or group with a common identity. As individuals become incorporated in the group and participate in mutual problem solving, an encompassing identity is created that is larger than the sum of the individual identities involved (Brown and Strawn 2017, p. 416). Individual cognitions are not simply exchanged, but as it were networked throughout the group, like computers might be networked to create a larger, more powerful processing unit. Thus, solutions produced in such a group by this mechanism of extended cognition cannot be simply attributed to one of the minds, but to the aggregate whole.

The perspective of embodied realism, then, portrays discernment as a somewhat fuzzy and intuitive, but also rational and relational process, based on our incorporation in a social group and our embodied participation in a particular context.

Rational, emotional and intuitive concerns each play their role in corporately constructing or adapting the interpretation of the situation in such a way that one or more courses of action open up for the group, and that a choice can be made for what appears at that moment to be most optimal.

Embodiment further implies that discernment is not primarily framed by institutional concerns and societal values, except in so far as they represent the social setting within which one participates. It also implies that authority figures have no special claim to discern better than other participants, except in so far as the authority figure is incorporated in the group in which the discernment process takes places. Discernment is a fuzzy and relational process in which all participants have an important role to play in contributing from their perspective as embodied participants.

4.3 Embodiment, Discernment and Leadership

Embodiment is beginning to impact leadership studies as well. In 2013, the journal *Leadership* published a special issue on "The materiality of leadership," creating a space for discussions on how embodiment effects the relationship between leaders and followers, on the gestures and aesthetics of leadership, on the effect of (material) place on leadership, on the embodiment of emotions and passion in (abusive) leadership, and on gender and transgressive bodies in leadership. In the same year, the International Leadership Association published a volume in its Building Leadership Bridges series on *The Embodiment of Leadership* (Melina et al. 2013). The introduction explains that great leaders are memorialized by statues, celebrating their bodies. These statues present a visible reminder that the leader is different from followers even in their bodies. Also, leadership involves a particular bodily performance of various tasks, and is experienced as embodied authority, control and/or empowerment (Melina et al. 2013, pp. xiii–xvi). To advance our argument about embodied spirituality and discernment, the question arises, How does embodied discernment affect our views of leadership?

In his contribution to *The Embodiment of Leadership*, David Holzmer offers a three-part conceptual framework to reconstruct leadership as embodied leadership in a context of rapid and continual change. The first concept, "liminality," focuses on experiences of "disruption and upheaval" which leaders can use "as an important and necessary condition ... to construct new narratives" (Holzmer 2013, pp. 49–50). This liminal period is not simply an insecure transition period through which leaders quickly navigate their constituency; rather, the leader is able to bear and hold fast this liminal insecurity in order to lead others in re-habituating their practices and remolding their identity. In Heifetz' theory of adaptive leadership, this is comparable to the holding environment that leaders are to create as they strive to harness and resolve conflict (Heifetz et al. 2009, pp. 149–157). The description of this "holding environment" indicates various physical and embodied features, so that people are, as it were, physically held together in one place to face the conflict or liminality. Liminality, then, is not a moment of cognitive confusion but a period of disorientation and change that is felt and experienced viscerally as well as cognitively. The holding space likewise is an embodied experience of being held together, not so much by force (although that might occur as well), but by factors such as persuasion, encouragement and empowerment by adaptive leaders to resist the tendencies that drive the group apart in order to find a constructive way forward. Although Heifetz et al. did not use the terminology of embodiment, Holzmer's analysis makes the embodied dimension manifest.

Holzmer's second concept, "performance," relates to how leaders present themselves and their body, and how their embodied leadership is experienced by subordinates. Typically, leaders embodied control and domination in a long history of leadership practice, but now leaders are called upon to openly acknowledge the hierarchical norms they embodied and to experiment with new forms of embodied leadership to create new ways of common action (Holzmer 2013, pp. 53–56). It has long been maintained that domination and hierarchy are simply rational ways of controlling and leading others, in a way that leaves the role of leadership bodies unexplored. However, in many ways, leadership is the performance of a particular social role in which social and cultural norms are enacted. This performance is more than just rational, and relates to the leader's presence and interaction with his or her followers. Occasionally, a leader's presence can be intensely felt in bodily fashion (Ladkin 2013, pp. 321–22). Thus, the way a leader uses his or her body is an essential part of leadership performance, highlighting the embodied nature of leadership.

Finally, Holzmer's third concept, "dialogue," focuses on the leaders' task to create "communicative space between people" so that the "transformative process" of dialogue can yield fruit (Holzmer 2013, pp. 57–58). In this perspective, leadership is not simply a rational process that directs the vision and actions of followers through disembodied discourse, but it becomes a rational, emotional and intuitive performance to create a safe holding environment for followers in spite of fears and insecurities. The concept of extended cognition, discussed above, can explain how such a dialogue in a safe holding environment can create a new sense of group purpose and identity. It creates cognitive connections between group participants that allow for a broader and more adequate way to process the challenges of liminality. This, in turn, creates the personal and organizational transformation necessary to stand strong in a fluid society. Evidently, dialogue in all its richness is an embodied process that cannot be managed purely rationally and cognitively.

Holzmer thus illustrates how leadership is an essentially embodied process in which discernment and dialogue are vital social practices to enable groups and organizations to determine fruitful courses of action.

5 Conclusion

In summary, based on theories about embodied and extended cognition, embodiment offers important epistemological insights that generate the perspective of embodied realism, a perspective that has gained significant attention in various disciplines.

Embodied realism implies that spirituality, as a concern with the divine-human encounter, is an embodied phenomenon, as practiced in religious rituals and as confessed in the Christian doctrine of the incarnation. This, then, allows us to consider discernment as not merely a rational or disembodied spiritual practice, but as a practice of seeing, listening and sensemaking that draws our embodied experiences, memories and perceptions together to arrive at a collective attribution of meaning and wise action. This, in turn, recasts the framework of leadership from one of vision casting and rational strategizing to embodied (social and institutional) performance, creating a safe but liminal space to enable the transformation of personal and collective identity, leading to renewed social and religious action.

Bibliography

Bass DC, Cahalan KA, Miller-McLemore BJ, Nieman JR, Scharen CB (2016) Christian practical wisdom: what it is, why it matters. Eerdmans, Grand Rapids

Benner PE (2000) The roles of embodiment, emotion and lifeworld for rationality and agency in nursing practice. Nurs Philos 1(1):5–19

Benner PE (2001) From novice to expert: excellence and power in clinical nursing practice (Commemorative ed). Prentice Hall, London. Original edition, Addison-Wesley Pub, Menlo Park, 1984

Berlinger LR, Tumblin TF (2004) Sensemaking, discernment, and religious leadership. J Relig Leadersh 3(1–2):75–98

Brown WS, Strawn BD (2012) The physical nature of Christian life: neuroscience, psychology, and the church. Cambridge University Press, Cambridge

Brown WS, Strawn BD (2017) Beyond the isolated self: extended mind and spirituality. Theol Sci 15(4):411–423

Browning DS (1991) A fundamental practical theology: descriptive and strategic proposals. Fortress, Minneapolis

Carman T (1999) The body in Husserl and Merleau-Ponty. Philos Topics 27(2):205–226

Cartledge MJ (2015) The mediation of the spirit: interventions in practical theology, Pentecostal manifestos. Eerdmans, Grand Rapids

Dooyeweerd H (1999) In the twilight of Western thought: studies in the pretended autonomy of philosophical thought. Strauss DFM (ed) Vol. B: 4, The collected works of Herman Dooyeweerd. Edwin Mellen, Lewiston

Eikema Hommes HJ van (1982) Inleiding tot de wijsbegeerte van Herman Dooyeweerd. Martinus Nijhoff, The Hague

Gill R, Hughson RT, Kaye PB, Percy VRPM (2013) Theology in a social context: sociological theology, Vol. 1, Ashgate contemporary ecclesiology series. Ashgate, Farnham

Graham EL (2002) Transforming practice: pastoral theology in an age of uncertainty. Wipf and Stock, Eugene. Original edition, Mowbray, Woonsocket, 1996

Grenz SJ (2001) The social God and the relational self: a trinitarian theology of the Imago Dei. Westminster John Knox, Louisville

Heifetz RA, Grashow A, Linsky M (2009) The practice of adaptive leadership: tools and tactics for changing your organization and the world. Harvard Business Press, Boston

Holzmer D (2013) Leadership in the time of liminality: a framework for leadership in an era of deep transformation. In: Melina LR, Burgess GJ, Lid-Falkman L, Marturano A (eds) The embodiment of leadership. Jossey-Bass, San Francisco

Ignatow G (2007) Theories of embodied knowledge: new directions for cultural and cognitive sociology? J Theor Soc Behav 37(2):115–135

Iyadurai J (2015) Transformative religious experience: a phenomenological understanding of religious conversion. Pickwick, Eugene

Kaak P, Lemaster G, Muthiah R (2013) Integrative decision-making for christian leadership: prudence, organizational theory, and discernment practices. J Relig Leadersh 12(2):145–166

Kahneman D (2011) Thinking, fast and slow. Farrar, Straus and Giroux, New York

Kahneman D, Lovallo D, Sibony O (2011) Before you make that big decision. Harv Bus Rev 89 (6):50–60

Ladkin D (2013) From perception to flesh: a phenomenological account of the felt experience of leadership. Leadership 9(3):320–334

Lakoff G, Johnson M (1980) Metaphors we live by. University of Chicago Press, Chicago. Reprint 2008 edn

Lakoff G, Johnson M (1999) Philosophy in the flesh: the embodied mind and its challenge to Western thought. Basic, New York

Liebert E (2015) The soul of discernment: a spiritual practice for communities and institutions. Westminster John Knox, Louisville

Luhrmann TM (2006) The art of hearing God: absorption, dissociation, and contemporary American spirituality. Spiritus J Christ Spirituality 5(2):133–157

Luhrmann TM (2012) When God talks back: understanding the American evangelical relationship with God. Doubleday, New York

McGuire MB (2007) Embodied practices: negotiation and resistance. In: Ammerman NT (ed) Everyday religion: observing modern religious lives. Oxford University Press, Oxford

McGuire MB (2008) Lived religion: faith and practice in everyday life. Oxford University Press, Oxford

Melina LR, Burgess GJ, Lid-Falkman L, Marturano A (eds) (2013) The embodiment of leadership. Building leadership bridges. Jossey-Bass, San Francisco

Merleau-Ponty M (1978) Phénoménologie de la perception. TEL Gallimard, Paris. Reprint by S.P. A.D.E.M., 1945 edn

Michener RT (2013) Postliberal theology: a guide for the perplexed. Bloomsbury, London

Michener RT (2016) Engaging deconstructive theology. Routledge new critical thinking in religion, theology and biblical studies. Routledge, London

Morris DE, Olsen CM (2012) Discerning God's will together: a spiritual practice for the church. Revised and updated edn. Alban, Herndon. Original edition, 1997

Murphy NC (2006) Bodies and souls, or spirited bodies? Vol. 3, Current issues in theology. Cambridge University Press, Cambridge

Osmer RR (2008) Practical theology: an introduction. Eerdmans, Grand Rapids

Root A (2014) Christopraxis: a practical theology of the cross. Fortress, Minneapolis

Roxburgh AJ (2015) Joining god, remaking church, changing the world: the new shape of the church in our time. Morehouse, New York

Ruijter K de (2005) Meewerken met God: ontwerp van een gereformeerde praktische theologie. Kok, Kampen

Scharen C (2015) Fieldwork in theology: exploring the social context of god's work in the world. Smith JKA (ed) The church and postmodern culture. Baker, Grand Rapids

Shleifer A (2012) Psychologists at the gate: a review of Daniel Kahneman's *Thinking, Fast and Slow*. J Econ Lit 50(4):1080–1091

Simon HA (1972) Theories of bounded rationality. Decis Organ 1(1):161–176

Simon HA (2000) Bounded rationality in social science: today and tomorrow. Mind Soc 1(1):25–39

Smith JKA (2009) Desiring the kingdom: worship, worldview, and cultural formation. 3 vols. Vol. 1, Cultural liturgies. Baker Academic, Grand Rapids

Smith JKA (2016) You are what you love: the spiritual power of habit. Baker, Grand Rapids

Teske JA (2013) From embodied to extended cognition. Zygon J Sci Relig 48(3):759–787

Thomas SP (2005) Through the lens of Merleau-Ponty: advancing the phenomenological approach to nursing research. Nurs Philos 6(1):63–76

Toadvine T (2016) Maurice Merleau-Ponty. In: Zalta EN (ed) The Stanford encyclopedia of philosophy. Stanford University Press, Stanford
Ven JA van der (1998) Practical theology: an empirical approach. Peeters, Leuven. Original edition, Entwurf einer empirischen Theologie. Translated by B. Schultz. Reprint ed
Vlaardingerbroek M (2011) Grensverleggend: hoe je als kerk opnieuw missionair kunt zijn. Medema, Heerenveen
Voestermans P, Verheggen T (2007) Cultuur & Lichaam: een cultuurpsychologisch perspectief op patronen in gedrag. Blackwell, Malden
Voestermans P, Verheggen T (2013) Culture as embodiment: the social tuning of behavior. Wiley, New York
Wenger E, McDermott RA, Snyder W (2013) Cultivating communities of practice: a guide to managing knowledge. Harvard Business Review, Boston

Jack Barentsen (Ph.D.) studied physics, philosophy and theology in the US, and moved to the Netherlands in 1988 as pastor and church planter. Working with new church plants provided opportunity to learn about discipleship and leadership development. This became an academic pursuit at the Evangelische Theologische Faculteit in Leuven (Belgium) by researching leadership development in early Christianity through the lens of modern leadership theory (Emerging Leadership in the Pauline Mission, W&S 2011). Since then, Barentsen teaches and researches the practice of pastoral and religious leadership in multiple countries, developing his own descriptive "Integrative Model of Pastoral Leadership." He serves as Full Professor and Chair of Practical Theology and as Senior Research Fellow of the Institute of Leadership and Social Ethics. He also holds an appointment as Extraordinary Associate Professor of New Testament and Practical Theology in the Faculty of Theology of North-West University, South Africa. He is married and has two grown-up daughters, with their own expanding family.

A Well-Played Life: Discernment as the Constitutive Building Block of Selfless Leadership

Stephan Joubert

Abstract Selfless leadership is a full-time calling, and a summons to be of service to others. It is a vocation, not as a position of power or an opportunity for self-enhancement. Selfless leaders know that discernment is not just another useful tool in the ever-expanding leadership toolkit to make their organisations more profitable, streamlined, or desirable. It is a gift, but also a learned ability to think, desire, know, feel, choose and do what is right for the present moment, and to influence future circumstances for the welfare and common good of others. Discernment is a habitual ability to read "the signs of the times" wisely and to act thereupon with clarity, wisdom and soberness. At the same time selfless leaders deliberately choose to focus on the potential, abilities, strengths and gifts of people in their organisation and on how to harness them to the best of their abilities, as well as to the advantage of their organisation. Just as any editor would ensure that an author produces the best possible manuscript by assisting him/her through all the phases of writing and rewriting, selfless leaders assist those within their spheres of leadership to become the best authors of their own and their organisation's stories. Their fine-tuned ability to discern the right paths to follow in planned and unplanned ways create safe spaces for good decisions, relational growth, creativity, the right kind of profitability, and healthy relationships.

1 Shifting to Interactive, Process-Oriented Forms of Leadership

In the previous century, those taken-for-granted assumptions regarding leadership such as that leaders should always be put on the centre stage, or that leadership is a function of a position are challenged from various angles nowadays. There is a clear shift away from the idea that officially appointed leaders are singlehandedly responsible for "engineering" the right working conditions and social environments in

S. Joubert (✉)
Contemporary Ecclesiology, University of the Free State, Bloemfontein, South Africa
e-mail: stephan@ekerk.org

© The Author(s) 2019   139
J. (Kobus) Kok, S. C. van den Heuvel (eds.), *Leading in a VUCA World*,
Contributions to Management Science, https://doi.org/10.1007/978-3-319-98884-9_9

order to enhance expected outcomes towards leadership as a process. More correctly, relational processes, or series of such interaction processes, which are co-produced by leaders and followers engaged in various relations of "mutuality," have now become prominent (cf. Karp 2013, pp. 17–18; Vlachoutsicos 2011, p. 124).

People can no longer be viewed as "human machines," nor should they be controlled by leaders and/or managers "to perform with the same efficiency and predictability" as machines (Wheatley 2007, p. 19). From this perspective, themes such as social capital, social awareness, as well as emotional and social intelligence have become part and parcel of the vocabulary and the theoretical jargon of new approaches to leadership. Individualised leadership, with a strong emphasis on high-quality reciprocal relationships between leaders and followers, is more than ever significant. Within such relationships, leaders, according to Van Dierendonck and Driehuizen (2015, p. 103ff.), should provide their colleagues with a sense of self-worth, whereas the colleagues should reciprocate by providing satisfactory performance and outcomes mutually agreed upon.

Recent transformational approaches to leadership, while sometimes still reflecting persistent undertones of heroism inherent in the classic ideal of that one significant individual leader at the top, have begun to shift their emphasis in the direction of leaders' effects on their followers' organisational commitments (cf. Avolio et al. 2009; Chan and Mak 2014). Nowadays, the focus on subordinates' personal and professional ambitions, as well as their striving for success and achievement, are understood in terms of leaders' sustained efforts at, among others, their followers' "intellectual stimulation, idealized influence, inspirational motivation, and individual consideration" (Holstad et al. 2013, p. 270). Thus, at present, it is all about authentic leadership, ranging from multi-faceted processes of "essentialising" leaders' selves to an emphasis on leaders' "self-awareness, relational transparency, balanced processing of information, and internalized moral perspective" (Alok 2014, p. 268; cf. also Avolio and Gardner 2005). At the same time, the nature and characteristics of followership is more important than ever. In this regard, Kellerman's (2008, p. xxi) influential research on followership as "a relationship between subordinates and superiors and a response of the former to the latter" has been expanded to include the characteristics, predispositions and attitudes of followers, their preferences of leadership styles, and so forth (cf. Alok 2014).

Hogg's (2001, p. 185) assertion that "leaders exist because of followers and followers exist because of leaders" may represent the current emphasis on the symbiotic relationships between followers and leaders as a process of mutual influence. In order to make this transition from old ways of regarding an organisation "as an imposed structure, plan, design, or role" to a new world where organisation "arises from the interactions and needs of individuals who have decided to come together" (Wheatley 2007, p. 26), leaders urgently need new narratives derived from an entirely new understanding of self, others and reality.

2   Leadership as a Summons, a Calling

Once you have reached that proverbial fork in the road, there is only one option available, left or right, except if your name is Yogi Berra. This famous American baseball player once remarked: "When you get to a fork in the road, take it!" At least he is right on one crucial point: you have to take some form of action when you have reached a crossroad. The ancient Greeks considered forks in the road so significant that they even had a specific goddess called Hekate who presided over them. Apart from guarding the graves by roadsides and the entrance to Hades (that is, the underworld), Hekate also protected crossroads. Women, in particular, relied on her guidance and wisdom when they reached certain "fork-road" stages in their lives (cf. Agha-Jaffar 2002, p. 77).

Making the right choices at those perilous crossroads in the life of any organisation is what leadership is all about, some would say. The popular leadership guru, John Maxwell, even states that approximately 95% of the decisions CEOs make could also be made by any intelligent high-school graduate. They get paid for the remaining 5%. Those are the tough calls, and the way in which leaders handle them is what separates them from everyone else (cf. http://www.execleadership.com/880/3-signs-youre-facing-a-tough-call.html). Still, effective leaders also know that it is not simply about the good choices. Indeed, these do matter, but leadership entails more than choices, positions, titles, power, successful enterprises, or bigger profits. Leadership is also about a "well-played" life (cf. Sweet 2014), one that is lived selflessly to the advantage of others within one's sphere of influence. Leaders who are "summoned to lead and to serve" in this manner do so from the heart, not merely from the mind. They never lead as part of their job description; they do so from their inner conviction.

At its core, leadership is deeply spiritual. Leadership is a full-time calling, a summons to be of service to others. It is a vocation, not a position of power or an opportunity for self-enhancement. A selfless leader's life would be miserable and unfocused if s/he did not respond to, and pursue this lifelong calling to serve. Over against the ambitious, majestic dreams of talented individualistic leaders, selfless leaders do not follow carefully scripted career paths in order to attain financial benefits or personal fame at the expense of others. They follow a lifelong vocation. Rather, their vocation chooses them. They are summoned to lead (cf. Sweet 2004); they are called! In fact, they have no choice in the matter. They know that such a calling of selfless service goes against the grain of the prevailing contemporary business culture, but they have no other option but to cultivate their gift and trained ability of discernment in order to be of service to others in their organisations.

Selfless leadership is not only a platform to help shape, but also a garden to help grow the lives of those within a leader's field of influence (cf. also Davenport 2015). It is an ongoing interactive process of assisting others in crossing those fixed mental and physical boundaries, which their social environments might have established in terms of the rules of business, the nature of competition, the tyranny of ever-increasing profits, or the selfishness of winning at all costs. Discernment is a prerequisite to step up to this type of leadership. It also requires a profound shift in understanding what leadership is all about. More to the point, it entails a *metanoia* of sorts, one that will lead to a lifelong investment in personal character growth and the social upliftment of others.

3   The *"metanoetic"* Nature of Selfless Leadership

Although the Greek term *metanoia* is mostly used to signify religious conversions, this term means more than a moral repentance, or a revisiting of the pains and wrongdoings of the past. As a matter of fact, *metanoia* probably never signified a moral turnabout by sinners based on fear of divine punishment, but rather a change of heart and mind, a border-crossing experience that brings one to a fresh understanding of reality (cf. Joubert 2013, p. 122). Through *metanoia* "one becomes what one is not ... *Metanoō*, I have had a change of heart, I have been transformed, made into something new ..." (Caputo 1999, p. 213). When using *metanoia* in terms of Jesus' new understanding of the concept, Moore (2009, p. 37) describes in detail the challenges posed by a *metanoetic* change of heart and mind: "... one of the most difficult things to do is to change the way you imagine your place in life. Nothing is more challenging. On the other hand, once this takes place, nothing could be more vitalizing. Truly, it's as if you are born a second time. Your eyes open to a different world ... *Metanoia* comes at a great cost. You are to give up an understanding of life that has been in place for a long time."

Leaders have crossed the divide from old leadership paradigms, where their identity is determined by cultures that are explicitly or implicitly linked to control over others and sometimes even to the reduction of subordinates' "working selves to disposable pieces of furniture" (Harding 2014, p. 409). They are now part of a subversive new reality where selflessness is the norm. This shift requires nothing less than a personal *metanoia*. No, this shift is not a regression into a weak, *laissez-faire* form of leadership without any rules or boundaries. To the contrary, selfless leadership is strong and focused. Such leaders deliberately choose to curb their selfish egos, share power and use their influence to the advantage, growth and development of others. As an ongoing process of personal metamorphosis, such a shift of mind and heart facilitates new forms of "complexity leadership, where leaders turn into sages who create fluid new structures to facilitate trusting relationships, and a new culture of respect in which followers/workers/subordinates thrive as they are given permission to work and operate in their respective flow states" (Joubert 2013, p. 218).[1]

---

[1]"Csíkszentmihályi is well known for his research on flow states, as a reference to any person's deep concentration and complete absorption with an activity at hand. This causes ... the person in flow not only forgets his or her problems, but loses temporarily the awareness of self that in normal life often intrudes in consciousness, and causes psychic energy to be diverted from what needs to be done (Csíkszentmihályi 1988, p. 33). This flow state is an optimal state of intrinsic motivation,

4   The Character of Selfless Leaders Is Grown in the Right Fertile Soil

Character is the matrix of internalised beliefs, norms and values that define and direct a person. According to Hauerwas (1983, p. 39), "character is not merely the result of our choices, but rather the form our agency takes through our beliefs and intentions . . . character is not a surface manifestation of some deeper reality called the 'self'. We are our character." Elsewhere, Hauerwas (1975, p. 203) mentions that "nothing is more nearly at the 'heart' of who we are than our character. It is our character that determines the primary orientation and direction which we embody through our beliefs and actions."

Character is not innate or automatic, as Brooks (2015) correctly argues. A strong moral character, which flows from a *metanoia* or a radical change in one's understanding of reality and which is expressed in a life of selfless service, has to be nurtured and cultivated. It has to be grown with both artistry and effort. As the English novelist James A. Froude would say: "You cannot dream yourself into character, you must hammer and forge one for yourself." Character needs the right fertile soil in which to grow. The fertilizers for this soil include:

(a) An unquenched curiosity, combined with a lifelong passion for learning;
(b) A child-like second naïveté;
(c) A strong sense of justice combined with deep empathy for others, as well as
(d) Ruthless honesty about personal blind spots and weaknesses.

Selfless leaders do not have big egos to feed or carefully crafted public personas to defend. They pursue a lifelong calling of service. As the philosopher Paul Ricoeur (1969, p. 349) would say: "[B]eyond the desert of criticism they wish to be called again." Such leaders are well aware of the fact that they swam across the river of complexity and self-enhancement only to discover a new route of childlike simplicity on the other side. No, they are not blind to the tough, day-to-day challenges of leadership, or deaf to the questions facing our fast changing global landscape, but they have embraced a second naïveté which allows them to deal with chaos, complexity and change from the fresh perspectives of curiosity and honesty. In this sense, quoting Carattini (2013), "true naïveté can thus describe one who shows absence of artificiality or unaffected simplicity of nature, one who has no hidden agendas or duplicitous motives."

Character should never be confused with talent (that is, the possession of certain repeatable skills). Modern-day society blindly celebrates talent over character. Far too easily talents, masked as so-called "résumé virtues," are sold off to the highest bidders in the corporate world. No wonder organisations are "overcrowded" with

---

marked by deep concentration, a distorted sense of time, and absorption. The person is fully immersed in what s/he is doing so that temporal concerns such as time, food or even the self are disregarded" (Joubert 2013, pp. 128–129).

many ambitious individuals who know how to climb the corporate ladder *en route* to formal leadership and managerial positions, but "understaffed" with character-driven individuals. The latter are passionate about forging a strong moral ethos in any organisation, one that delivers sustainable outputs while also sustaining the personal growth of others. Character-driven people pull organisations through. When wrong decisions are taken and relationships in the workplace suffer, brute talent will never save the day. Character-based leadership is what is called for then . . . and always!

5   Discernment Flows from the Hearts of Selfless Leaders

Discernment is not simply another useful tool in the ever-expanding toolkit of leaders to make their organisations more profitable, streamlined, or desirable. Discernment is a gift, but also a learned ability to think, desire, know, feel, choose and do what is right for the present moment, and to influence future circumstances for the welfare and common good of others. It is the habitual ability to read "the signs of the times" wisely and to act thereupon with clarity, wisdom and soberness. In the words of Howard (2000, p. 10), "discernment is a noetic verbal noun . . . the term nearly always has something to do with 'knowing'. Terms like 'awareness,' 'interpret,' 'examine,' 'recognize,' all give indication of the activity of discernment being cognitional. Whether the individual of community 'mind' is operative, whether the focus is external or internal, discernment itself refers to a distinguishing which is a process/product of cognition—a kind of 'knowing'."

Discernment should not be confused with that never-ending pressure on the shoulders of leaders of "constantly getting it right." It is not so much decision-and-outcome driven, but rather the outflow of a deepened ability to notice and choose what is the right way of being present and being of service to others in the "everydayness of our lives—those very places we often overlook as important for discernment" (Liebert 2008, p. xi). Linear processes of reasoning alone do not suffice in this instance. A constant interplay of heart and mind is what is needed, one that is influenced by a strong awareness of the social, situational, and immediate contexts within which leaders find themselves.

Discernment cannot be switched on or off at will. It is a way of life, fuelled by a personal commitment to pay attention to the needs of others and to facilitate their growth. Selfless leaders are well aware of the interconnectedness of people. Keen observation, creative thinking, practical wisdom, and openness to the input of others are key components in their discernment-driven leadership arsenal. Their interactions and decisions are never pragmatic, but flow from an inner clarity regarding the right routes to be pursued to the advantage of others. Hence, discernment in their presence is an art, but also a learned ability to align their perceptions and decisions with their inner character, which also aligns with the well-being of others. "Discernment discovers what is the reasonable thing to do by engaging not only in the head but also in the heart. In and around the linear flow of discursive reasoning, discernment is an experienced perception involving the back-and-forth, around-and-about movement of intuition, affective sensibility to values, and subtle assessments of the relationships of multiple factors" (Gula 1997, p. 50).

6 Character-Based Discernment Translated into the Roles of Sages and Editors

As part of their reading and shaping the culture of their organisations, selfless leaders intuitively know that it is never about individualism versus the group, but about reciprocally facilitating the unique individuality of members of their organisation to give shape to new forms of "belonging." "This is part of the fluid 'leadership dance', or the ability to understand that currently it is about both individuality and the group, about speeding up and slowing down, and solidity and fluidity" (Joubert 2013, p. 130). Selfless leaders have deliberately stepped down as "professional specialists" and "accountants" whose function it is to constantly keep subordinates "accountable." In their new self-understanding as "editors," leaders assist colleagues, subordinates, followers, clients and customers to write (and rewrite!) their own life stories along the lines of selfless service, respect and generosity. Over against dated routes of accountability leadership, where the emphasis is mostly on past performances of subordinates (or the lack thereof!), selfless leaders choose to focus on the potential, abilities, strengths and gifts of people in their organisation and on how to harness them to the best of their abilities, as well as to the advantage of their organisation. Just as any good editor would ensure that an author produces the best possible manuscript by assisting him/her through all the phases of writing and rewriting, selfless leaders assist those within their spheres of leadership to become the best authors of their own and their organisation's stories. During these different phases, the discernment skills of both leaders-as-editors and subordinates-as-authors are sharpened by their interactions and their shared learning experiences.

At the same time, selfless leaders also perceive themselves as sages who are constantly engaged in mastering "the ways and means of planning, managing and understanding a good life" (Baltes and Staudinger 2000, p. 124). Their rich knowledge of what a well-played life in service of others entails, allows them to "deal[ing] successfully and ethically with people, and also with difficult and ambiguous questions" (Baltes and Staudinger 2000, p. 124). They walk their talk by modelling a life of sincerity, respect and generosity. Narcissism, that "inflated sense of self-importance and grandiosity" (Greaves et al. 2014, p. 341), is never cultivated in their proximity, since they know that it is damaging to personal relationships and the general welfare of others in their organisations. Selfless leaders have sufficient practical wisdom to constantly modify their strategies and plans. They know how to think on their feet and build aeroplanes in mid-air. Uncertainty and chaos do not scare them. As a matter of fact, complexity and ambiguity are conducive to their abilities to discern.

The very nature and practical application of selfless leaders' gifts and fine-tuned abilities to discern flow from their self-understanding as sages and editors. These roles are the formative lenses through which they view reality, approach others, grow relationships, manage day-to-day business, and so forth. Thus, the operational mode of selfless leaders is a route of wisdom and editorship where good decisions and right choices are determined by, and judged on the merits of how any possible course of action, or any business deal for that matter, would assist others within their sphere of influence to be of service to their organisations, and how they could reach their full human potential during the course of such processes.

7 Discernment Is Fine-Tuned by a New Sense of "We-ness," or Community

All processes of discernment should be based on, and measured by actions that facilitate the reshaping of the core of any organisation from a "me to we"-based culture. In this instance, personal motives and selfish options are deliberately set aside in favour of mutually benefitting ones as a non-negotiable core value. In this instance, people are never left adrift in a dangerous sea of subjectivity at the mercy of a single leader who controls the direction of their organisation. Good discernment never takes place in social isolation, or within hierarchically structured contexts. In a world where all are constantly threatened with suffocation by an avalanche of information and a never-ending barrage of choices, discerning leaders are definitely not updated versions of the Lone Ranger or Rambo. They are not "one-man" or "one-woman" bands trying to singlehandedly save or advance their organisations. They surround themselves with wise people. More to the point, they passionately embrace the value of community; hence, they constantly forge strong and positive relationships with others. In order to foster such a healthy discernment culture, people on all levels of responsibility in their organisations are treated with the same dignity and respect. In turn, this embodied value translates into others also being entrusted with a distinct awareness of, and a practical responsibility for the growth of a relationship-based culture, as well as for specific outcomes during the course of decision-making processes. Undoubtedly, "the process of discernment is slow and messy. But it is neither arbitrary nor authoritarian. The same cannot be said for all other methods of decision making" (Johnson 1983, p. 33).

Selfless leaders are tasked not only with displaying an awareness of the talents, character, needs and responsibilities of others, but also with facilitating adequate responses thereto by building platforms for them on which to prosper (cf. also Gabriel 2015). In such environments, discernment is not only about discriminating, determining, deciding or distinguishing between right and wrong, yes and no, or between the best possible course of action, as the word would literally imply. Of course, leaders' rational abilities to think matters through and to apply a healthy dose of common sense and sound reason to day-to-day decision-making activities should never be negated. Strategic thinking and good planning are part and parcel of any form of good leadership, but at the same time it must also include a constant willingness and the fine-tuned ability to approach day-to-day challenges from relational angles, which includes constant input from others.

8 Generosity as Lens

One of the big mind shifts that selfless leaders have to make, is towards a new understanding of resources and profit as the means with which to serve and not only as treasures to be stockpiled. In other words, generosity is what is called for. Attitudes of "limited good" are never allowed to grow in such contexts. Limited good, as understood by the anthropologist George M. Foster, proposes that all tangible and intangible entities exist in finite quantities. Everything is available in limited amounts or measures, including food, work, property, money, health, and safety to trust and loyalty, although such scarcity is represented "on a continuum in which the poles are 'more limited' and 'less limited'" (Foster 1972, p. 59). "In all limited good contexts, selfless generosity is uncommon, since without reciprocity, any person who takes from others without giving back anything of equal value is considered a thief, and his/her deeds are conceived of as socially destabilising" (Joubert 2013, p. 125–126). However, in selfless leadership contexts, the values of kindness and hospitality are never finite, since numerous stories of service, care, second miles, and so forth disclose the pervasive presence of generosity. Whereas the greedy live by the unspoken rule that for them to have, others should have less, generous people live their lives and do their work in the prosperity of others.

Selfless leaders work constantly at creating a new ethos of generosity in their organisations. They imprint the conviction in others to collectively participate therein, among others by shared affirmations, mutually rewarding interactions, as well as the constant sharing of narratives that reflect the distinct generosity culture of their organisations. Success on their scoreboard is registered in terms of the liberal sharing of resources and knowledge to the benefit of others. In this instance, wealth is measured by the growth in generosity and by a newly found freedom to share and serve responsibly, since this is one of the discernment-based lenses whereby all options are evaluated and all decisions made.

9 When Criticism Comes. . .

As a "me to we"-based process that grows in the fertile soil of mutual respect and generosity, discernment should never be confused with low expectations regarding the output and high quality of the work of others. These values can never be compromised, neither should the route of straightforward honesty be set aside when problems and conflicts arise. The opinions of all matter in selfless leadership environments, but never at the expense of the greater good of the organisation, the well-being of others, or the responsibilities of the leaders themselves. Clashes of opinion, criticism, and conflict will be a daily reality, but when criticism comes, good leaders will know not to count but to weigh it, and to address it directly.

The biggest dangers in any discernment-based culture is that of the so-called "anxious risk-avoiding leader" and those destabilizing "weakest human links" who have forced themselves into becoming the strongest ones actually! A risk-avoiding leader is someone who is more concerned with "good feelings than progress, someone whose life revolves around the axis of consensus, a 'middler' ..." (Friedman 2007, p. 13). Well-differentiated selfless leaders are not autocrats. They have clarity regarding their leadership calling and goals. They do not get lost in the entrapments of various emotional processes that sometimes swirl about in their organisations. As Friedman (2007, p. 18) notes: "A leader must separate his or her own feelings from that of his or her followers while still remaining connected. Vision is basically an emotional rather than a cerebral phenomenon, depending more on a leader's capacity to deal with anxiety than his or her professional training ..." Such leaders accept responsibility for their own emotional well-being, while not allowing the "weakest human links" in their organisations to hold others captive with their own emotional baggage and selfish agendas—all under the guise of consensus or unity. Safety and certainty do not motivate selfless leaders; rather, new ways of thinking and acting hold the key for them. It is not about trying harder, or doing more of the same, but by reframing questions, changing the nature, value and flow of information, and eliminating previous dichotomies. In this process, selfless leaders refuse to facilitate reactivity, blame displacement, or a quick fix mentality to determine outcomes, even if they have to face conflict, unpopularity and outright rejection.

Good leaders are able to separate themselves from surrounding emotional processes, especially from those negative ones when relationships and/or decision-making processes are imaginatively gridlocked. They intuitively know that more thinking or talking about problems will not suffice, neither will any naive accommodating of weakest human links. Within such situations, decisiveness, clear boundaries, a raised threshold for criticism, and persistence in the face of inertial resistance help sidestep toxic forms of anxiety, which is systemic in many corporate cultures at present (cf. Friedman 2007, p. 89).

10 Fin

Contrary to popular understandings of discernment as decision and action, or at best as a process that must always lead to the correct tangible results, it actually entails a way of life. Discernment is a never-ending relational and rational process. It is always in progress. It is relational motion, as some of the terms associated with discernment, such as "awareness, examination, interpretation, discovery, decision, response, action" would imply. Thus "discernment can be comprehended in toto as a process or act of knowing" (Howard 2000, p. 10), that is, relational insight and knowing. Such leaders constantly embrace their calling of selfless service to others. Their empathetic responsiveness to the feelings, giftedness, abilities and strengths of people does not overrule their abilities to make good decisions and to remain constantly true to their inner selves. Their fine-tuned ability to discern the right paths to follow in planned and unplanned ways create safe spaces and the right contexts for good decisions, relational growth, creativity, the right kind of profitability, and intimate relationships.

Bibliography

Agha-Jaffar T (2002) Demeter and Persephone: lessons from a myth. McFarland, London
Alok K (2014) Authentic leadership and psychological ownership: investigation of interrelations. LODJ 35(4):266–285
Avolio BJ, Gardner WL (2005) Authentic leadership development: getting to the root of positive forms of leadership. Leadersh Q 16:315–338
Avolio BJ, Walumbwa FO, Weber TJ (2009) Leadership: current theories research and future directions. Annu Rev Psychol 60(1):421–449
Baltes PB, Staudinger UM (2000) Wisdom: a metaheuristic (pragmatic) to orchestrate mind and virtue toward excellence. Am Psychol 55(1):122–136
Brooks D (2015) The road to character. Random House, New York
Caputo JD (1999) Metanoetics: elements of a postmodern Christian philosophy. In: Ambrosio FJ (ed) The question of Christian philosophy today. Fordham University Press, New York, pp 189–224
Carattini J (2013) http://rzim.org/a-slice-of-infinity/second-naivete/. Posted on 17 July 2013
Chan SCH, Mak WM (2014) Transformational leadership: pride in being a follower of the leader and organizational commitment. LODJ 35(8):674–690
Csíkszentmihályi M (1988) The flow experience and its significance for human psychology. In: Csíkszentmihályi M, Csíkszentmihályi IS (eds) Optimal experience: psychological studies of flow in consciousness. Cambridge University Press, Cambridge, pp 15–35
Davenport B (2015) Compassion, suffering and servant-leadership: combining compassion and servant-leadership to respond to suffering. Leadership 11(3):300–315
Foster GM (1972) A second look at limited good. Anthropol Q 45:57–64
Friedman EH (2007) Failure of nerve: leadership in the age of the quick fix. Seabury, New York
Gabriel Y (2015) The caring leader: what followers expect of their leaders and why? Leadership 11 (3):316–334
Greaves CE, Zacher H, McKenna DR (2014) Wisdom and narcissism as predictors of transformational leadership. LODJ 35(4):335–358
Gula RM (1997) Moral discernment. Paulist, New York
Harding N (2014) Reading leadership through Hegel's master/slave dialectic: toward a theory of the powerlessness of the powerful. Leadership 10(4):391–411
Hauerwas S (1975) Character and the Christian life: a study in theological ethics. Trinity University Press, San Antonio
Hauerwas S (1983) 'The peaceable kingdom': a primer in Christian ethics. University of Notre Dame Press, Notre Dame
Hogg MA (2001) A social identity theory of leadership: personality and social psychology. Leadership 5(3):184–200

Holstad TJ, Korek S, Rigotti T, Mohr G (2013) The relation between transformational leadership and follower emotional strain: the moderating role of professional ambition. Leadership 10 (3):269–288

Howard EB (2000) Affirming the touch of God: a psychological and philosophical exploration of Christian discernment. University Press of America, Lanham

Johnson LT (1983) Scripture and discernment: decision-making in the church. Abingdon, Nashville

Joubert SJ (2013) Not by order, nor by dialogue: the metanoetic presence of the Kingdom of God in a fluid new world and church. Acta Theol 33(1):114–134

Karp T (2013) Studying subtle acts of leadership. Leadership 9(1):3–22

Kellerman B (2008) Followership: how followers are creating change and changing leaders. Harvard Business Press, Boston

Liebert E (2008) The way of discernment: spiritual practices for decision-making. Westminster/ John Knox, Louisville

Moore T (2009) Writing in the sand: Jesus and the soul of the Gospels. Hay House, Carlsbad

Ricoeur P (1969) The symbolism of evil (trans: Buchanan E). Beacon, Boston

Sweet L (2004) Summoned to lead. Zondervan, Grand Rapids

Sweet L (2014) The well-played life: when pleasing God doesn't have to be that hard work. Tyndale Momentum, Bonita Springs

Van Dierendonck D, Driehuizen S (2015) Leader's intention to support followers' self-worth. LODJ 36(2):102–119

Vlachoutsicos CA (2011) How to cultivate engaged employees. HBR 89(9):123–126

Wheatley M (2007) Finding our way: leadership for an uncertain time. Berrett-Koehller, San Francisco

Stephan Joubert is an Extraordinary Professor of Contemporary Ecclesiology at The University of the Free State, South Africa, as well as a Research Fellow at Radboud University, Nijmegen, The Netherlands. At the same time he is the editor of ekerk, a large cyberchurch that sends out more than 2.5 million emails to subscribers annually, a church consultant, speaker and author of more than Christian books, three international academic books, and close to 50 academic articles in various journals and books. He has a daily column in Beeld, the largest Afrikaans newspaper, as well as monthly columns in two South African magazines.

Discerning Spirituality for Missional Leaders

C. J. P. (Nelus) Niemandt

Abstract The concept of *missional church* represents a confluence of ideas on spirituality, discernment and leadership. The very idea of participating in the *missio Dei* implies a spiritual journey and underlying spirituality, and discernment is widely described as the "first step in mission." The missional church recognises the importance of leadership to envision, shape, and facilitate missional transformation. This chapter acknowledges the urgency and importance of discourses on spirituality and discernment, because of the context of the church finding itself in a complex world. The church *is* a complex system and finds itself in a dynamic reality where the dynamism also entails complexity—to the extent that Friedman (Thank you for being late: An optimist's guide to thriving in the age of accelerations. Allen Lane, London, 2016) typifies our age as the "age of accelerations." The research will introduce the idea of missional leadership and its relevance in the light of the renewed attention to concepts of missional church in South Africa, in many other contexts, and in ecumenical organisations. Defining missional leadership as *the Spirit-led transformation of people and institutions by means of meaningful relations to participate in God's mission*, the chapter will attend to an appropriate understanding of spirituality. This will be against the background of a shift of spiritual formation from knowing and believing, to hungering and thirsting. In the final section, discernment will be described as entering into a trialogue: the discerning interaction between church, culture, and biblical narrative—to seek, discover, understand, and share in what the Holy Spirit is involved in the close-to-the-ground particulars of the church's engagement in, with, against, and for the world.

C. J. P. (Nelus) Niemandt (✉)
Department Religion Studies, Faculty of Theology, University of Pretoria, Pretoria, South Africa
e-mail: nelus.niemandt@up.ac.za

1 Introduction

We live in complex times, in an age of acceleration. Friedman (2016, pp. 26–27) coined the concept of the "age of accelerations" to describe the rapid acceleration in globalisation where the flow of information and knowledge leads to a hyper-connected world; where the acceleration in climate change leads to biodiversity loss and the restructuring of mother nature; and the acceleration in computing power and smart technology to seamless complexity. These accelerations combine to form the "Great Acceleration," transforming almost every single aspect of modern life. This is a time where institutions that survived for ages are under pressure, and where even resilient institutions such as churches and universities face unprecedented challenges. It is not only a question of an increase in the rate of change, but an issue of dislocation because the rate of change exceeds the ability of mankind to adapt to change. Friedman argues that the world is not just rapidly changing. Societal structures are failing to keep pace with the rate of change, and the world is starting to operate differently (Friedman 2016, p. 28).

Although Friedman writes from a particular Western and developmental perspective, recent contributions on super-diversity[1] (Vertovec 2016) affirm the complexity of society, more so in South Africa. South Africa is indeed a country of complex diversity: it has 11 official languages; a multitude of ethnic groups; widely diverging histories; all major religions are present; it experienced various phases of colonialisation and decolonialisation; it hosts many formal and informal economic approaches; many stories compete for attention.

Friedman's approach provides an entry point to engage with the complexities of South Africa, especially in terms of leadership studies: "A shifting world opens a new leadership challenge" (Terry 2001, p. 143). The age of accelerations challenges leaders in all facets of society and raises important questions on core competencies of leaders, such as discernment, the ability to formulate appropriate mission, vision and forming teams that are able to transform institutions and communities. The age of accelerations demands a new wisdom culture (*vis a vis* the focus on leadership skills) and more than "outside the box" thinking—but "thinking without a box" (Friedman 2016, p. 14). It demands a discerning spirituality from missional leaders.

This research focuses on leadership in the church and, more specifically, missional leadership. It is certainly limited by the scope of a single chapter and the fact that the researcher represents a particular facet of the complex denominational and religious landscape in South Africa, but attempts to contribute a perspective that can enhance the ability of the system to adapt to the changing context that equips leaders to act with more agility. This is typically the task of missional leaders, and a discerning spirituality will equip and assist missional leadership in this journey.

---

[1]Super-diversity is a term denoting a transformation of population patterns, especially arising from shifts in global mobility. Around the world over the past three decades, there have been increasing movements of people from more varied national, ethnic, linguistic and religious backgrounds.

Missional leadership recognises the fact that big systems, such as denominations, have "traders" and "gatekeepers" that determine the flow of ideas, the pace of transformation and orientation on the identity of systems. The life and actions of a complex system such as denominations are influenced by the relationship between traders and gatekeepers. Gatekeepers are the guardians of the *status quo*. They must ensure stability, fidelity and control. Their mission is to slow the pace of change and to bring stability to the system by leaning back into the past. Yes, any system needs a focus on the past, but then in a particular way with the aim to build on the best in the history of the system (such as is being prepared with Appreciative Inquiry [AI]). The gatekeeping function is appropriate in an age of accelerations, to preserve that of the past worthy of taking into the future (Terry 2001, p. 73). It is to drive forward but keeping an eye on the rear view-mirror. Leadership is rooted in the wisdom of the past: "You live in the present from the past forward" (Sweet 2004, p. 138).

The art of leadership is not to focus on the rear-view-mirror but to journey into the future. Leadership wisdom includes matching the best of knowledge and experience to the current reality and accelerations (see Terry 2001, p. 407). Leadership in an age of accelerations needs the posture of traders. Traders are at the forefront of change. They are the "innovators" and "early adopters" in the system (Keifert 2006, p. 55). Traders ring in changes and introduce new grammar, ideas, and innovation. Traders try to direct accelerations and incorporate a culture that embraces change. Friedman (2016, p. 306) makes a compelling case for what I label as traders, when he says that the most resilient countries and systems are those that are able to absorb many alien influences and incorporate them into the system while maintaining overall stability.

Missionaries are typical traders. They are focused on finding creative solutions and prone to be caught up in a mission to expend their talents for a self-transcending cause—they are people convinced that God has entrusted creation to human beings not merely as caretakers of a past condition but as co-creators with a God of the future (Haight 2014, p. 55).

The church, and especially denominations, find themselves in the midst of the age of accelerations and serve as a case study of the interaction between leadership, discernment and spirituality. The church needs missional leaders able to apply the wisdom of traders on the journey into an unsure and undefined future.

2 Focus on Missional Church

The concept of missional church is particularly relevant due to the renewed attention it receives in many contexts, including South Africa, and in important ecumenical organisations. The concept of missional church is also perhaps the best expression of ecclesiology to address the contextual challenges posed by the age of acceleration, especially since ideas such as contextualisation, welcoming the stranger, and faithful presence in the midst of chaos, are part and parcel of the missional church.

A number of South African churches made important policy decisions to facilitate the transformation towards missional church—to name but a few:

- The Dutch Reformed Church (DRC)—The executive of the DRC decided, at the very first meeting of their term, to prioritise the continued missional transformation of the DRC as its most important strategic goal (Nederduitse Gereformeerde Kerk 2015, p. 14).
- The Uniting Presbyterian Church in Southern Africa stated at its 2012 General Assembly that "supporting the development of missional congregations" is one of the mission priorities of the denomination (Uniting Presbyterian Church in Southern Africa 2012).
- The Anglican Church embarked on a process of renewal and revival labelled "Anglicans Ablaze" to build up the church and serve God in the world (Anglican Church of Southern Africa n.d.).
- The Netherdutch Reformed Church (NHKA) attended to a missional ecclesiology at its 2013 general assembly, and committed itself to a process of missional transformation (Nederduitsche Hervormde Kerk van Afrika 2013, p. 313–314).
- Gereformeerde Kerke in Suid-Afrika (GKSA) also focuses on the missional calling of local congregations (Gereformeerde Kerke in Suid-Afrika 2014).
- The same can be said in a global context of a number of other denominations—the Church of England and the Methodist Church in the United Kingdom with the Fresh Expressions initiative; The Protestant Church in The Netherlands (PKN)—with changes in the church polity to express this missional re-orientation[2]; the Christian Reformed Church with the dream that "our congregations will flow like streams into their communities."[3] For the Reformed Church in America the big picture is about being transformed and transforming.[4]

The issue has received significant attention in ecumenical meetings since 2010:

- The World Council of Churches published a new mission affirmation, *Together towards life* (Keum 2013). This affirmation attends to the missional calling and renewal of the church (Keum 2013, p. 7) and concludes: "Thus the churches mainly and foremost need to be missionary churches" (Keum 2013, p. 22).
- The Cape Town Commitment (Lausanne 2010), a meeting of the Lausanne Movement, acknowledged the mission of the church and the importance of the church participating in God's mission (Lausanne 2010, p. 5).

---

[2]The Kerkorde states: "2. *Levend uit Gods genade in Jezus Christus vervult de kerk de opdracht van haar Heer om het Woord te horen en te verkondigen. 3. Betrokken in Gods toewending tot de wereld, belijdt de kerk in gehoorzaamheid aan de Heilige Schrift als enige bron en norm van de kerkelijke verkondiging en dienst, de drie-enige God, Vader, Zoon en Heilige Geest.*"

[3]The CRC states: "Our congregations will flow like streams into their communities. We will meet our neighbors at community events and gathering places, listening to each other, learning from each other, and serving each other. By our presence we will become channels for the love of Christ and the Holy Spirit's life-giving transformation."

[4]This includes spiritual formation to be more like Jesus in loving God and neighbours, and making the world a better place.

- The Edinburgh 2010 mission conference, celebrating the great mission conference of 1910, emphasised the missional nature of the church and the fact that the church is the result of God's mission (Niemandt 2014, p. 66).
- The World Communion of Reformed Churches (WCRC) recognises the calling of the church to participate in the mission of the Triune God and urges members with the following:

> The missional identity and engagement of the churches and of our communion is the *raison d'être* (reason for being) of WCRC, is essential to its Reformed identity, and therefore, must be reflected in its structures, use of resources and programmatic actions (WCRC 2010, p. 164).

It is clear that the idea of missional church has captured the imagination of a significant, if not critical, amount of South African mainline denominations and local congregations. The missional church sees itself within God's mission (the *missio Dei*), and seeks "to re-enter [the world] as a missionary presence. . .living adventurously as a subversive movement, realising afresh its total reliance on the Lord" (Gibbs 2000, p. 51). Missional ecclesiology builds on the *missio Dei*, the active presence of the Triune God in his creation and the life-changing invitation to participate in this mission of God. N'kwim Bibi-Bikan (2016, p. 2) applies this to the church in Africa as well when he states that the mission of the church in Africa should be the mission of God in Africa. It is important to understand to focus on God's mission: "Mission is the result of God's initiative, rooted in God's purposes to restore and heal creation and to call people into a reconciled covenantal relationship with God" (Hesselgrave and Stetzer 2010, p. 24).

The concept of missional church does not only raise interest due to the ecumenical and denominational focus it receives, but also because it represents a confluence of ideas on spirituality, discernment and leadership. The very idea of participating in the *missio Dei* implies a spiritual journey and underlying spirituality, and discernment which is widely described as the "first step in mission." A missional church is a community of followers called by the Spirit on a journey of discernment. The active presence of the Triune God in his creation presupposes discernment as the way to understand where God is working so that God's people can join in with the Spirit and participate in God's mission. The missional church recognises the importance of leadership to envision, shape and facilitate missional transformation. To be transformed and to nurture a transforming presence in communities and the world at large requires a new kind a leader.

3   Context of Acceleration and Complexity

Discourses on spirituality and discernment are important because the church finds itself in a complex world. This is also and perhaps particularly true of the church in South Africa. The church *is* a complex system. Whether one refers to local congregations or huge denominational structures—they are all complex systems, and complexity theory provides interesting answers to new questions and challenges that churches face. More than that—the church finds itself in a dynamic reality where the dynamism also entails complexity. Some of the characteristics mentioned by Friedman seems to be quite evident in the South African landscape, such as the acceleration of globalisation, climate change, connectivity and interdependence (Friedman 2016, pp. 26–27).

Complexity enhances acceleration, and acceleration feeds complexity. The interplay between complexity and acceleration results in a situation described by Friedman (2016, p. 91) as a situation where complexity became, "fast, free, easy for you, and invisible." Computing power, increased connectivity and powerful programmes are changing the world and the way society operates: "It is making the world not just flat but fast. Fast is a natural evolution of putting all this technology together and then diffusing it everywhere" (Friedman 2016, p. 93).

The combination of acceleration and complexity creates a totally new context for the church. The importance of contextualisation in mission has been underscored by Bosch in his argument that contextualisation is an affirmation that God has turned towards the world, and that the world is a constitutive element in our understanding of mission (Bosch 1991, p. 426). This shows the importance of the context of acceleration and complexity for the church. Mission as praxis is about concrete transformation; it is specifically about transformative encounters: amongst people, and between the living God and his people (Kritzinger and Saayman 2011, pp. 49–52). This necessitates a new understanding of contextualisation. Friedman (2016, p. 312) pleads for an openness of cultures to adapt when faced with big changes in the environment. *Deep contextualisation*,[5] an expansion of contextualisation, might assist in this process. Mission as deep contextualisation will attempt to proclaim the gospel and actualise the good news in the particular circumstances brought about by globalisation and a shifting understanding of history, including "deep history" (Gregersen 2013, pp. 370, 376) and the age of accelerations. Deep contextualisation assists with the re-orientation of the history of mission on a deeper understanding of history. It also embraces the complexity and rapid evolution of society and the existence of vast ungoverned spaces in cyberspace.

4 Missional Leadership

What kind of leadership will assist the (missional) church on the journey of deep contextualisation in the context of acceleration and complexity? Perhaps the discussion on leadership must start with an introduction of Scharmer's (2009, loc. 356) definition of leadership—he describes leaders as "all people who engage in creating change or shaping their future, regardless of their formal positions in institutional structures." This can be expanded with the insight that the role of the leader is, "to help people face reality and to mobilize them to make change" (Heifetz n.d.). Leadership gives direction and cohesion to a group of people or an organisation (Noordt et al. 2008, p. 285). Direction implies change and transformation, a movement or journey to new places or experiences.

---

[5]For a more comprehensive explanation of deep contextualisation, see Niemandt (2017).

The issue of leadership is of particular importance in the process of transformation to a missional church. The church needs an appropriate missional understanding of leadership, in order to organise and transform the church into missional life, and to participate in the transformation of communities to be able to share life in its fullness (Niemandt 2016a, p. 91). The missional imperative of deep contextualisation adds perspective to the kind of leadership needed—it must guide participants with wisdom to face the deep contextual changes and assist the transformation of the church and membership to embrace and participate in God's presence in an age of complexity and acceleration. Missional leadership is *the Spirit-led transformation of people and institutions by means of meaningful relations to participate in God's mission.* Missional leadership is a turn towards discernment by God's pilgrim people. As Hendriks (2004, p. 30) puts it: "The solution to faith communities' questions about how to participate in God's missional praxis is a critical, constructive dialogue or correlation between their interpretations of the realities of the global and local context and the faith resources at their disposal."

Leadership includes helping people to adapt to change and changing contexts. The challenge lies in the understanding of change, especially if the nature of change has changed! Friedman (2016, p. 32) argues that the rate of change has accelerated and now exceeds the ability of mankind to adapt to change. "...Our societal structures are failing to keep pace with the rate of change" (Friedman 2016, p. 33). South Africa and the churches in South Africa are not immune to these global changes. But we cannot resist the invitation to be co-creators of the future. The argument by Haight (2014, p. 55) comes to mind when he describes the "Anthropology of Constructive Action":

> God has entrusted creation to human beings not merely as caretakers of a past condition but as co-creators with God of the future. This formula corresponds with the recognition that being is not static but in process, and that human beings were created by God not simply to enjoy creation but, as part of the universe, to work with the processes of evolution and to assume responsibility for its historical movement (Haight 2014, p. 55).

The leadership challenge in the age of acceleration is to reimagine and reinvent social technologies. Friedman (2016, p. 200) argues that we will need a better understanding of the way people and society operates, and we will need to find ways to accelerate the adaptability and evolution of institutions (certainly including churches), organisations and society at large. The church as a relational organism is deeply dependant on social technologies and the ability of the members to cope with and flourish in a new era. Mathewes (2015, loc. 1203–1205) argues that churches "...are those institutions that aim to give us a communal and personal, intellectual and affective, structure to help cultivate joy, our cultivation of which is their ultimate purpose."

Missional leadership responds to these challenges by focusing on the Spirit-led transformation of people and institutions by means of meaningful relations to participate in God's mission. It is a kind of leadership that facilitates changes and transformation, more so in the face of complexity and acceleration. Mpinga (2014, p. 184) states that missional leadership will have the responsibility to discern, to disclose, to teach, to expose and to develop missional identity. Cordier and Niemandt (2014), reflecting on research carried out in the South African context, concluded that missional leadership is not in the first place about strategic planning or management, but on cultivating within the missional community the capacities needed for spiritual discernment and formation: "What is needed, is not the training of religious technicians, but the formation of spiritual leaders" (Cordier and Niemandt 2014). Missional leadership requires new capacities and new paradigms.

5 Missional Spirituality

Missional leadership can only facilitate transformation and guide church members to a flourishing life in a new age of complexity and acceleration if it is deeply imbedded in a missional spirituality. In this section, the discussion on missional spirituality will, first of all, be achieved from the perspective of broader discourses on spirituality. What does spirituality really mean? Haight (2014, loc. 269–270) defines spirituality as the way persons and groups live their lives with reference to something that they acknowledge as transcendent. He argues that spirituality is a form of behaviour. It consists in the sum total of a person's actions as he or she moves along in life: ". . . spirituality is intrinsically developmental. Spirituality is a living thing that grows through time and through the life cycle of human experiences" (Haight 2014, loc. 280–281). Heifetz (n.d.) makes a strong case for the need of a sanctuary. He argues that leaders need a sanctuary, a place where they can go to get back in touch with the worth of their life and the worth of their work. This is not necessarily a physical place or an extended sabbatical. Maybe Heifetz refers to a kind of spirituality that will sustain a leader—the formation of habits and the cultivation of spaces where a leader can create daily rhythms or moments that helps leaders to "stay alive."

Terry (2001, p. 383, see also Sweet 2004, p. 110) recognises the importance of spirituality in leadership literature and states that the concept plays a role in many books, even to the extent that it is central to many leadership theories. His argument is even more appropriate in the age of complexity and acceleration:

> When we are in the midst of chaos and devastation, the past looks clear and sensible, the future unclear, even senseless. Yearning for order and meaning, we want to know that whatever is worthy of our faith and belief is present to inform, support, sustain, and encourage us (Terry 2001, p. 413).

For him spirituality equals with creating a meaning of life. Spirituality refers to the ultimate values we hold and meanings we make in relation to that which is deemed ultimately important (Terry 2001, p. 385).

The broader description of spirituality created the context for a more focused description of Christian spirituality. Wright (2015, p. 121) argues that Christian spirituality is:

> —an awareness of the loving and guiding presence of God, sorrow for sin and gratitude for forgiveness, the possibility and challenge of prayer, a love for God and for our neighbors, the desire for holiness and the hard moral work it requires, the gradual or sudden emergence of particular vocations, a lively hope for God's eventual new creation—is generated by the

good news of what has happened in the past and what will happen in the future. All this and much, much more is what is meant by the good news in the present.

Mpinga (2014, p. 197) describes missional spirituality as the Christian way of living derived from the encounter with God in Christ, the fellowship with him, and his mission in the world. Christian spirituality gives a particular content to the transcendent and acknowledges the life-giving presence of the Triune God. The ability to find meaning in life is a gift from the Spirit and ultimate values flow from the ultimate self-revelation of God in Jesus Christ. Haight says:

> Every revelation and religion has some medium or set of symbols and practises that define the form and content of its faith. According to this formula, the logic of Christian faith is Christomorphic. This means that, by definition, Christians find their way to God through faith in Jesus of Nazareth, who is acknowledged to be the Messiah or anointed one of God or Christ (Haight 2014, loc. 2138–2141).

Missional leaders are centred in and fuelled by their immersion in the body of Christ. Spiritual leadership involves two aspects closely related to each other: (1) *Spiritual discernment*—The spiritual leader possesses the ability to discern and to establish *spiritual discernment* as a practise amongst the leadership team and the congregation; and (2) *Faith formation and discipleship*—The spiritual leader lives a lifestyle of discipleship and focuses on the *spiritual coaching and formation of members* within the congregation towards biblical formation and discipleship (see also Cordier and Niemandt 2014).

With this background in mind, the focus now moves to missional spirituality. Mission is to live in the active presence of the Triune God and to participate in this mission of God. Missional spirituality is Trinitarian. Christian leadership finds its deepest ground, orientation, and direction from the God who is worshipped (Niemandt 2016a, p. 93). Missional spirituality is the discovery of God's rhythms, and the ability to align one's life to those rhythms. It is about rhythms of life, or habits, which integrate the sacred and secular. It is to join God's dance of mission (Niemandt 2016a, p. 89). Missional spirituality is imperative during transformation (Helland and Hjalmarson 2011, loc. 107) and thus completely appropriate in the context of an age of complexity and acceleration. For Helland and Hjalmarson (2011, loc. 559, 239) a missional spirituality is a spirituality embodied in daily life that forms and feeds mission. They argue that, "spiritual disciplines will form us, and doing the Father's work in community will feed us" (2011, loc. 239–240). It is about spiritual formation. Formation is an attitude that aligns the church with the kingdom of God, and that forms the basis for a spirituality that changes lives.

This also means a shift of spiritual formation from knowing and believing to hungering and thirsting, because our wants and longings and desires are at the core of our identity, the wellspring from which our actions and behaviour will flow (Smith 2016, loc. 103). Smith (JKA, loc.167) criticises modernism with its intellectualist approach that reduces human beings to mere intellect—one that treats us as if we're only and fundamentally thinking things. He builds his argument on his conviction that to be human is to be a liturgical animal, a creature whose loves are shaped by worship (Smith 2016, loc. 434). It is a transformation or re-orientation of the heart that happens from the bottom up, through the formation of our habits of desire. We are teleological creatures (Smith 2009b, p. 52), formed by habits that constitute the fulcrum of desire (Smith 2009b, p. 56). We act according to habit or dispositions that are formed in us through practises, routine, and rituals (Smith 2009b, p. 62). Smith (2016, loc. 465) concludes: "Learning to love (God) takes practise."

Ungerer et al. (2013, pp. 48–64)—South African researchers from various disciplines, provide a framework and creative perspective to develop habits for a transformative, missional spirituality. Niemandt (2016a, pp. 85–103) applied the insights of Ungerer et al. (2013) to missional spirituality and practises.

Ungerer et al. (2013) describe the following six virtues, where a virtue is defined as moral excellence, righteousness, and a particularly good (or beneficial) quality. Each of these virtues has a social, or relational dimension, as well as a personal, or emotional dimension. They developed reflective routines (habits) to facilitate inner transformation and personal knowing, and include the art of reflective learning (Ungerer et al. 2013, p. 33).

- Transcendence, which includes appreciation of beauty, gratitude, hope, humour, and religiousness.
- Humanity, which includes the social competencies of kindness, love, and social intelligence.
- Wisdom and knowledge, which include the cognitive competencies of creativity, curiosity, open-mindedness, and love of learning.
- Courage, which includes the personal and emotional competencies of bravery, persistence, and zest.
- Justice, which is associated with fairness, leadership, and teamwork.
- Temperance, which include the competencies of forgiveness, modesty, prudence, and self-regulation.

Niemandt (see 2016a, pp. 94–100) developed missional spiritual practises that relate to each of these virtues. They are summarised for the sake of brevity:

Virtue	Missional practise
Transcendence	Solitude—a ritual to find one's identity in Christ. Solitude is to step away from people for a period of time, in order to encounter God and rediscover one's true identity in Christ. Solitude is about creating space to listen—it is to open up for God, mostly in the context of a community of followers of Christ. It entails a disposition to discern
Humanity	Kindness/compassion to all, even those who anger us. The exercise involves not only reflecting on a situation of anger and withdrawing from it, but also active acts of compassion and understanding. It values relations more than theological barriers Hospitality to the stranger is a typical missional response and expression of love. Gospel hospitality has always been at the heart of Christian life. One can say that missional spirituality is characterised by welcome and hospitality
Wisdom and knowledge	This refers to a wisdom-shaped spirituality that focusses on a faithful presence in all contexts

(continued)

Virtue	Missional practise
	Sparks et al. (2014, p. 46) understands faithful presence as taking your bodies, your location and your community very seriously, as seriously as God in Christ took them. Faithful presence invites you to act on the belief that God is giving you what you need to be formed as disciples within your location. Wisdom and knowledge develops ways to be faithfully present Meylahn (2012, p. 40) states that "being church, doing theology is about listening to the narratives of a particular local context and then seeking to interpret these narratives within their cultural, social, political narrative setting, with the help of other disciplines. . ."
Courage	Taking risks. Frost and Hirsch (2011, p. 24) write: "The church should be one of the most adventurous places on earth—the locus of all quests, the highly adaptive Jesus community at the very forefront of what God is doing in the world." Courage refers to the willingness to break with traditional ideas and convention and agreement in faith communities that mistakes and experiments will be tolerated and even celebrated. In terms of missional leadership, play is important. Play is the oxygen for creativity, and creativity ignites missional innovation. Smith (2009a, pp. 47–49) argues: "We play because our God is good. Grace is sufficient for us. God wants us to be full of joy, and play is a way to experience the goodness of God and the richness of life"
Justice	Ungerer et al. (2013, p. 55) states that the virtue of justice is associated with fairness, leadership, and teamwork. Life in mission means creativity, generosity, and reconciliation. Missional leadership is orientated on the cross. The cross of Christ reveals a missional, justifying, justice-making God and creates a missional, justified, justice-making people. Enjoying flourishing life as a gift of the Trinity is a celebration of righteousness and justice (Niemandt 2016b, p. 5). Smith (2016, loc. 87–88) gives an excellent description of the relationship between spirituality and justice: "If you are passionate about seeking justice, renewing culture, and taking up your vocation to unfurl all of creation's potential, you need to invest in the formation of your imagination. You need to curate your heart. You need to worship well. Because you are what you love" (Smith 2016, loc. 87–88)
Temperance	Temperance is about forgiveness, modesty, prudence and self-regulation. This entails a "kenotic" spiritual and missional ritual, where missional leaders can practise humility by dwelling in the Word (on a text such as Phlp 2, pp. 5–11). One can ask questions such as: "How can I imitate Christ's humility?" or "Share a story where you misuse the power of the gospel and what you learned from that." Transformational missional spirituality focuses on mutual service and interdependence, and on vulnerability. Shared stories create a safe space to practise this kenotic missional ritual

It is important to underscore the perspective that a missional spirituality embraces deep contextualisation. It is a spirituality where church, culture and biblical narrative constantly interact and the missional church dwells in the Word and in the culture (world). It is a movement in the power of the Spirit, where listening to the biblical narratives leads the listener closer to God and where the deepening relation with the Triune God leads to a deeper involvement with culture and context. Although transcendence focuses on the ultimate presence of God, God is never present in a way that ignores humanity and context. Courage, justice, temperance and wisdom plays out in real life.

6 Discernment

Discernment flows from spirituality and nurtures wisdom—it is about making wise choices. It is one of the most important qualities of leadership and emphasises wisdom and an awareness of that which is deemed ultimately important, and thus God's presence in all of reality. In his argument for the church's mission in Africa, N'Kwim Bibi-Bikan (2016, p. 26) says: "Every local church needs to discern what God wants it to be and to do." Discernment is about entering into the trialogue: the discerning interaction between church, culture and biblical narrative—to seek, discover, understand and share in what the Holy Spirit is up to in the close-to-the-ground particulars of the church's engagement in, with, against and for the world. Discernment is the first, and most decisive, step on this missional journey. Mission is joining in with the Spirit in the *missio Dei*. Discernment is the process of being aware of where the Spirit is working. Van Gelder (2007) summarises this discussion as follows:

> A missional ecclesiology understands congregations as being the creation of the Spirit. As communities are created by the Spirit, so also congregations seek to be led by the Spirit. They do this by engaging in some form of discernment process in order to understand their purpose (mission), and how they are being called through this purpose to participate in God's mission in the world... (Van Gelder 2007, p. 107).

It is a core practise of Christian leadership and spirituality. Mpinga (2014, p. 85) says the missional church will use discernment in order to find out a way of reaching out to the community in which it is working. It is the art of reading the times and signs—opening yourself up to the context and to God's involvement in the context (Niemandt 2016a, p. 90). Quaker communities can serve as an excellent example of communal missional discernment (see Love and Niemandt 2014).

Discernment involves listening. Sweet (2004, p. 17) argues that leadership is an acoustical art. Heifetz (n.d.): "...leaders must want to listen. Good listening is fuelled by curiosity and empathy: What's really happening here? Can I put myself in someone else's shoes? It's hard to be a great listener if you're not interested in other people." Meylahn (2012, p. 38) says that the church is no longer an institution—created and sustained by the proclamation of a truth, and the correct administration of the sacraments—but a hermeneutical space of listening and discerning. This is especially true of the missional church. Van Gelder and Zscheile (2011, p. 149) makes a strong case that the missional church is, "...a habit of mind and heart, a posture of openness and discernment, and a faithful attentiveness to the Spirit's presence and to the world that God so loves." Cordier and Niemandt (2015) describe the importance of listening in missional congregations as, first, the capacity to listen others into free speech. This refers to the skill of listening to others and articulating the insights. The second is the cultivation and facilitation of discerning processes in the congregation, which include the cultivation of four unique and related listening skills: to listen to God, to listen to the Word, to one another, and to the context (Cordier and Niemandt 2015).

In terms of listening to God and the Word, many missional communities found the practise of dwelling in the Word very valuable in the process of missional discernment

(Nel 2013). Dwelling in the Word is the practise of a repeated communal listening to a passage of Scripture over long periods of time in order to enable a Christian community to undertake its decisions and actions in line with biblical meta-narrative. The aim of dwelling in the Word is to discover the preferred and promised future of God for a specific faith community (see Nel 2013, pp. 1–2).[6]

Discernment connects leadership, communal life and missional spirituality, especially in the safe space of worship and liturgy. Rossouw (2016, p. 390) talks about *liturgical listening*. He says it is where the *missio Deo* and *coram Deo* meet. Liturgy creates an open, patient, rhythmic approach to discernment. Love and Niemandt (2014, p. 1) refer to the Quaker communities, where discernment is not simply about making decisions or finding your vocation but, at its heart is an act of worship. For them, seeking participation in the Divine life and will is an act of worship. They intentionally make a place for God to be an active participant in the discernment process (Love and Niemandt 2014, p. 7). The liturgy of worship flows into the liturgy of life when a missional community focuses on finding God in the neighbourhood and broader community. Many in the missional church movement calls this dwelling in the world. Dwelling in the world entails a process of dialogue and engagement with the contexts in which the missional community finds itself (see Niemandt 2010, p. 9). The participants ask: "What is God up to?" in their particular contexts.

---

[6]Nel (2013, p. 6) found that dwelling in the Word teaches and confirms the followings skills, attitudes and behaviour:

- Group members practice reaching out and sharing their faith with people they do not necessarily know well (the "reasonably friendly-looking stranger" in the group).
- Interpreting the text becomes the responsibility of all in the community, and not only of those considered experts in exegesis.
- Members practice the skill of listening to others and articulating their partners' insights.
- The communicative playing field is intentionally levelled. Those who are naturally reluctant to speak in groups are helped to do so by not having to share their own personal thoughts, whilst those who tend to dominate discussions are constrained by their having to share the insights of others.
- Strong emotions are negated as all insights are stated in the third person.
- Reading, discussing and reflecting on the Word become more important than concluding the "business" part of church meetings.
- The repeated reading of a specific text creates a shared sense of purpose and willingness to take risks for the sake of their faith amongst the practitioners of dwelling in the Word. Over time dwelling in the Word shapes a group's collective imagination. It defines who they are in relationship to one another and sometimes who they are over against everyone else in the world.
- Word-dwelling develops the skill of interpreting the Word with others and provides a language for sharing thoughts with each other. Although it is a metaphoric dwelling, it manages to create a sense of community and shared culture. Certain words begin to remind the dwellers of certain things and verbal shorthand develops.
- The sharing with another is the first filter for esoteric, way-out interpretations of Scripture.
- Honest reporting and fair access to the conversation builds trust.

7 A Hermeneutic of Love

I agree with Meylahn that the church is a hermeneutical space of listening and discerning. But this underscores the importance of reflecting on the nature of appropriate hermeneutics. Heath (2008) writes, in *The mystic way of Evangelism*, that the church will have to learn to look differently at the world. We need to look with a hermeneutic of love. A hermeneutic of love brings together the essential characteristics of a missional spirituality as well as a lens for discernment. The argument flows in the same direction in Helland and Hjalmarson's (2011, loc. 524) conviction that Christian spirituality is relational and formed in love. Faithful presence must be shaped by love. Sparks et al. (2014, p. 82) also makes a strong point that God is love, and mission is the loving expression of God being God: "Your longing to be a church comprised of love and faithful presence needs to be the primary motivation for the mission of the church."

When we dwell in culture and the world, as part of deep contextualisation, a hermeneutic of love changes the approach. Heath asks:

> What if we looked at our world...'with pity and not with blame'? What if we heard God's call to evangelize out of love instead of fear, hope instead of judgment? What if we saw sin for the complex mixture it is, grounded in wounds and unmet needs? What if we automatically tried to see the 'total fact' of others? In short, what would it mean to read our world with a hermeneutic of love? (Heath 2008, p. 119).

I was surprised to read Friedman's response to the age of complexity and accelerations. He labels this as a time of unprecedented freedom: "Cyberspace is the place we are all connected and no one is in charge" (Friedman 2016, p. 339). Complexity and accelerations create vast new ungoverned spaces with super-empowered individuals. It is a world where a small group of individuals are able to kill, not only another person or thousands of others, but are able to kill everyone. It is a time of daunting freedom and responsibility. Hyper-connectivity and cyberspace changed the perception of freedom. Friedman (2016, p. 339) states that there is no place where you encounter the freedom to choose more than in cyberspace. It is a place where all mankind can be unified and be totally free (Friedman 2016, p. 340). It reminds me of Haight's (2014, loc. 1825) argument that God bestowed on humans freedom and creativity through the mechanism of evolution. Created reality is an open system that includes a vast range of possibilities and unpredictable novelty. This brings mankind before a moral fork of epic proportions—"where one of us could kill all of us and all of us could fix everything if we really decided to do so" (Friedman 2016, p. 342). Friedman's answer to this challenge? He pleads that we need to find a way to get more people to practise the Golden Rule—love your neighbour as you love yourself, or do to others as you would wish them to do to you (Friedman 2016, p. 348). He echoes much of the sentiment of Heath and countless other wise people. To love others constitutes a simple effective moral guide, able to guide us in the most complex situations. It is ever adaptive and applicable to every imaginable situation. Friedman (2016, p. 348) reasons: "When the world is already complex, you don't want to make it more complicated. Make it simple." A hermeneutic of love forms the basis of a missional spirituality and guides discernment in the ever more complex world.

Deep contextualisation reminds us that this open system is a network in which human beings are an intrinsic part of the evolutionary network of life and the incomprehensible cosmos. We need to listen to and discern God's loving presence in the whole of creation and we need to seek "Christ's crucifixion in that context which opens what is for the kingdom still to come" (Meylahn 2012, p. 72). A hermeneutic of love allows deep contextualisation—embracing the age of complexity and acceleration. Niemandt (2016b, p. 6) argues that Christian joy is an embodied awareness of holy presence and extravagant love, and pleads that Christians must become an embodying presence of Christ's love (a contextualisation of God's presence). Love, and not faith, is indeed the final criterion for missional leadership.

8 Conclusion

Complexity and the age of accelerations impact on the church, society at large and thus also on leadership. This research focussed on missional leadership, defined as *the Spirit-led transformation of people and institutions by means of meaningful relations to participate in God's mission.* Missional leadership recognises the fact that big systems have "traders" and "gatekeepers" that determine the flow of ideas, the pace of transformation and orientation on the identity of systems. Gatekeepers are the guardians of the *status quo.* They must ensure stability, fidelity and control. Leadership in an age of accelerations needs the posture of traders. Traders are at the forefront of change. They are the "innovators" and "early adopters." Missionaries are typical traders, focused on finding creative solutions.

Discernment and spirituality are of the utmost importance, because spiritual leadership involves spiritual discernment and faith formation and discipleship. Missional spirituality is the discovery of God's rhythms, and the ability to align one's life to those rhythms. It is about rhythms of life, or habits, which integrate the sacred and secular. A number of habits for a transformative, missional spirituality were developed. Discernment connects leadership, communal life and missional spirituality, especially in the safe space of worship and liturgy. A hermeneutic of love allows deep contextualisation—embracing the age of complexity and acceleration.

References

Anglican Church of Southern Africa (nd) Anglicans ablaze. http://www.anglicansablaze.org/about-us.aspx. Accessed 15 Apr 2017
Bosch DJ (1991) Transforming mission: paradigm shifts in theology of mission. Orbis, Maryknoll

Cordier GS, Niemandt CJP (2014) Core capacities for the minister as missional leader in the formation of a missional congregational culture. J Missional Pract 5. http://journalofmissionalpractice.com/core-capacities-for-the-minister-as-missional-leader-in-the-formation-of-a-missional-congregational-culture-part-1-role-of-a-minister/. Accessed 1 May 2017

Cordier GS, Niemandt CJP (2015) Core capacities for the minister as missional leader in the formation of a missional congregational culture. Part 2: Capacities and conclusions. J Missional Pract 5. http://journalofmissionalpractice.com/core-capacities-for-the-minister-as-missional-leader-in-the-formation-of-a-missional-congregational-culture-part-1-role-of-a-minister/. Accessed 1 May 2017

Friedman LT (2016) Thank you for being late: an optimist's guide to thriving in the age of accelerations. Allen Lane, London

Frost M, Hirsch A (2011) The faith of leap: embracing a theology of risk, adventure and courage. Baker [Kindle], Grand Rapids

Gereformeerde Kerke in Suid-Afrika (2014) Missionale aktiwiteite van die GKSA. http://www.gksa.org.za/Deputate/sending-deputate. Accessed 29 July 2014

Gibbs E (2000) Church next: quantum changes in how we do ministry. InterVarsity, Downers Grove

Gregersen NH (2013) Cur deus caro: Jesus and the cosmos story. Theol Sci 11(4):370–393

Haight R (2014) Spirituality seeking theology, Modern spiritual masters series. Orbis, Maryknoll

Heath EA (2008) The mystic way of Evangelism. A contemplative vision for Christian outreach. Baker [Kindle Edition], Grand Rapids

Heifetz R (n.d.) The leader of the future. http://www.thierryschool.be/solar-system/starship-II/artemis/h8qAf2te9aja.htm. Accessed 15 April 2017

Helland R, Hjalmarson L (2011) Missional spirituality: embodying God's love from the inside out. InterVarsity [Kindle], Downers Gove

Hendriks HJ (2004) Studying congregations in Africa. LuxVerbiBM, Wellington

Hesselgrave DJ, Stetzer E (2010) Missionshift: global mission issues in the third millennium. B & H Academic, Nashville

Keifert P (2006) We are Here Now: A New Missional Era, a Missional Journey of Spiritual Discovery. Allelon, Eagle

Keum J (ed) (2013) Together towards life. Mission and evangelism in changing landscapes. World Council of Churches, Geneva

Kritzinger JNJ, Saayman W (2011) David J Bosch. Prophetic integrity, cruciform praxis. Cluster, Dorpspruit

Lausanne (2010) The Cape Town commitment. A confession of faith and a call to action. Proceedings of the Third Lausanne Congress on World Evangelization, Cape Town, October 16–25, 2010. http://www.lausanne.org/docs/CapeTownCommitment.pdf.r Accessed 15 April 2017

Love CR, Niemandt CJP (2014) Led by the Spirit: missional communities and the Quakers on communal vocation discernment. HTS Teol Stud/Theol Stud 70(1). https://doi.org/10.4102/hts.v70i1.2626

Mathewes C (2015) Towards a theology of joy. In: Volf M (ed) Joy and human flourishing: essays on theology, culture, and the good life. Fortress [Kindle], Minneapolis

Meylahn JA (2012) Church emerging from the cracks: a church IN, but not OF the world. SunPress, Stellenbosch

Mpinga A (2014) Francophone churches in the cities of Johannesburg and Pretoria (Tshwane): a missiological perspective. DTh dissertation, UNISA

Nederduitsche Hervormde Kerk van Afrika (2013) Notule van die 70ste Algemene Kerkvergadering van die NHKA. NHKA Kerkargief, Pretoria

Nederduitse Gereformeerde Kerk (2015) Notule van die Eerste Vergadering van die Algemene Sinode Moderamen, 16–18 November 2015. NG Kerk, Pretoria

Nel MJ (2013) The influence of dwelling in the Word within the Southern African Partnership of Missional Churches. Verbum et Ecclesia 34(1):1–8. https://doi.org/10.4102/ve.v34i1.778

Niemandt CJP (2010) Five years of missional church—reflections on missional ecclesiology. Missionalia 38(3):397–413

Niemandt CJP (2014) Emerging missional ecclesiology in the Dutch Reformed Church in South Africa and church polity. In: Jannsen AL, Koffeman LJ (eds) Protestant church polity in changing contexts I: Ecclesiological and historical contributions. Proceedings of the international conference, Utrecht, The Netherlands. Lit Verlag, Zurich

Niemandt CJP (2016a) Transformative spirituality and missional leadership. Mission Stud 33: 85–103

Niemandt CJP (2016b) Rediscovering joy in costly and radical discipleship in mission. HTS Teol Stud/Theol Stud 72(4). https://doi.org/10.4102/hts.v72i4.3831

Niemandt CJP (2017) Mission as breaking down walls, opening gates, and empowering traders—from contextualisation to deep contextualisation. HTS Teol Stud/Theol Stud 73(1). https://doi.org/10.4102/hts.v73i1.4621

N'Kwim Bibi-Bikan R (2016) The mission of the church in Africa for the 21st century. Paradigm Shifts and challenges. Les Editions Du Vin Nouveau, Kinshasa

Noordt G, Paas S, de Roest H, Stoffels S (eds) (2008) Als een kerk opnieuw begint: Handboek voor missionaire gemeenskapsvorming. Boekencentrum, Zoetermeer

Rossouw PF (2016) Inclusive communities: a missional approach to racial inclusivity within the Dutch Reformed Church. Stellenbosch Theol J 2(1):381–396

Scharmer CO (2009) Theory U: learning from the future as it emerges. Berrett-Koehler [Kindle], San Francisco

Smith JB (2009a) The good and beautiful life: putting on the character of Christ. Lux Verbi BM, Cape Town

Smith JKA (2009b) Desiring the kingdom: worship, worldview and cultural formation. Baker, Grand Rapids

Smith JKA (2016) You are what you love: the spiritual power of habit. Baker [Kindle], Grand Rapids

Sparks P, Soerens T, Friesen DJ (2014) The new parish: how neighborhood churches are transforming mission, discipleship and community. InterVarsity [Kindle], Downers Grove

Sweet L (2004) Summoned to lead. Zondervan, Grand Rapids

Terry R (2001) Seven zones for leadership: acting authentically in stability and chaos. Davies-Black, Palo Alto

Ungerer M, Herholdt J, Le Roux J (2013) Leadership for all: virtue practices to flourish. Knowres, Randburg

Uniting Presbyterian Church in Southern Africa (2012) UPCSA Mission and Vision. http://unitingpresbyterian.org/mission-vision/upcsa-mission-and-vision/. Accessed 15 Apr 2017

Van Gelder C (2007) The ministry of the missional church. Baker, Grand Rapids

Van Gelder C, Zscheile DJ (2011) The missional church in perspective: mapping trends and shaping the conversation. Baker, Grand Rapids

Vertovec S (2016) Super-diversity. Routledge, London

World Communion of Reformed Churches (2010) Proceedings of the Uniting General Council 2010, Grand Rapids

Wright NT (2015) Simply good news: why the gospel is news and what makes it good. HarperCollins [Kindle], London

Nelus Niemandt (D.D.) is professor in Missiology and Head of the Department Religion Studies of the Faculty of Theology at the University of Pretoria, South Africa. His D.D. thesis, which he wrote at the University of Pretoria, focused on ethics and multiculturality. He is a rated researcher of the National Research Foundation. He does research on missional church, missional leadership, ecumenism and missional theology. He is the author of two books, numerous chapters in books and more than 50 articles in South African and international peer-reviewed journals. He is the promotor of 16 Ph.D. and supervisor of 45 M-degrees completed under his supervision. He is a member of several national and international academic organisations and research consortia, and vice-editor of *Missionalia*. Before his tenure as lecturer he ministered in the Weltevreden congregation for 25 years and also served as chaplain in Johannesburg, South Africa.

Challenging the New "One-Dimensional Man": The Protestant Orders of Life as a Critical Nuance to Workplace Spirituality

Steven C. van den Heuvel

Abstract While recognizing the increased attention to spirituality in the workplace as being a good development overall, this chapter focuses on some problematic aspects of this new emphasis. In particular, three problems are identified: (1) the danger of instrumentalization and narcissistic misdirection; (2) the adoption of pragmatism in solving conflicts between conflicting spiritualities in the workplace, and (3) the dominance of radical social constructivist approaches, which don't take into consideration the metaphysical claims inherent in many (especially religious) forms of spirituality. Together, these problems amount to a new "one-dimensionality," referring to the famous description of modern society by Herbert Marcuse. In order to address these problems, I make recourse to the Protestant concept of the different orders of life, particularly as developed by the German theologian Dietrich Bonhoeffer. In this chapter, I focus on three characteristics of his concept and argue that they can help in addressing the problems with the new emphasis on workplace spirituality that I have identified.

1 Introduction: The New Quest for Spirituality in the Workplace

The background to this volume is the enormous increase in the attention being paid to the theme of spirituality in the workplace. This upsurge can be understood in a number of different ways. On the one hand, it can be seen as an expression of the dramatic changes taking place in the nature of work, especially in the West. From the predominantly repetitive and mechanical work in factories during the era of

The original version of this chapter was revised. A correction to this chapter is available at
https://doi.org/10.1007/978-3-319-98884-9_13.

S. C. van den Heuvel (✉)
Department of Systematic Theology, Evangelische Theologische Faculteit, Leuven, Belgium

Extraordinary Researcher at the Faculty of Theology, North-West University, Potchefstroom, South Africa
e-mail: steven.vandenheuvel@etf.edu

J. (Kobus) Kok, S. C. van den Heuvel (eds.), *Leading in a VUCA World*,
Contributions to Management Science, https://doi.org/10.1007/978-3-319-98884-9_11

industrialization, the West has moved towards a service economy, and is currently moving increasingly towards an information economy. This dynamic has been noted by many researchers. Thomas Friedman, for example, speaks about the current era as being the "age of accelerations" (Friedman 2016).[1] Spirituality, as a quest for unity and meaning, can be seen as the desire for an answer in this context of fraction and change. This renewed focus on the individual makes the personal and spiritual wellbeing of the employee vitally important to the competitive success of an organization in a way that has not been widely recognized before (see, for example, Holman et al. 2005). Many studies show how a focus on spirituality is positively correlated with greater worker performance. They demonstrate how workers who score well on the indicators of spiritual wellbeing can deal better with workplace stress and job overload and enjoy more job satisfaction.[2]

A second reason for the upsurge in spirituality in the workplace is a genuine interest on the part of both employers as well as employees, an interest that goes beyond the instrumental use of spirituality as a way of boosting employee performance. In fact, many people with an interest in spirituality might say that such an instrumental view betrays the very intention with which they seek to develop their spiritual growth—this intention will most often be characterized as genuine, non-instrumental value-directed-ness. As such, renewed spirituality in the workplace is the expression of an old and profound realization, namely that one's place of work is not just a way of making money to fund a life lived outside of the organization. This latter view can best be understood, in fact, as a result of the mechanization and dehumanization of work in the industrial era. It is conceivable that work loses its meaning for the factory worker who has to perform monotonous tasks over and over again, day in day out. That worker might try to find meaning elsewhere, or, more likely, drown its loss—quite literally—in the café. As mechanical and dehumanizing labor has almost disappeared in the West, it has become possible for the majority of people to once more seek a connection between their work and their spirituality. In that sense the new quest for spirituality is really not that new, to be understood primarily as a reaction, but is rather the re-emergence of an age-old endeavor.

While recognizing the genuine interest in workplace spirituality, in this chapter I nevertheless take a critical distance, discerning several problems with this interest. I will focus on three in particular: (1) the danger of instrumentalization and narcissistic misdirection, (2) the use of pragmatism as a framework for solving conflicts between spiritualities, and (3) the social constructivism inherent in many pleas for workplace spirituality. I then attempt to address these problems by means of the uniquely Lutheran concept of the different orders of life, specifically as set out by the German theologian, Dietrich Bonhoeffer. In particular, I focus on his proposal of the different "mandates," which represents his interpretation of the Lutheran concept of the orders

---

[1]See also the chapter "Discerning Spirituality for Missional Leaders" by Nelus Niemandt in this volume.

[2]Some examples are Atlaf and Awan (2011); Marques and Dhiman (2014); Gupta et al. (2014); and Moran (2010). For an overview, see Lambert III (2009).

of life. I will argue that consideration of these mandates can help address the problems identified with contemporary appeals for workplace spirituality. First, the mandates can act as a restraint on attempts to instrumentalize and abuse workplace spirituality. Second, the mandates form an alternative way of appropriating spiritual pluralism. Thirdly and finally, they allow for a constructionist approach to workplace spirituality, while similarly helping to resist radical social constructivism.

2 Problems with the Appeal for a "New Spirituality"

The contemporary appeal for spirituality in the workplace is understandable—indeed, for the reasons given above it is almost inevitable that spirituality will end up high on the agenda. Yet while understandable, and mostly commendable, the existence of different motives for this contemporary interest nevertheless also gives rise to difficulties and dangers. In particular, I identify three problems.

2.1 The Danger of Instrumentalization and Narcissistic Misdirection

As already suggested, organizations—especially in competitive businesses—may have a less-than-genuine interest in stimulating the spiritual development of their employees. They might be primarily interested in increasing the productivity rates of their employees by paying more attention to workspace spirituality, with the expected benefit of increased resistance to stress and excessive workload, as well as increased creativity and originality. This motive has been explored by Tourish and Pinnington, amongst others, who speak cynically about transformational leadership, corporate cultism, and the spirituality paradigm as being a new "unholy Trinity," whose aim is to create a false sense of consent among workers and to fire them on to work more, and harder (Tourish and Pinnington 2002).

   While some degree of commercialization or instrumentalization of spirituality may seem inevitable, it becomes a different story when requirements for spiritual investment are put up front as a precondition for work at the organization; and when, consequently, an employee's spiritual reservoir is tapped by the organization—sometimes until it is empty. There is a certain naïveté about this danger in the writings of some management gurus. Peter Block, for example, expressly asks employees to put themselves in the vulnerable situation of owning the organizational processes in which they are involved, as if they actually did control or own them. He identifies this posture as stewardship (Block 1993). While he clarifies that this attitude isn't one of meekness, but rather of fortitude—he makes approving references to the philosophy of Friedrich Nietzsche in this context, for example—it is nevertheless clear that it could expose the employee to considerable stress if they feel responsible for processes that they ultimately don't control.

There is a further danger: passionate calls for spiritual investment in an organization can easily become part of the toolbox of the manipulative and the narcissistic leader. The much-studied example of Steve Jobs is a good example of someone who demanded from his staff a deep personal and spiritual commitment to Apple and to the products the company was developing. While he indeed managed to greatly inspire many employees, getting them to give their best, there was also a very dark side to this management style, one that Walter Isaacson refers to as his "reality distortion field" (Isaacson 2011, *passim*). While hugely inspiring on the one hand, Jobs was also instrumental in the psychological breakdown of a number of employees, due to his demanding and manipulative leadership style.

Instances such as these point to the potentially very negative consequences of a deep entanglement between the spirituality of employees and that of a company. History provides many disturbing examples of these consequences. Vladimir Tarassenko, for example, points out that in the Soviet Union workers were urged to invest deeply and personally in the state endeavors for which they were enlisted. The rhetoric around such appeals sounded sincere and innocent, but in reality it was a means to overcome any internal resistance the "workers" might have had against the communist imperialism that tried to swallow them up whole (Tarassenko 2006, 2008).[3] Similar attempts at overcoming the distinction between personal and organizational spiritual goals were made in Nazi Germany (see Van den Heuvel 2017b).

2.2 Pragmatism as the Solution to Conflicting Spiritualities

People differ widely in their definition of spirituality, as well as in the way they practice it. Although in literature much care is taken to distinguish between religion and spirituality (see, for example, Mitroff and Denton 1999; Phipps and Benefiel 2013), in practice there is a large overlap between religious belief and spirituality in the workplace. This case has been made strongly by Douglas Hicks—he argues that religion is wrongfully overlooked in discussions of spirituality in the workplace (Hicks 2003; this point is also made by Zinnbauer and Pargament 2005). This of course raises the question of how to negotiate religious conflict at the workplace. Focusing particularly on this question, Hicks develops his theory of "respectful pluralism." Central to this theory are the concepts of *respect* and of *human dignity*. He gives these guidelines a personalist basis—according to him, "[p]ersons simply have dignity and deserve to be accorded respect because they are human" (Hicks 2003, p. 167). The third guiding principle, undergirding those of respect and dignity, is that of *equality*—according to him, ". . . all human beings possess *equal* dignity and thus deserve *equal* respect" (Hicks 2003, p. 167, italics original). Furthermore, Hicks assumes that a certain legal context exists in relation to the workplace.

---

[3]For a fuller engagement, see Kessler (2016) and Van den Heuvel (2017b).

Gotsis and Kortezi, while being sympathetic to Hicks's proposal, note that his proposal for dealing with conflicts over spirituality in the workplace is based on a consequentialist foundation (Gotsis and Kortezi 2008). This is indeed the case: because while Hicks does, in part, include substantive accounts in defense of human dignity, for instance, his framework, as such, is not based on such substantive claims. Instead, it is an open-ended and mostly procedural attempt to reach *consensus* in conflicts over workplace spirituality. Hicks says: "I offer the framework of respectful pluralism in the hope that some or many readers will find it convincing and that those who disagree will offer a superior approach that addresses the circumstances of the contemporary workplace" (Hicks 2003, p. 166).

Gotsis and Kortezi deem such a consequentialist framework to be insufficient, and in reply they consider alternative foundations to workplace spirituality, making recourse to the other main schools of normative ethics, namely value ethics, deontological ethics, and virtue ethics. According to them, consideration of these other schools results in a richer approach to conflicts between differing spiritualities in the workplace. However, they don't concretize how the alternatives they offer would specifically achieve this enrichment, nor do they outline how potential differences arising from the application of these different approaches should be negotiated.

Furthermore, an important problem with Hicks's proposal, as well as with the response to it by Gotsis and Kortezi, is that the norms for deciding on spiritual practices do not derive from the spiritual journeys themselves, but come "from outside."[4] That is a major stumbling block for working with this approach in a spiritually diverse environment. Even though the approach hinges on the ability of the parties involved in the conflict to recognize their mutual equal dignity, and subsequently, the right of the other to respect, insufficient effort is made to make a case for this attitude that is based on the internal sources of the various spiritualities.

2.3   Spirituality: A Social Construct?

Connected to this is a third problem, namely the tendency by social scientists to primarily study spirituality within the framework of social constructivism (just one example is Hyde et al. 2014). Social constructivism as an approach is still in the process of forming, drawing on a number of disciplines, in particular psychology, history, and philosophy. Berger and Luckman's 1966 book *The Social Construction of Reality*, has been seminal. In it they claim that

> There is only human nature in the sense of anthropological constants (. . .) that delimit and permit man's socio-cultural formations. But the specific shape into which this humanness is moulded is determined by those socio-cultural formations and relative to their numerous variations. While it is possible to say that man has a nature, it is more significant to say that

---

[4]In fact, Hicks himself recognizes the problem of such an approach when he critically discusses Rousseau's views on the civil religion. See Hicks (2003, p. 116).

man constructs his own nature, or more simply, that man produces himself (Berger and Luckman 1991 [1966], p. 67).

This approach is a clear break with the view that human and social nature have a metaphysical basis, grounded, for example, in Christian theism. The methodological presuppositions of social constructivism have an immanent basis, which is exemplified in a further definition by Fiona Hibberd, according to whom "social constructivism emphasizes the historicity, the context-dependence, and the socio-linguistically constituted character of all matters involving human activity" (Hibberd 2005, p. viii; quoted in Sremac 2010, p. 10). This approach is suited to explicating many internal spiritual processes, again using psychology, for instance. But the often-unstated presupposition is that these constructions are all there is. As John Swinton and Harriet Mowat note: "The meaning and definition of reality is . . . flexible, and open to negotiation depending on circumstances, perception, knowledge, power, structures and so forth" (Swinton and Mowat 2006, p. 36; quoted in Sremac 2010, p. 10).

This social constructive view on spirituality may resonate with those who accept that their own spirituality is indeed such a conditioned phenomenon.[5] Most people, however, especially if they are theistic believers, will have difficulty accepting a social constructivist way of looking at their innermost beliefs and practices. Beyond such personal objections, there are also serious theological objections to be made against a purely social constructionist understanding of spirituality. Mark Wallace, for example, while generally positive about the potential of social constructivism for theology, nevertheless warns that this new school has a certain "tone deafness to the importance of *alterity* in the formation of self-hood" (Wallace 2002, pp. 108–109, italics original). He continues: "If subjectivity is reducible to culture, is there any place for the sometimes unique and distinctively 'other' voice of 'the good within' to tear apart the fabric of one's social relations in an effort to work out the meaning and truth of one's *ownmost, radically individualistic, and oftentimes antisocial sense of the good?*" (Wallace 2002, p. 109, italics original).[6]

It is important to be nuanced here. Steven Engler has pointed out that many studies on the relationship between social constructivism and the study of religion are too superficial, either because they misrepresent social constructivism as necessarily relativistic, or because they take the theory for granted to such an extent that it is no longer deemed necessary to explicate its workings (Engler 2005). When criticizing the dominance of social constructivism, it is especially important to be mindful of that first pitfall of unjustly equating social constructivism with relativism. In this connection, it is imperative to realize that as a working theory in the social sciences, social constructivism deliberately functions *etsi Deus non daretur*—it is a paradigm to be used in a specific context, without purporting to offer a total explanation of social and human life. As such, it is comparable with the paradigm of *homo economicus*, for example. Yet it still is the case that often the study of spirituality is in danger of the

---

[5]An example is the neuroscientist and well-known atheist Sam Harris—in his book, *Waking Up*, he is quite outspoken about his purely pragmatic choice for "stream of consciousness" (Harris 2014).
[6]For other criticisms, see for example Glaserfeld (2000).

second pitfall, namely absolutizing the social constructivist paradigm, granting it more explanatory power than it warrants.

2.4 Summary: The New "One-Dimensional Man"

Together, a cynical use of calls for spirituality by some leaders who see it as a free (or at least relatively cheap) productivity boost, combined with a primarily utilistic way of dealing with spiritual differences, and underpinned by a radical application of the social constructivist framework, exacerbate the possibility that spirituality contributes to the creation of what Herbert Marcuse in his well-known 1964 book famously calls "the one-dimensional man" (Marcuse 1964). Marcuse claims that through the machinations of rationality and management, modern industrial societies seek to control human beings, especially their freedom, creativity, and initiative. Society, Marcuse says, is obsessed with control, seeking to make life manageable and one-dimensional. At the time, this book reverberated widely in Western societies. Marcuse's argument should now extend to the attention being paid currently to workplace spirituality—the reasons outlined above warrant that a critical "hermeneutics of suspicion" be applied. This is not to negate the importance of spirituality, but it is a recognition that the processes of commodification and control threaten genuine spirituality, as well as the richness and necessary multi-dimensionality of life, precisely by coopting the language of spirituality.

3 The Different Spheres of Life: Contributions from a Protestant Concept

In order to assist the related processes of *discernment* and *leadership* in this area, I want to help address the problems I have identified with the contemporary focus on spirituality in the workplace. In doing so, I focus on a Protestant theological concept, namely that of the different orders, or spheres of life, specifically as expounded by the German theologian Dietrich Bonhoeffer.

Martin Luther's conception of the *Stände* is an important source of the Protestant concept of the different orders of life. At its core, this doctrine claims that God rules the world through three different orders (*Stände*). As Luther describes in a key formulation in the 1528 *Great Confession Concerning the Holy Supper*: "But the holy orders and true religious institutions established by God are these three: the office of priest, the estate of marriage, the civil government" (Luther 1999, p. 364). Going back to older medieval concepts, Luther had already developed this doctrine before his break with Rome,[7] and it forms an important cornerstone in his social ethics especially. In particular, it can be seen as a further specification of his important two-kingdom theory (on this, see Schirrmacher et al. 2001). The aim of this concept is to find a middle way between natural and theological ethics, or, in other words, between "the relative autonomy and immanence of Thomistic social ethics, in which nature is elevated and perfected by grace," and "the transcendental philosophical position according to which nature is not elevated but given greater profundity by grace ..." (Bayer 1998, pp. 146–147). Specifically, it allowed Luther to identify three different orders that structured social reality, discerning that each was governed by different laws which must be respected. In identifying these orders, Luther echoes distinctions found in Scripture—simultaneously, his concept echoes the world of the late Middle Ages, with "the estate of priest" encompassing the Church and the religious life, "the civil government" denoting the state, and "the estate of marriage" referring to the concept of *oeconomia*, which encompasses the often-intertwined spheres of "work" and "family life" (an example would be a farm, where the spheres of family life and work are deeply interwoven).

Much scholarship surrounds Luther's concept of the three orders of life.[8] It is important to stress just how influential the Protestant concept of the different orders of life has become in the social history of the West. As Charles Taylor comments: "What is important for my purpose is this positive side, the affirmation that the fullness of Christian life was to be found within the activities of this life, in one's calling and in marriage and the family. The entire modern development of the affirmation of ordinary life was, I believe, foreshadowed and initiated, in all its facets, in the spirituality of the Reformers" (Taylor 1989, p. 218; quoted in Saarinen 2005, p. 195).[9]

In this chapter, I would like to focus particularly on how the Protestant concept of the orders of life is developed in the works of the German theologian Dietrich Bonhoeffer (1906–1945). While he has become best known for his role in the resistance against the Nazi regime, Bonhoeffer himself looked beyond the context of Nazism, considering the question of how Germany should be rebuilt after the war.

To help answer that question, he wrote his magnus opus, *Ethics*, which was intended to offer moral blueprints for the post-war society (Bonhoeffer 2005). In various of the *Ethics* manuscripts, Bonhoeffer makes recourse to the Lutheran concept of the different orders of life, seeking to revive that doctrine.[10] In doing so, he suggests an alternative to the word *Stände* itself, arguing that it has lost its original meaning. In its place, he suggests the word *Mandat* (mandate). As well as

---

[7]Adam Francisco points out that by 1519 Luther has already discerned three basic orders of ordinary life. See Francisco (2007, p. 134).

[8]See, for example, Wingren (2004), Lohse (1995), Duby (1980), and Maurer (1970).

[9]On the significance of Luther's concept, see also Montover (2012, p. 113). An example of a thorough contemporary ethical appropriation of Luther's concept of the *Stände* is Ulrich (2005).

[10]Especially the manuscripts "Christ, Reality, and Good" (Bonhoeffer 2005, pp. 47–75) and "The Concrete Commandment and the Divine Mandates" (Bonhoeffer 2005, pp. 388–408). For more on Bonhoeffer's interaction with Luther, see DeJonge (2017, esp. pp. 130–131).

the word changing, the concept itself also changes: instead of Luther's three orders, Bonhoeffer proposes four such orders: namely those of work, marriage, government, and church (Bonhoeffer 2005, p. 68). This means that the order of *oeconomia* is divided into two separate orders: the order of work, and the order of marriage. This change reflects the Industrial Revolution, in which for most people "work" was more distanced from family life—work for the office worker, the factory worker, or the miner was no longer as integral a part of their family lives.[11]

Like Luther, Bonhoeffer's intention with the concept of the divine mandates is to overcome the tension between living in the kingdom of God and simultaneously living "in the world," or, in Bonhoeffer's language, between the "worldly" and the "spiritual." He stresses that we have to live in both realities in the same time—the mandates are a heuristic tool to structure this living. As he says: "There can be no retreat . . . from a 'worldly' into a 'spiritual' 'realm.' The practice of the Christian life can be learned only under these four mandates of God" (Bonhoeffer 2005, p. 69).

Much critical debate surrounds Bonhoeffer's concept of the divine mandates,[12] and it continues to be employed regularly in theological ethics.[13] In what follows, I will draw out three particular characteristics of his concept, indicating how they can contribute to solving the problems with the contemporary emphasis on workplace spirituality that have been identified.

3.1   The Mandates as a Restraint Against "Overstepping the Limit"

Bonhoeffer's primary intent in developing the concept of the divine mandates is to protect the multicentered character of human and social life. In a key citation, Bonhoeffer asserts that "[o]nly in their being with-one-another [Miteinander], for-one-another [Füreinander], and over-against-one-another [Gegeneinander] do the divine mandates of church, marriage and family, culture, and government communicate the commandment of God as it is revealed in Jesus Christ" (Bonhoeffer 2005, p. 393). The direct context of this assertion is the Nazi policy of *Gleichschaltung*, which attempted to bring all spheres of life into line with the powerful Nazi state. That meant, for example, that children in the *Hitlerjugend* were encouraged to give their loyalty to the Party first, rather than to their families. But the state also sought to intervene directly in the Church, as well as in other sectors of socio-economic life. Contrary to these developments, Bonhoeffer strongly asserted the relative

---

[11]This change is commented on by Ulrich Duchrow, who also notes that apart from that, Bonhoeffer's and Luther's concepts are identical. See Duchrow (1983).

[12]See, amongst others, the studies of the concept offered by Moltmann (1967), Mayer (1992), and De Lange (1996).

[13]See Scott (2007); and Van den Heuvel, "Bonhoeffer's Theology of Responsibility and the Social Dimension of Environmental Ethics," in Van den Heuvel (2017a, pp. 207–261).

independence of each mandate, identifying this with God's creational intention of making the world a habitable place.

Although the context is very different, attempts at the instrumentalization of (organizational) spirituality, as well as narcissistic misdirection of this spirituality, can amount to a similar overstepping of the limits between the different spheres of life. In that context, the recognition of different spheres of life can be important in two regards. First, when "work" is concerned, the employee's orientation is not so much on the leader, but on the right ordering of their work—that is to say: to the structure, context, and directionality of that work, in the organization of which he or she is a part. Any organization seeks to attain certain goals, using certain means, within a specific context. Those boundaries are not just important for the essential self-identification of the organization, but also define the specific sphere and form of spirituality within that context. The leader is, in the end, not the only thing that counts, in that particular context, nor is the spiritual fulfilment of the employee—rather, within the specific context of the workplace, the goals, means, and context of the organization play a leading role (see Verkerk 2014).

Secondly, the recognition of the different spheres of life helps with the understanding of any organization—even one as venerable as a church, for example— as just one part of a rich, multidimensional reality; and it invites us not to find just one focal point for our spirituality—be it family, church, or the workplace; each is necessary for a rich, multifaceted spiritual existence. This may seem like stating the obvious, but there is a value in exploring further how the concept of orders can be a newer and better way of uncovering the dangerous and creeping tendencies of one-dimensionality. This leads me to the second contribution that the concept of the divine mandates can make.

3.2   The Mandates as a Means to Appropriate Spiritual Pluralism: The Pragmatist Solution Revisited

The grammar of the divine mandates also represents a way of negotiating conflicts between differing spiritualities. I have suggested above that pragmatist attempts, such as Hick's, that try to resolve such conflicts from the outside could be problematic. Bonhoeffer's doctrine of the divine mandates, on the other hand, represents an insider perspective—at least for many Protestant Christians. As I have stated, Bonhoeffer's key assertion about the divine mandates is that they are not to rule over each other. Specifically, this means that the state shouldn't try to dictate to the Church how it should organize itself; it also means that the Church is not to dictate how the economy should be run.

Bonhoeffer recognizes God's design in this system of orders that keep each other in check—he deliberately grounds his proposal in biblical texts (see, for example, Bonhoeffer 2005, p. 69). While one may argue about the solidness of this foundation, or about the definition Bonhoeffer gives to them, his concept—as a further development of Luther's concept—represents an attempt to negotiate the different spheres in life, as well as the tension between the "kingdom of God" and the "kingdom of the world." As a genuine "insider perspective," the doctrine of the divine mandates can help—at least from a Christian perspective—to appropriate differences in the spiritualities expressed in the workplace (on this, see also Kessler 2016).

The attitude to these will still be helpfully described by means of Hick's "respectful pluralism," but rather than being an outsider perspective, the Bonhoefferian concept of the divine mandates offers a more direct way for Christians to embrace this concept—it allows Christians to recognize that not all their deepest faith convictions are communicated in the same way in every sphere of life. The organization for which one works is not the same as one's church—and consequently, one's spirituality is expressed differently there. Not to recognize this can be criticized as trying to shortcut or overcome the world as it is, as happened in the Radical Reformation.

3.3 The Mandates as a Middle Way Between Onto-Theology and Radical Social Constructivism

Thirdly, Bonhoeffer's concept of the divine mandates can also assist in, on the one hand, appropriating a constructionist approach to spirituality, while on the other hand resisting its radical interpretation. Bonhoeffer asserts strongly that the different orders of life are not merely social constructs alone, but derive from God, from "above." He states:

> By "mandate" we understand the concrete divine commission grounded in the revelation of Christ and the testimony of scripture; it is the authorization and legitimization to declare a particular divine commandment, the conferring of divine authority on an earthly institution. A mandate is to be understood simultaneously as the laying claim to, commandeering of, and formation of a certain earthly domain by the divine command (Bonhoeffer 2005, p. 389).

This assertion of the divine origin of the mandates may seem a blunt refusal of the validity of the whole project of investigating the social constructive dimension of religious beliefs and practices. However, Bonhoeffer doesn't revert to what Wallace calls an indefensible onto-theological conception of social reality "as it is" (Wallace 2002, p. 96). In contrast, Bonhoeffer grounds his concept of the divine orders simultaneously as structures brought about by God's will, as well as in the observation of reality itself.[14] In the citation above, the primacy is on the commanding word of God—but at the same time there is a clear relationship between this

---

[14]Interestingly, Wallace, to whom I have just referred, recognizes in Bonhoeffer an example of someone whose life and theology pose a challenge to social constructivism. He argues that "[t]he life and work of Dietrich Bonhoeffer is a ... counterexample to the constructionist emphasis on selfhood as a social predicate" (Wallace 2002, p. 109). Further on he explicates: "In fidelity to conscience, one may find oneself running the risk of violating social values and incurring personal guilt in pursuit of the responsible action in service to the neighbor" (Wallace 2002, p. 109).

commandment and what Bonhoeffer calls the "earthly domain"—this means that while God's commandments come firmly "from above," there is a clear relationship with the "below," and the word of God does not function in isolation from that.

This is recognized by Moltmann, who emphasizes that the very nature of the mandates as *commandments* of the living God opens up the possibility for change within the mandates. As he puts it: "The negative rigidity which has been the object of complaint might be removed by integrating them into the living history of God. And then, finally, we shall see the law in the hand of the Lawgiver and the mandate in the hand of the God who commissions men to his service" (Moltmann 1967, p. 94). This is indeed correct, and it led Bonhoeffer to revise Luther's conception of the *Stände*, by breaking up the *oeconomia* into the different mandates of "work" and "family"—it also led him to muse about the possibility of a fifth mandate, in prison.[15]

Theologically speaking, Bonhoeffer thus occupies a middle position between the radical position of Karl Barth on the one hand, where all the emphasis is on the inbreaking word of God,[16] and the reason-based Roman Catholic position on the other hand.[17] Yet this middle-position of Bonhoeffer is not to be understood as an attempt to carefully delineate between the "religious" and the "secular," but precisely to overcome such attempts. Bonhoeffer's desire, fleshed out more fully in other manuscripts in his *Ethics*, is to speak about the world theologically and at the same time from a perspective *etsi Deus non daretur*, giving both their full due.

This dynamic of giving both perspectives their due can also be fruitful in relation to the question of how a social constructionist approach to spirituality can be appropriated. Adopting Bonhoeffer's "both-and" approach, one can say that spirituality isn't to be purely understood either as "God's work and nothing else," nor simply as a social construct. Rather, it recognizes the dynamic interplay of both elements at once, thus resisting both the negation, as well as the radical application of social constructivism.[18]

---

[15]He does so in a letter to Renate and Eberhard Bethge, dated January 23, 1944 (Bonhoeffer 2010, pp. 264–271). In this letter, Bonhoeffer muses about adding a fifth mandate, namely that of "culture" (*Kultur*), a realm of freedom. As he puts it: "Someone who doesn't know anything of this sphere of freedom can be a good parent, citizen, and worker, and probably also be a Christian, but whether such a person is a full human being (and thus also a Christian in the fullest sense) is questionable to me" (Bonhoeffer 2010, p. 268).

[16]See Edward van't Slot, who comments: "... Barth prefers a more 'actualist' or 'eschatological' approach than Bonhoeffer in his ongoing quest for permanence in an ethics of God's commandment" (Van't Slot 2015, p. 206).

[17]Cf. Brian Brock, who says: "The mandates are thus not properly understood as metaphysical axioms, ethical blueprints, or programs; they are Christologically keyed signposts indicating the features of reality that allow us to encounter Christ" (Brock 2007, p. 90). See also Abromeit (1991, p. 135).

[18]Bonhoeffer's concept of the divine mandates is not the only way in which Christian thinking can overcome the false juxtaposition of onto-theology and constructionism. Within the tradition of Reformed Philosophy, for example, as developed by Dooyeweerd and others, an alternative has been developed. See Verkerk (2014).

4 Conclusion

In this chapter I have presented the increasingly loud call for workplace spirituality as a double-edged sword. While recognizing its validity, as well as its promise for the contemporary workplace, I have drawn particular attention to the significant potential risks involved for the employees. Appeals for spiritual investment in the workplace can be used by manipulate and narcissistic leaders. Conflicts between different spiritualities are often superficially resolved, primarily making recourse to pragmatism for a solution. And, furthermore, radical social constructionist interpretations of spirituality do not do justice to the actual experience of (religious) spirituality.

In this context, I have made recourse to the Protestant concept of the different orders of life, as introduced by Luther and particularly as developed by Bonhoeffer. As a general concept, the idea of the different orders corresponds to the foundational human insight that, while we may strive for unity in our lives, in order to live full lives, we also need multidimensionality—we need to live in different "keys," corresponding to different spheres of life.

I have argued that the idea of the different mandates that Bonhoeffer puts forward is helpful with regards to the challenges identified. First, the recognition of the different spheres of life can illuminate attempts to manipulate workers into investing too much of their spirituality in the company—it may also help to deter manipulative and narcissistic leaders from demanding too much of their followers. Second, the mandates provide an answer on to how to deal with differences in spirituality, encountered in the workplace. Rather than accepting a pragmatic solution to these, the concept of the divine mandates provides an insider perspective to the appropriation of these differences, by recognizing the sphere of "work" to be different from that of the "church," thus urging a respect for pluralism that is founded in Christianity itself. Third, the concept of the mandates provides a way of accepting both the claim of deep authenticity of spirituality, as well as social constructivist appropriations of it.

In short, the concept of the different orders of life, as developed by Bonhoeffer, can function as a heuristic tool by means of which to correct some dangers to the current drive for more workplace spirituality. As such, this chapter contributes to the wider goal of this volume to contribute to the tasks of leadership and discernment with regards to the promising upsurge in spirituality.

Acknowledgements I would like to thank the participants in the conference "Leadership, Discernment and Spirituality," as well as two anonymous reviewers, for their comments on an earlier version of this chapter. Furthermore, I would like to thank Kay Caldwell for her help with the language editing of this chapter.

References

Abromeit HJ (1991) Das Geheimnis Christi: Dietrich Bonhoeffers erfahrungsbezogene Christologie. Neukirchener Beitrage zur Systematischen Theologie 8. Neukirchener, Neukirchen-Vluyn

Atlaf A, Awan MA (2011) Moderating affect of workplace spirituality on the relationship of job overload and job satisfaction. J Bus Ethics 104:93–99

Bayer O (1998) Nature and institution: Luther's doctrine of the three orders. Lutheran Q 12 (2):125–159

Berger PL, Luckman T (1991) The social construction of reality: a treatise in the sociology of knowledge. Penguin, London

Block P (1993) Stewardship: choosing service over self-interest. Berrett-Koehler, San Francisco, CA

Bonhoeffer D (2005) Ethics, Dietrich Bonhoeffer works 6. Green CJ (ed). Fortress, Minneapolis, MN. Translated by Reinhard Krauss, Charles C. West and Douglas W. Stott

Bonhoeffer D (2010) Letters and papers from prison, Dietrich Bonhoeffer works 8. de Gruchy JW (ed). Fortress, Minneapolis, MN. Translated by Isabel Beste, Lisa E. Dahill, Reinhard Krauss, and Nancy Lukens

Brock B (2007) Singing the ethos of god: on the place of Christian ethics in scripture. Eerdmans, Grand Rapids, MI

DeJonge MP (2017) Bonhoeffer's reception of Luther. Oxford University Press, Oxford

Duby G (1980) The three orders: feudal society imagined. University of Chicago Press, Chicago, IL. Translated by Arthur Goldhammer

Duchrow U (1983) Dem Rad in die Speichen fallen—aber wo und wie? Luthers und Bonhoeffers Ethik der Institutionen im Kontext des heutigen Weltwirtschaftssystems. In: Gremmels C (ed) Bonhoeffer und Luther: Zur Sozialgestalt des Luthertums in der Moderne. Internationales Bonhoeffer Forum: Forschung und Praxis 6. Kaiser, Munich, pp 16–58

Engler S (2005) Two problems with constructionism in religion. Revista de Estudos da Religião 4:28–34

Francisco AS (2007) Martin Luther and Islam: a study in sixteenth-century polemics and apologetics. Brill, Leiden

Friedman TL (2016) Thank you for being late: an optimist's guide to thriving in the age of accelerations. Farrar, Straus and Giroux, New York

Glaserfeld E von (2000) Problems of constructivism. In: Steffe LP, Thompson PW (eds) Radical constructivism in action: building on the pioneering work of Ernst von Glasersfeld. Routledge/Falmer, London, pp 1–9

Gotsis G, Kortezi Z (2008) Philosophical foundations of workplace spirituality: a critical approach. J Bus Ethics 78(4):575–600

Gupta M, Kumar V, Singh M (2014) Creating satisfied employees through workplace spirituality: a study of the private insurance sector in Punjab (India). J Bus Ethics 122(1):79–88

Harris S (2014) Waking up: a guide to spirituality without religion. Simon & Schuster, New York

Heuvel SC van den (2017a) Bonhoeffer's Christocentric theology and fundamental debates in environmental ethics, Princeton theological monograph series 217. Wipf & Stock, Eugene, OR

Heuvel SC van den (2017b) The dangers of charismatic leadership: a perspective from the theology of Dietrich Bonhoeffer. In: van den Heuvel SC, Barentsen J, Lin P (eds) The end of leadership? Christian perspectives on leadership and social ethics 4. Peeters, Leuven, pp 125–139

Hibberd FJ (2005) Unfolding social constructionism. Springer, Dordrecht

Hicks DA (2003) Religion and the workplace: pluralism, spirituality, leadership. Cambridge University Press, Cambridge

Holman D, Wall TD, Clegg CW, Sparrow P, Howard A (eds) (2005) The essentials of the new workplace: a guide to the human impact of modern working practices. Wiley, Chichester

Hyde B, Ota C, Yust K-M (2014) The deconstruction and social (re)construction of spirituality. Int J Child Spirituality 19(1):1–3

Isaacson W (2011) Steve Jobs. Simon and Schuster, New York

Kessler V (2016) Bonhoeffer's doctrine of four mandates as a framework for decision-making within different contexts. In: Barentsen J, Kessler V, Meier E (eds) Christian leadership in a changing world: perspectives from Africa and Europe, Christian perspectives on leadership and Christian ethics 3. Peeters, Leuven, pp 61–76

Lambert L III (2009) Spirituality, Inc.: religion in the American workplace. New York University Press, London

Lange F de (1996) 'Miteinander, Fureinander, Gegeneinander': Bonhoeffers Mandatenlehre in einer pluralistischen Gesellschaft. Lecture, Siegen, September 27. http://home.kpn.nl/delangef/artdbmandatduits.pdf. Accessed 14 Aug 2017

Lohse B (1995) Luthers Theologie in ihrer historischen Entwicklung und in ihrem systematischen Zusammenhang. Vandenhoeck & Ruprecht, Göttingen

Luther M (1999) Word and sacrament III, Vol. 37 of Luther's works. Pelikan JJ, Oswald HC, Lehmann HT (eds). Fortress, Philadelphia, PA

Marcuse H (1964) One-dimensional man: studies in the ideology of advanced industrial society. Beacon, Boston, MA

Marques J, Dhiman S (eds) (2014) Leading spiritually: ten effective approaches to workplace spirituality. Palgrave Macmillan, New York

Maurer W (1970) Luthers Lehre von den drei Hierarchien und ihr mittelalterlicher Hintergrund. Bayerischen Akademie der Wissenschaften, Munich

Mayer R (1992) Die Bedeutung von Bonhoeffers Mandatenlehre für eine moderne politische Ethik. In: Mayer R, Zimmerling P (eds) Dietrich Bonhoeffer heute: Die Aktualitat seines Lebens und Werkes. Gießen, Brunnen, pp 58–80

Mitroff II, Denton EA (1999) A study of spirituality in the workplace. Sloan Manag Rev 40(4):83–92

Moltmann J (1967) The lordship of Christ and human society. In: Moltmann J, Weissbach J (eds) Two studies in the theology of Bonhoeffer. Scribner, New York

Montover N (2012) Luther's revolution: the political dimensions of Martin Luther's universal priesthood. James Clarke, Cambridge

Moran DJ (2010) ACT for leadership: using acceptance and commitment training to develop crisis-resilient change managers. Int J Behav Consult Ther 6(4):341–355

Phipps K, Benefiel M (2013) Spirituality and religion: seeking a juxtaposition that supports research in the field of faith and spirituality at work. In: Neal J (ed) Handbook of faith and spirituality in the workplace: emerging research and practice. Springer, Dordrecht, pp 33–43

Saarinen R (2005) Ethics in Luther's theology: the three orders. In: Kraye J, Saarinen R (eds) Moral philosophy on the threshold of modernity, The new synthese historical library 57. Springer, Dordrecht, pp 195–219

Schirrmacher T, Vogt T, Peter A (2001) Die vier Schöpfungsordnungen: Kirche, Staat, Wirtschaft, Familie—bei Martin Luther und Dietrich Bonhoeffer. VTR, Nürnberg

Scott PM (2007) Postnatural humanity? Bonhoeffer, creaturely freedom, and the mystery of reconciliation in creation. In: Nielsen KB, Nissen U, Tietz C (eds) Mysteries in the theology of Dietrich Bonhoeffer: a Copenhagen Bonhoeffer symposium. Vandenhoeck & Ruprecht, Gotingen, pp 111–134

Slot E van't (2015) Negativism of revelation? Bonhoeffer and barth on faith and actualism. Dogmatik in der Moderne 12. Mohr/Siebeck, Tubingen

Sremac S (2010) Converting into a new reality: social constructionism, practical theology and conversion. Nova Prisutnost 8(1):7–27

Swinton J, Mowat H (2006) Practical theology and qualitative research. SCM, London

Tarassenko V (2006) Kniga Bizness-Peremen: 64 Strategemy. Genesis, Moscow

Tarassenko V (2008) Ostorozno Stiven Kovi. Dobraia Kniga, Moscow

Taylor C (1989) Sources of the self. Cambridge University Press, Cambridge

Tourish D, Pinnington A (2002) Transformational leadership, corporate cultism and the spirituality paradigm: an unholy Trinity in the workplace? Hum Relat 55(2):147–172

Ulrich H (2005) Wie Geschöpfe Leben: Konturen Evangelischer Ethik. Lit, Berlin

Verkerk M (2014) Spirituality, organization and leadership: towards a philosophical foundation of spirit at work. In: Nullens P, Barentsen J (eds) Leadership, innovation, and spirituality, Christian perspectives on leadership and social ethics, vol 1. Peeters, Leuven, pp 57–77

Wallace MI (2002) Losing the self, finding the self: postmodern theology and social construction. In: Hermans CAM, Immink G, de Jong A, van der Lans J (eds) Social constructionism and theology, Empirical studies in theology 7. Brill, Leiden, pp 93–111

Wingren G (2004) Luther on vocation. Wipf & Stock, Eugene

Zinnbauer BJ, Pargament KI (2005) Religiousness and spirituality. In: Paloutzian RF, Park CL (eds) Handbook of the psychology of religion and spirituality. Guilford, London, pp 21–42

Steven C. van den Heuvel (Ph.D.) studied Pastoral Ministry at the Christelijke Hogeschool Ede, the Netherlands. He then went on to study theology at the Evangelische Theologische Faculteit (ETF), Leuven (Belgium), receiving his Th.M. in 2010, followed by his Ph.D. in 2015, as part of a joint doctorate with the Theologische Universiteit Kampen, the Netherlands. His dissertation was entitled *Bonhoeffer's Christocentric Theology and Fundamental Issues in Environmental Ethics* (Wipf and Stock, 2017). He is currently Postdoctoral Researcher in the department of Systematic Theology and Ethics at ETF and Senior Research Fellow of the Institute of Leadership and Social Ethics. Furthermore, he is Extraordinary Researcher at the Faculty of Theology at North-West University, South Africa.

From Spirituality to Responsible Leadership: Ignatian Discernment and Theory-U

Patrick Nullens

Abstract In its desire to build a bridge between self-awareness and morally responsible leadership, this chapter seeks to contribute to the theory of authentic leadership. The central thesis of this chapter is that Ignatian spiritual discernment is a valuable resource for making this connection. Ignatian Spirituality is directed at the world, the world beyond the self and the world beyond our primary experiences. It is inherently aimed at the common good and is therefore an interesting source when contemplating moral leadership. We will discuss the Spiritual Exercises of humility, silence, and detachment, the prevalence of emotions and imagination, ethical evaluation, and journaling and mentoring as means for increasing self-awareness. We will do this in dialogue with the new Theory-U. This, too, is an approach where societal meaning is fundamental and seeks to increase awareness and genuine openness to the future by letting go of the self. This makes for an interesting dialogue, leading to a deeper understanding of spiritual discernment.

1 Ignatian Spiritual Discernment and Addressing Our Blind Spot

The volatility, uncertainty, complexity, and ambiguity (VUCA) we are faced with in today's world demand that we make fast decisions and to get it right. In this highly competitive world, there is no room for trial and error, nor will we get a second chance. In plain language the managerial acronym VUCA means "Hey, it's crazy out there!" (Bennett and Lemoine 2014). It describes the sense that, even with all our technological power, we are not in control and the future is unpredictable. VUCA can also mean: "Hey, it's crazy in my head!" Volatility, uncertainty, complexity, and ambiguity are not only to be found in the world around us, they also become the

P. Nullens (✉)
Evangelische Theologische Faculteit, Leuven, Belgium

North-West University, Potchefstroom, South Africa
e-mail: patrick.nullens@etf.edu

© The Author(s) 2019   185
J. (Kobus) Kok, S. C. van den Heuvel (eds.), *Leading in a VUCA World*,
Contributions to Management Science, https://doi.org/10.1007/978-3-319-98884-9_12

storms within us. In this turbulence, we feel a need for a space where time stands still and where we can experience the present. How do we calm our internal storms? How do we make mental space for discernment when it comes to strategic life decisions? The greatest challenge is not the process of quieting our minds and becoming more mindful in body, thinking, and emotions; even more challenging when it comes to leadership is to create a deeper awareness that results in making the right decision to the benefit of others. What we desperately need is a form of authentic leadership, resulting from deeper awareness and from addressing the blind spot, the inner source from which we act (Scharmer 2016, p. 22). Authenticity requires rootedness in ourselves, in our story, and in our faith traditions.

This chapter hopes to contribute to the authentic leadership theory, one of the newest areas of leadership research which makes ethics the center of leadership (Hannah et al. 2011; George et al. 2015).[1] According to Avolio, its central premise is "that through increased self-awareness, self-regulation, and positive modeling, authentic leaders foster the development of authenticity in followers. In turn, followers' authenticity contributes to their wellbeing and the attainment of sustainable and veritable performance" (Avolio and Luthans 2005, p. 317). There are many ways to create this bridge between a deeper self-awareness and morally responsible leadership. As one optional pathway, we'll look at the Ignatian model of spiritual discernment. This chapter focusses on the individualistic aspect of Ignatian discernment. The interaction between leadership theory and Ignatian spirituality is of course not new (Moberg and Calkins 2001; Darmanin 2005; Rothausen 2017). There is also an increased interest in different kinds of spiritual discernment. The dialogue between Ignatian and secular forms of discernment, however, does remain largely unexplored (Bouckaert 2017, p. 16). Referring to Ignatius's *Spiritual Exercises* (*Sp.Ex.*), Moberg and Calkins have pleaded for more room for reflection, and not just decision making, in the curriculum of business schools . Reflection means bending back on oneself, allowing more space for emotions and the imagination (2001, p. 258).

At the outset of our quest, we'll observe the growing appreciation of spiritual intelligence, spiritual vitality, and workplace spirituality. This new research interest within the social sciences makes way for more spiritual approaches to decision making in leadership. A broad leadership model that can relate easily to this new quest is Theory-U (Scharmer 2016). In the second part of this chapter I will present Theory-U in broad brushstrokes. The chapter pleads for a Christian approach, more specifically the Ignatian way of discernment as it might be helpful for making decisions. This is the central thesis of this chapter, and its main focus. The argument is not theological[2] nor apologetic, as if this were the only true and valid model, but

---

[1]Four behavioral components are crucial to this theory: self-awareness, internalized moral perspective, balanced processing, and relational transparency (Northouse 2016, pp. 193–223).

[2]In this essay I haven't opted for a critical theological engagement. The publications on this specific topic of comparative spirituality are limited (Richter 1955; Lafontaine 2011). For instance, the comparison between Ignatius and the Calvinist puritan Richard Baxter on meditation is interesting (Hinson 2007). It is a myth that the Jesuits were established to fight the reformation. This was a later development, which occurred after Ignatius (see Maryks 2014). More practically, there are also

rather that it is a reliable method that has been tested over many hundreds of years. Discernment is an implicit part of Christian spirituality—it is clearly present in the writing of St Paul. However, there are relatively few explicit instructions on discernment. By far the most accessible and comprehensive of these systems is that found in the Spiritual Exercises. However, I am aware that some readers might prefer a more generic form of spiritual discernment, not grounded in a particular religious tradition. In my opinion, the main problem here is the common but deceitful disconnection of spirituality and religion that often functions as a secular dogmatic presupposition. It suggests that being rooted in one particular religious tradition, be it Christian, Jewish, or Muslim, diminishes mental openness and our capacity for discernment. In the third paragraph I make a case for the re-connection of faith and spirituality, which have been artificially separated. In the three sections that follow, I try to establish Ignatian discernment as a valid form of Christian discernment in leadership. To a limited extent, I will make some connections with Scharmer's Theory-U. In Theory-U, societal meaning is obviously robust. It is my contention that the theological particularity and Christian character of the Ignatian model does not negate this broader impact. It is the interesting dialogue between the new and the old which leads to a deeper understanding of spiritual discernment as an intrinsic part of authentic leadership.

2 Spiritual Intelligence and Discernment

At the beginning of the twenty-first century the spiritual dimension of leadership is widely recognized (Fry 2003; Fry and Nisiewicz 2013; Scharmer 2016; Dhiman 2017). According to some scholars, the successful transformational leadership theory was all too limited to the service of institutional practices and goals and weak in core values and service to the common good (Rothausen 2017, p. 7). In addition to the concept of "emotional intelligence," which came to the fore near the end of the twentieth century (Goleman 2014) and which underpins the transformational leadership theory, the concept of "spiritual intelligence" (SI or SQ) appears on the horizon of our postmodern age (Zohar and Marshall 2001; Wigglesworth 2014; Dhiman 2017). SI is the intelligence of our inner source, our true self, our transcendental capacities. As one might expect, a plethora of definitions circulate. A broad working definition is:

> Spiritual intelligence is concerned with the inner life of mind and spirit and its relationship to being in the world. Spiritual intelligence can be defined as the ability to create meaning based on deep understanding of existential questions, and awareness of and the ability to use multiple levels of consciousness in problem solving. (Vaughan 2002, p. 30).

---

protestant-evangelical books appropriating the Spiritual Exercises (Wakefield 2006; Warner 2010). However, this doesn't mean there are some serious points of difference, for instance the call for radical obedience to the Roman Catholic church in the *Spiritual Exercises* (pp. 353, 358, 365 etc.) is highly problematic for a protestant Christian, including the author of this chapter.

In popular leadership theory SI is appropriated by Stephen Covey. In his recent *8th Habit*, Covey mentions four types of intelligence: Physical intelligence (PQ), which corresponds with the body; mental intelligence (IQ) corresponds to the mind; emotional intelligence (EQ) corresponds to the heart and finally there is spiritual intelligence (SQ), which is connected to the spirit. Spiritual intelligence is our drive for meaning and connection with the infinite. According to Covey "spiritual intelligence is the central and most fundamental of all the intelligences, because it becomes the source of guidance for the others" (Covey 2014, p. 53).

The organizational value of spiritual intelligence is well documented. For instance, Laura Reaves has reviewed 150 studies showing the clear consistency between spiritual values and practices and effective leadership. According to Reave, spirituality helps leaders to inspire trust, motivate followers, create a positive ethical and relational climate, and achieve organizational goals. The impact of spirituality is not only present in this soft area, it also increases productivity, lowers rates of turnover, and improves employee health and sustainable development (Reave 2005). In this chapter we focus on just one aspect of this spiritual dimension: the reflective practice which includes self-examination and/or communication with God. This is a practice that increases managerial effectiveness. Spiritual vitality is a strength for managers since it gives them a more global view of life and makes them less dependent on current situations (Quick et al. 2000).

Along with the appreciation of spiritual intelligence there is a growing interest in "workplace spirituality" (Neal 2012; Giacalone and Jurkiewicz 2015). Employees are looking for meaning in their jobs. Yet again, definitions vary widely. A possible working definition for workplace spirituality is:

> ...aspects of the workplace, either in the individual, the group, or the organization, that promote feelings of satisfaction through transcendence. To elaborate, that the process of work facilitates employees' sense of being connected to a nonphysical force beyond themselves that provides feelings of completeness and joy (Giacalone and Jurkiewicz 2015, p. 15).

Jody Fry deals with spiritual leadership as a moral source in the business world. His model of spiritual leadership is based on vision, altruistic love, hope/faith, and intrinsic motivation (Fry 2003). According to Fry, values such as trust, the value of human life, and altruistic love are found in the major world religions as well as in secular models. The ethical call of the triple bottom line of a company is coupled with spiritual leadership, which creates a vision and organizational culture that transcends egoistic self-interest and fosters a value-driven stakeholder approach (Fry and Nisiewicz 2013). According to Fry, a sustainable economy requires a spiritual approach through which we can overcome our desires for short term profits.

The quest for joy, completeness, and wellbeing typical of the Western stressful and fast-changing world, leads to renewed interest in meditation and inner resourcing. The success of mindfulness as a method for stress reduction, shows the present need for space, time, and internal rest (Chiesa and Serretti 2009). The young science of positive psychology values spirituality as part of a healthy life, as it strengthens our agency and daily functionality. "The capacity to envision, seek, connect to and hold on to, and transform the sacred may be what makes us uniquely human" (Pargament and Mahoney 2011, p. 616). There is a noticeable sociological and demographic shift from materialist to post-materialist societal values: an increased desire for fulfillment, freedom, a sense of community, self-expression, and meaning. It is expected that, globally, post-materialists emphasizing self-expression values will soon outnumber materialists; organizations and businesses need to take this new reality into account (Inglehart 1997; Inglehart and Welzel 2005; Giacalone and Jurkiewicz 2015).

The practice of discernment in order to make the best decision about the future of an organization, one's career, or new opportunities goes beyond the classical cognitive social and emotional processes. This is evidenced by the rising interest in spiritual intelligence, workplace spirituality, the search for meaning, and stress reduction. A deeper awareness and a sense of the future are vital to making the right decisions. This in turn raises a renewed interest in the Ignatian method of discernment as well as some newer models, generally rooted in Eastern philosophy.

3   Theory-U and Leadership Spirituality

In light of the broad shift towards more awareness and post-materialist societal values, Theory-U is a notable model, especially because of the paradigmatic changes it proposes. Theory-U was developed by C. Otto Scharmer at the Massachusetts Institute of Technology. It found its way to management, health care, education, economics, and organizational sciences.[3] We are confronted with some serious global challenges, such as climate change, poverty, violence, and the income gap. It is essential for Theory-U that our complex problems need solutions that do not come from the old paradigms that created them in the first place. Scharmer makes a call for a new consciousness and a fresh approach to leadership.

According to Scharmer, we often observe the behavior of leaders, the strategies and processes they deploy. But there also seems to be a blind spot, blindness to the inner place, the source from which leaders act and from which effective leadership and social action come into being (Scharmer 2016, p. 21). And what is true for individual leaders is also true for groups and society: "Blind spots appear in individuals, groups, institutions, societies, and systems; they reveal themselves in our theories and concepts in the form of deep epistemological and ontological assumptions." (Scharmer 2016, p. 21) The attention of Theory-U goes to the inner center of our being as essential for leadership; what really counts is where you're coming from, inside your deepest being: "the success of an intervention depends on the interior condition of the intervener." (Scharmer 2016, p. 27) It is the inner place of the leader, mysterious as it is, that ultimately defines the outcome. Scharmer is convinced that we have to work and train more inside-out. What is required is a shift

---

[3]See www.presencing.org

in consciousness from ego-system to eco-system awareness (Scharmer and Kaufer 2013).

Most of our knowledge is a result of a superficial "downloading," instead of a careful experience of a future as it emerges. Scharmer proposes a learning theory in the form of a "U," based on the attitudinal stages of letting go, "presencing," and letting come.[4] The neologism "presencing" is a blending of the words "presence" and "sensing." "It means to sense, tune in, and act from one's highest future potential—the future that depends on us to bring it into being." (Scharmer 2016, p. 8) More concretely, presencing is a journey with five movements or a matrix of five dimensions: We move down the left side of the U, all the while connecting to the world that is outside of our well known structures. Reaching the bottom of the U we connect to the world that emerges from within. And as we move up on the right side of the U, we've reached the "letting come": embodying and bringing forth the new into the world. The movement of the U shouldn't be seen as linear stages, but as dimensions or a matrix of perceiving reality. It is a dance with the situation you are dealing with (Scharmer 2016, pp. 44, 45).

On that journey, at the bottom of the U, lies an inner gate that requires us to drop everything that isn't essential. This process of letting go (of our old ego and self) and letting come (of our highest future possibility: our Self) establishes a subtle connection to a deeper source of knowing. The essence of presencing is that these two selves, our current self and our best future self, meet at the bottom of the U and begin to listen to and resonate with each other. The task of discernment is to catch the future as it comes to us. There is a process of an open mind, an open heart and an open will. Retreating and letting go for a time of reflection becomes the basis for later action. Once an individual or a group crosses this threshold, nothing remains the same. People begin to operate with a heightened level of energy and increased sense of future possibility. Often, they then begin to function as an intentional vehicle for an emerging future.

4   Spirituality and Religion Connected

Before we enter the religious world of Ignatian spirituality, a word needs to be said about the relationship between spirituality and religion. Scharmer is critical of "a faith-based spirituality," since it can mean a conservative retro-movement and even fundamentalism (Scharmer 2016, p. 4).[5] Being oriented by a faith system is the very opposite of being open to the future. For Scharmer, there is barely space for religion at all.[6] And as is often

---

[4]For figures see www.prescencing.com

[5]Scharmer describes fundamentalism as a particular form of "absencing," opposite of "presencing." He briefly discusses three forms of fundamentalism: religious, economic, and political (Scharmer 2016, pp. 244–245).

[6]His main intellectual sources are Buddhism, Rudolf Steiner, Edmund Husserl, Martin Buber, Martin Heidegger, Jurgen Habermas, Johan Galtung, Friederich Glasl, Francisco Varela (p. 104).

the case, spirituality is disconnected from religion, as if we are dealing with some Kantian universal scientific model that stands above all particularities of ideals and religions.

It is often argued that throwing spirituality into the mix adds up to uncertainty and ambiguity. But in fact, it can go both ways, as is the case with religion: it may obscure the functioning of some people, but it makes others more effective. The distinction between religion and spirituality is widely accepted. Generally speaking, religion refers to the external dimension such as institutions, dogma, practices, symbols. Spirituality on the other hand, refers to the inner life, the subjective, experiential, and emotional dimension.

In psychological terms, spirituality is broadly described as something that gives meaning to life and the experience of being part of a larger whole. For instance, Sandra Schneiders defines: "Spirituality is the actualization of the basic human capacity for transcendence . . . defined . . . as the experience of conscious involvement in the project of life-integration through self-transcendence toward the horizon of ultimate value one perceives" (in Holder 2005, p. 16). From this point of view, spiritual discernment is mainly about life-integration and reconnecting to one's own value system. Such a broad interpretation may lead to the conclusion that faith systems are redundant.

In contrast, we opt for an integration of spirituality and lived religion. While both terms are useful in order to distinguish between the subjective and objective dimension, the two cannot be disconnected from one another. Kees Waaijman rightfully critiques the quasi-dogmatic separation between spirituality and religion that dominates the social sciences. He states that by the disconnection from the original philosophical-theological perspective on spirituality, the conceptual depth of spirituality gets lost (Waaijman 2007, p. 88). If religion is a lived religion it integrates conceptual views of faith (as content) and spiritual experiences.[7] Particularly when faced with the challenge of discernment, conceptual framing, a concrete religious community, a faith tradition, and textual sources all play a significant role. Moreover, this religious framing is not a limitation, it is a concretization or manifestation of spirituality.

In the same way, Kenneth Pargament defines spirituality as "the search for the sacred" (Pargament and Mahoney 2011, p. 612). The term "search" indicates that spirituality is always a process, "one that involves efforts to discover the sacred, hold on to the sacred once it has been found, and transform the sacred when necessary" (Pargament and Mahoney 2011, p. 612). The sacred is a broad term, which could be interpreted theistically or as a transcending ideal that we experience as sacral.[8]

---

[7]In theology we distinguish *fides qua*, our act of believing, from *fides quae creditor*, the content of this belief. The two cannot be separated.

[8]For the idea of "the Holy" or the numinous we can also refer here to Rudolf Otto's classical *Das Heilige* (1917 [ET:1959]). The sacred is irreducible, a manifestation of the "ganz Andere." [The "ganz Andere" is a (famous) way in which Barth describes God—it is not, however, how Otto conceptualized "das Heilige" (note his use of "das" instead of "der"): for Otto, "das Heilige" is the "numinous," not necessarily a personal conception of a God/gods.

Equally important is the realization that there are many potential pathways for this life-search. To put it metaphorically: spirituality provides the paint, brushes, and a canvas, but lived religion draws the picture, diverse as it might be. Whether we consider the picture to be a piece of art or rubbish, is another question. This is where the theological argument will take place. Moreover, Waaijman points out, experiences in and of themselves are blind and need critical feedback from an ethical perspective. Therefore, spirituality is not only connected to a faith system, but also to a specific configuration of virtues or character (Waaijman 2007, p. 6). The focus of this chapter is Christian spirituality that Holmes defines briefly as "the lived experience of Christian faith and discipleship" (Holder 2005, p. 5). As a concrete type of "lived experience" it is a form of spirituality, and therefore it is profitable to connect with broader studies of spirituality from other disciplines, such as, for instance, Theory-U. As a lived experience it has its own language and traditions. So whereas in the broader context one may bring in new words such as "presencing," with the lived experience of Christianity one picks up the old language of faith. Johan Verstraeten sees this openness to different language as a prerequisite for true moral reflection on one's business practice. We don't use the common managerial vocabulary of control, efficiency, institutions, and measurement, but a language of meaning, metaphors, and narratives (Verstraeten 2014).

5 The Spiritual Exercises of Ignatius of Loyola

Ignatius of Loyola (1491–1556), the founder of the *Societas Jesu* (1539) is the subject of much debate, and the heritage of the Jesuits is not without blemish. This chapter is not the place for a hagiography, not even a biography.[9] But, however briefly, we need some facts to put his new approach to spirituality in context. Ignatius (Iñigo) was a military officer of noble birth. His family was from the Basque region, in the north of Spain. In his youth, he is described as a vain person, living the worldly lifestyle of a nobleman, obsessed by heroic stories. In a losing battle against the French, he was hit in the knee by a cannonball. During his long recovery Iñigo read books about the life of Jesus and the lives of the saints. This was the beginning of his "search for the sacred," a long and intense journey. These experiences were the basis of a short handbook for meditations written in Spanish, entitled *Spiritual Exercises* (1522–24).[10] Ignatius began to share his spiritual principles because he believed the exercises could also help others and the *Spiritual Exercises* have become fundamental for the Society of Jesus and far beyond.

---

[9]A classic biography is the one by Philip Caraman (1990). A well-documented biography written from a psychoanalytic lens is the one by W. Meissner (1994).

[10]Most of the Spanish text was finished by 1541. With papal approval, a Latin translation was published in 1548. In this article the 1951 translation of Louis J. Puhl is used, available at http://spex.ignatianspirituality.com/SpiritualExercises/Puhl#pre01. Accessed 15 January 2018.

For a good understanding of the *Spiritual Exercises* (*Sp.Ex.*) we need to read them against the background of Ignatius's wider corpus of texts, for instance his *Constitutions*, *Autobiography* and *Spiritual Diary* (Ignatius et al. 1997). Equally important are his many letters (about 7000) containing pastoral and practical advice (Ignatius et al. 2006). The *Sp.Ex.* are a particular literary genre consisting of a compilation of prayers, meditations, and contemplative practices, intended to help people deepen their relationship with God. In style it is brief, with dense wording, sometimes even cryptic. The *Spiritual Exercises* are not meant as a devotional book for a wide public, rather they are written as a handbook for spiritual directors to use in the context of a 4-week (30 days) or shorter (8 days) retreat in solitude and silence. The purpose of all spiritual exercises is an examination of conscience and a training in spiritual discernment (*discretio*), the discernment of good from evil spirits. The *Sp.Ex.* combine three interconnected elements: first, praying with the gospel texts, a focus (visualization) on the life of Jesus; second, an intense examination of one's own conscience and finally, as a form of synthesis, to discern and come to a spiritual decision. Its purpose is the pedagogy of the best choice, wherein the higher greater glory of God is always the ultimate purpose. It is really a practical handbook for exercises, not just devotional writing to be read and meditated on. In the opening words of Ignatius himself:

> By the term "Spiritual Exercises" is meant every method of examination of conscience, of meditation, of contemplation, of vocal and mental prayer, and of other spiritual activities that will be mentioned later. For just as taking a walk, journeying on foot, and running are bodily exercises, so we call Spiritual Exercises every way of preparing and disposing the soul to rid itself of all inordinate attachments, and, after their removal, of seeking and finding the will of God in the disposition of our life for the salvation of our soul. (*Sp.Ex.* 1.)

To use the terminology of Theory-U, a continued training is required to overcome superficial listening (downloading), suspend judgment, abandon cynicism and fear and to go to generative listening. It is not a onetime event, but a training; repetitive exercises that lead to a change of habits. Theory-U, much like Ignatian spirituality, qualifies as a leadership development practice in the sense of "a coherent set of activities that is intentionally and regularly enacted by an individual" (Rothausen 2017, p. 4).

6   Ignatian Spirituality for the World and Beyond the World

The art of discernment and decision making is only part of an overall spiritual formation, so it is important to understand how the decision-making process fits into the wider context of a practical spirituality. The Jesuit priest James Martin wrote a popular book, playfully entitled: *The Jesuit Guide to (almost) Everything* (2010). Martin summarizes four essential characteristics of Ignatian Spirituality:

1. Finding God in all things
2. Becoming a contemplative in action
3. Looking at the world in an incarnational way

4. Seeking freedom and detachment

These four concepts are a faith-based approach that does not close off our experience of the world around us, but rather the supports opening up to one's surroundings. Finding God in all things and experiencing the world as a manifestation of God makes us sensitive to the meaning of little events around us. An important corrective on Martin's otherwise apt summary, is that they all take shape with Christ in the center. Christ himself is the norm of all discernment. Experiencing God's unconditional love in Christ, the power of the cross, reconciliation, and Christ's healing, and the resulting desire to be his disciple, is the main topic of the first week of Spiritual Exercises.

An important characteristic of Ignatian spirituality, especially in comparison with other traditions, such as for instance the Benedictine tradition, is that Jesuit spirituality is oriented towards the world outside the walls of the cloister. Here we see a similarity with the strong moral component of Theory-U, which wants to lead us out of ego-system into eco-system economics, a shift from wellbeing of the individual to the wellbeing of the whole. Spirituality is connected with contemporary challenges in economics, politics, and society (Scharmer and Kaufer 2013). Ignatian spirituality is missional: inner growth must lead to a change in society. Only limited attention is paid to contemplation: Jesuits are traditionally socially oriented and devoted to the promotion of the common good. The disengagement from society the *Spiritual Exercises* create, allows for a greater engagement with the self and with God. Its ultimate purpose is to enable better functioning in society. The adage "finding God in all things" makes Ignatian spirituality a way of living in the world. Martin summarizes it this way: "Instead of seeing the spiritual life as one that can exist only if it is enclosed by the walls of a monastery, Ignatius asks you to see the world as your monastery" (2010, loc. 165, 166). There is a deep commitment to advocating justice and the common good, and caring for the vulnerable (O'Brien 2011, p. 4). It is also called a "frontier spirituality," for those who want to be active on those risky frontiers where the church meets our secular and pluralistic world (Heiding 2012, p. 150).

Next to this immanent focus of Ignatian spirituality, there is also a transcendental side, the other-worldly dimension, the beyond. But first of all discernment is focused on the "movements of spirits" where "spirits" have a very broad meaning. Discernment is a form of interpreting what Ignatius calls "motions of the soul." These interior movements consist of desires, feelings, thoughts, imaginings, emotions, repulsions, and attractions. Discernment of spirits involves becoming sensitive to these mental movements, meditating on them, and understanding their sources and purposes. Spirits can include the Holy Spirit and the enemy of our human nature, but also includes the pulls from other interior and exterior impulses. Actually there is in this profundity or beyond no clear divide between natural and supernatural.

In a Christian faith system, this "beyond" is not merely an emerging future or a broad connecting with the planet, it is also, but not only, a supra-natural reality that is knowable beyond our natural senses.[11] It sounds strange to most contemporary readers to hear about the continuous battle between that which comes from God and what comes from "the enemy." Of course, this metaphor of a battle fits well with Ignatius's former interest in the military, but the duality between God and devil is also deeply rooted in the New Testament worldview.[12] According to the New Testament the world is dual, a world of matter and spirit, and that which is unseen is nevertheless real (Bonnie Thurston in Holder 2005, p. 56). For many Christians this is a very real conflict between two personal entities. Yet in a secularized worldview, for those living in a scientific and disenchanted world, this open view on transcendent reality is bizarre. For those, this spiritual battle can be explained as the continuous conflict between good and evil in one's personal self. However, this is merely one dimension of discernment. In most cases it is simply about discerning the good from the best in the motions of the soul.

Creating in a leader a moral center that goes beyond institutional goals is one of the major challenges we face today and requires more than a company list of core values, desired behaviors, and norms (Rothausen 2017). Scharmer regularly refers to Aristotle's *Nicomachean Ethics* and the five different ways of knowledge. First is science (*episteme*), exact knowledge determined by necessity, limited to the things that cannot be otherwise than they are. The other four ways of grasping truth are broader and apply to all other contexts of reality and life. They are art or creating (*techne*), practical wisdom (*phronesis*), theoretical wisdom (*sophia*), and intuition or the capacity to grasp first principles or sources (*nous*). It is by developing the *sophia* and *nous* that we overcome our obsession with the what (*episteme*) and how (*techne*). "It is that blind spot that sets apart master practitioners and leaders from average performers" (Scharmer 2016, p. 16).

7 Principles for Spiritual Discernment

This chapter isn't a comprehensive treatise about Ignatian spiritual discernment, [13] rather we will discuss some key issues that are helpful for discerning in a "VUCA-world."[14] There is a strange paradox in Ignatian spirituality that is relevant to the

---

[11]This is an ontological as well as an epistemological claim. For extensive theological and philosophical arguments within a Jesuit tradition see the many works of Karl Rahner (Endean 2009).

[12]According to Alfred Darmanin it is less the military metaphors than the "organization as a body metaphor" which is dominant (2005, p. 10). Taking Ignatius's actual phrasings in *Spiritual Exercises* and his pre-conversion obsessions for the military into account, I find Darmanin's argument unconvincing.

[13]For a more extensive treatment of spiritual discernment, see the works of Timothy M. Gallagher (2009, 2012, 2013).

[14]It is also based on limited personal experience, not as a Jesuit, not even a Roman Catholic, but as an evangelical-protestant inspired by this type of frontier spirituality. In a more protestant

postmodern experience of the VUCA-world. On the one hand, the Ignatian principles create an awareness that the future is not in our hands; they are intended to help a person live in the moment and deal with unpredictable events, and to survive in a volatile and uncertain environment. On the other hand, there is a commitment to reflect profoundly on one's choices and to consider all the options. Spiritual discernment is often oriented towards making choices, in particular the hard life-changing choices. Or it can be discerning to allow the active choice to continue and to become recommitted. In the choice also lies the paradox, we can't choose just everything and some choices that have been made can't be undone. Acceptance of the unchangeable, whatever this may be, is a presupposition for discernment.[15]

7.1 Humility and Telos

Perhaps the most important rule for spiritual discernment is the conditional virtue of humility, as it is arrogance which blinds and misleads us. Ignatius suggests we start our process of discernment in the following way: "A step or two away from the place where I will make my contemplation or meditation, I will stand for the (time)length of an Our Father [prayer 1 min.]. I will raise my mind and think how God our Lord is looking at me, and other such thoughts. Then I will make an act of reverence or humility." (*Sp.Ex.* 75) We start with a moment of awareness (the length of time that the Lord's Prayer lasts). We experience the way in which God looks at us in a loving way, more loving than we can love ourselves. It is crucial that we don't start with self-love, but rather from the love of God bestowed on us. The whole spiritual exercise and discernment process is considered to be an exercise in humility. God blesses the poor in spirit, the beggars (Mat. 5: 3).

According to Scharmer, a leader can't advance to a higher level of performing without humility, or a selfless self. We won't touch our essential core, our emerging future Self (capital S), if we refuse to go deep down. Scharmer calls it "going through the eye of the needle." "We must learn to drop our ego and our habitual 'self' in order for the authentic Self to emerge" (Scharmer 2016, p. 42). It is interesting that Scharmer makes direct reference to Jesus' words to the rich, that it is as hard for them to enter into the Kingdom of God, as it is for a camel to go through a small gate called "the needle." The camel driver had to unload his animal before he could enter: "Likewise, at the bottom of U there is an inner gate that requires us to drop everything that isn't essential" (Scharmer 2016, p. 187). According to Scharmer, there are three inner voices of resistance which

---

vernacular, the spirituality of Dietrich Bonhoeffer has the same focus on calling and "Christ in the world." The Ignatian spirituality fits this type of engagement with society (Nullens 2011).

[15] According to the catholic priest Ignatius, "there are things that fall under an unchangeable choice, such as priesthood, marriage, etc." even "if the choice has not been made as it should have been" (*Sp.Ex.* 171). Marriage and priesthood are sacramental and therefore involve an ontological change that can't be altered. Most people nowadays will disagree with this, but it remains a fact that some things can't be changed.

block the gate to the open mind: the voice of judgment, the voice of cynicism, and the voice of fear (Scharmer 2016, pp. 43, 44). Arrogance is part of the voice of cynicism, as it refuses to become vulnerable. Nevertheless, one wonders why the blocking voice of hubris isn't mentioned here, since presencing also means an absence of manipulative behavior and the creation of a connection with the beings who surround us. This intense spiritual experience is described differently by various religious traditions, for Christians it is God, Christ, and the Holy Spirit (Scharmer 2016, p. 185). In this experience, which takes place at the bottom of the U, it is common that the personal ego is diminished and the connection with beings who surround us is increased.

The ethical challenge is serious. It is widely documented that many senior leaders, especially in the highly competitive business world, have a narcissistic tendency (Johnson 2011, p. 47) or "swollen egos" (Scharmer, p. 73). Narcissism has helped them get to the top: in those that are successful, self-centeredness is combined with charisma, high energy, and intelligence. They can be efficient and effective, but their moral compass tends to be underdeveloped. Characteristics of these types of leaders are arrogance, amorality, feelings of inferiority, an insatiable need for appreciation, hypersensitivity and anger, lack of empathy, irrationality and inflexibility, and even paranoia (Sankowsky 1995; Rosenthal and Pittinsky 2006). In a VUCA-world they may actually flourish, but often at great cost to all stakeholders in the organization. And as Craig Johnson observed, their self-centeredness blocks innovation and growth: "Ego-driven leaders ignore creative ideals and valuable data that come from outside their circle of influence" (Johnson 2011, p. 46). For this reason, the so-called "great man theory of leadership" fundamentally collides with the essence of Ignatian spirituality, which teaches one has to become small and make a conscious choice to serve (Greenleaf 2002, pp. 27, 28).

Humility is also a helpful virtue when we try to disconnect ourselves from people's opinions of us. As a disposition, it is closely related to the experience of leaving behind the focus on ourselves. The first week opens: "Man is created to praise, reverence, and serve God our Lord, and by this means to save his soul. . . . Our one desire and choice should be what is more conducive to the end for which we are created" (*Sp.Ex.* 23). The purpose of life is God's greater glory.[16] Nonbelievers understandably might have difficulty with this. At the same time, it is important for fostering our altruism that we leave our own ego behind. A retreat can start with turning in on oneself but should eventually lead to a transcendence of oneself and experience of oneself within a larger network. "This approach makes room for the integration of development built on a foundation of ego-transcendence, love, or God. It also leaves to each leader to discern, in interaction with other organization members, which organizational missions to forward (ends) and how (means)" (Rothausen 2017, p. 2).

---

[16]This reminds us of the first question of the Westminster Shorter Catechism: "1. What is the chief end of man? Man's chief end is to glorify God, and to enjoy him forever."

7.2   Silence, Detachment and Indifference

Spiritual exercises are inconceivable without times of solitude, silence, and detachment. We practice being still with God, just to be in His presence, in much the same way as silent company is part of any profound relationship. We learn to be disconnected from our lower superficial self, rediscover our deepest desirers, the voice of the inner self where God speaks, then refocus, and finally reconnect with society. In a turbulent world of constant noise and stimulation, several days of silence can be an odd experience. It is in silence that we create room for encountering God in our very depths. Many managers describe their activities as "getting things done," "keeping everyone in the loop," "putting out fires," "react and navigate," "have impact," "call Mr. x and mail Mss. y" etc. Taking time for reflection and detaching oneself from daily pressures seems to be a luxury, only available to the elite. Yet those who have managerial responsibilities need this profoundly (Moberg and Calkins 2001, p. 257). Through silence one develops a receptive attitude, an openness to experiencing the beauty of nature as incarnated beauty. In short, one develops a contemplative receiving attitude towards reality instead of a manipulative or controlling attitude (Verstraeten 2014, p. 89). It is only through silence that one comes in contact with one's deeper self, one is able to listen to one's own consciousness. Finally, one develops the skill of listening, indispensable for leading an organization.

The experience of detachment is also mainly caused by the experience of silence and the minimalism of a retreat setting. As stated before, the heart of Ignatian spirituality is freedom and detachment. Humility is detachment from the agenda of the self, silence from the surrounding multitude of information. According to Ignatius, the detachment of a pilgrim on this earth yet living out of another reality, is a fundamental attitude. For discernment one needs to become detached from all kinds of desires and needs. Indeed, it is through detachment that one becomes open to new possibilities. Before making any important decision, our general spiritual state should be to "make ourselves indifferent to all created things" (*Sp.Ex.* 23). In this context, "indifference" has a particular meaning. It relates to the attitude of freedom and detachment. It is a mental state in which you can take sufficient distance from your own condition, views, and prejudices, and this is hard to achieve. Is absolutely everything becoming an option in your mind? Are you really free to serve God in everything? "Indifference is another way of describing spiritual freedom. It is a stance of openness to God: we look for God in any person, any situation, and any moment. Indifference means that we are free to love and serve as God desires" (Martin 2010, p. 210). In contemporary words we might call this a "zero calibration," to ensure that our "mental needle" reads zero, every option becomes possible.

Some key words in Theory-U are "open mind" and "state of fundamental freedom." For Scharmer the social technology of presencing is essentially a technology of freedom (Scharmer 2016, p. 184). We need to create a mental space for letting go of the old and everything that isn't essential before we can co-create the new.[17] For this profound experience we need to find a sacred place of silence or deep listening. Only here do we allow the inner knowing to emerge. Through silence one feels connected with others and new creative ideas emerge (Scharmer 2016, p. 237).

7.3   The Primacy of Emotions and Imagination

Spiritual Exercises reflects on the moods of our soul, our longings, and feelings. "Discerning the spirits" has a broad meaning and implies affective stirrings of our heart, the experience of emotions such as anxiety, sorrow, joy, peace, or hope, as well as the thoughts related to these feelings. The purpose is to identify which emotions are from God and which are not (Gallagher 2013, loc. 365–367). Two opposite affective states are crucial: consolation and desolation. We imagine our decisions and ask ourselves what comforts or discomforts us in light of our journey through life. "I call it consolation when an interior movement is aroused in the soul, by which it is inflamed with love of its Creator and Lord, and as a consequence, can love no creature on the face of the earth for its own sake, but only in the Creator of them all . . . I call consolation every increase of faith, hope, and love" (*Sp.Ex.* 316). "And the opposite desolation, as darkness of soul, turmoil of spirit, inclination to what is low and earthly, restlessness rising from many disturbances and temptations which lead to want of faith, want of hope, want of love. The soul is wholly slothful, tepid, sad, and separated, as it were, from its Creator and Lord" (*Sp.Ex.* 317). The whole reflective process is about ordering our confused desires. It is important not to make any important decisions in times of desolation, but at such times to "preserve in patience" (*Sp.Ex.* 321). God alone can give consolation of the soul (*Sp.Ex.* 330).

Ignatius speaks about three stages or modes. In the first mode, one knows exactly what choice God calls us to make, it is merely a matter of obedience (*Sp.Ex.* 175). In the second stage, we investigate more deeply our emotional experience of consolations and desolations (*Sp.Ex.* 176). The third mode is about making a rational choice by thinking through all the options and weighing the pros and cons (*Sp.Ex.* 176). It is when the affective is unclear that the rational takes priority. And even then, one has to come back to the affective to see whether the rational choice gives consolation. In short, the *Spiritual Exercises* prioritize the emotional dimension over the rational decision process (O'Sullivan 1990). The exercitant is encouraged "to probe the netherworld of non-cognizant knowledge" (Moberg and Calkins 2001, p. 265). To be clear: we are not referring to a chaos of emotions and intuitions, but to ordered

---

[17]Scharmer interacts with the famous cognitive scientist Francisco Varela who studied the process of becoming aware. For the transcript of the often-used interview https://www.presencing.org/#/aboutus/theory-u/leadership-interview/francisco_varela

affections as a basis for discernment.[18] Lennick and Kiel make a case for moral intelligence in leadership. They rightfully pay a lot of attention to emotions and to reflecting on our emotions with the purpose of recognizing patterns in our responses to situations. In times of reflection one should ask: "During what experiences in my past have I felt happy, excited, hopeful, angry, sad, or fearful?" (2011, p. 170).

This leads us to another point: the ordering of our affects through imagination and creativity. In Theory-U, imagination and creativity are also treasured. Creativity, individual as well as collective creativity, is the ultimate source for all capital and value creation (Scharmer and Kaufer 2013). They offer visual practice programs as well as a presencing theater.[19] In Theory-U the self, being bodily connected to others and the world around us, is the main source for creativity.

In Ignatian discernment, imagination and creativity are related to the experience of Scripture. Scripture is used as an external source for our inner ordering. A combination of meditation (reflection) and contemplation (imagining) is arrived at (Gallagher 2008). Imagination enables us to see things in a new light and can be a pathway to innovation (Verstraeten 2014, p. 86), and an important part of the Ignatian meditation exercises is picturing gospel scenes. The object of these meditation exercises is to focus on the life, passion, and resurrection of Jesus. Our imagination is not only a visual activity, but also involves feeling, smelling, tasting, and experiencing with all the senses, just as if one were there. One is creating a drama and participates in the performance. Martin gives as an example the passage of Jesus in the storm: "even here in the boat, you might imagine tasting the saltwater spray. Now that you have used your senses and 'composed the place,' you have the scene set. At this point you can just let the scene play out in your mind, with you in the picture" (Martin 2010, loc. 2510–2513). The exercise of imagination is not impulsive or random, but based on an assignment given by the spiritual director. This intense focus on Christ breaks with our tendency for self-absorption (Moberg and Calkins 2001, p. 264). Biblical stories can help us to integrate our work with our lives, or as Verstraeten formulates it: "contribute to the narrative reconfiguration of a leader" (Verstraeten 2014, p. 88).[20]

The power of imagination is not only used for contemplating Scripture, it is also used to imagine different circumstances and the decisions one can make. Through imagination, a person's social network comes into the picture: husband, children, friends, colleagues etc. Imaginative prayer thus has a socially constructed content (Moberg and Calkins 2001, p. 264). In leadership studies, there is an awareness of the importance of the skill of imagination and talent of telling vivid stories, for innovation as well as for creating a common vision in an organization (Liu and Noppe-Brandon 2011).

---

[18]In Christian ethics, especially within the Protestant tradition, the role of emotions and experiences has been vastly undervalued and the power of cognitive reasoning overvalued (Van den Heuvel et al. 2018).

[19]See for both https://www.presencing.org

[20]We are not autonomous self-sufficient identities but are configured by the other (E. Levinas), not only concretely, but also by the otherness of the text (P. Ricoeur). Cf. Verstraeten (2014).

7.4   The Two Standards and Ethical Evaluation

With the power of imagination in mind, one comes to the exercise of "imagining the Two Standards." Ignatius's former love of the battlefield presumably plays an important role in the imagination exercise of the two banners during the second week (*Sp.Ex.* 136–148). The retreatant imagines two armies, each with a flag, banner or standard. On one side we see the army of Christ, on the other the army of Satan. This conflict metaphor goes back to the conflict between Jerusalem and Babylon as we find it in the New Testament, another example of it can be found in Augustine's City of God and City of Satan. This meditation on the Two Standards refers to the battle within ourselves, between that which moves us toward God and that which moves us away from Him. That which moves us toward God is the good spirit, and that which moves us away from Him is the evil spirit. Christ the King is calling us to choose his side and leave behind the riches and honors calling from the other side. Discernment is the art of distinguishing between those two forces. It requires acquaintance with the voice of Christ, as well as insight in the subtle strategies and seductions of evil.[21] Jesus is calling us to choose the more demanding path, the one asking for *imitatio Christi,* which involves suffering, poverty, humility, service and contempt. Ignatius describes evil as "Lucifer, the deadly enemy of our human nature" (*Sp.Ex.* 136). In contrast, according to him, Jesus empowers us to embrace our humanity in all of its beautiful complexity and transforms us according to his image, into loving and serving people. In present-day language, we might investigate our desires and ask ourselves what is humane or inhumane about them. In this part of the exercise, the moral dimension of discernment is at the forefront. We are confronted with our own fixations on power, possessions, esteem, etc.

The investigation of our desires and decisions is particularly important in business and leadership ethics. In dealing with a sense of purpose and the discernment between good and evil we come to the very heart of authentic leadership. This part of discernment is similar to what George calls "discovering your true North." It is the internal compass, based on your deeper self and life story, which leads us on in a tumultuous world (George et al. 2015).

As the ethicist Craig Johnson states: all leadership has a dark and a light side. The question is: do we cast light or shadow? (Johnson 2011). In order to answer this question, we must start with a reflective practice which goes beyond following a set of rules, but which is about mastering our inner drives and attachments. The answer thus lies in well-developed basic trust (Verstraeten 2014, pp. 92, 93). To be engaged in this type of meditation also means that one consciously scrutinizes the defining moments of our past practices. Did we really act in accordance to what we believe is good and in line with our moral compass and goals? The exercise of the Two Standards is similar to what we now refer to as reflecting on the big picture and reframing the situation (Lennick and Kiel 2011, pp. 174, 175).

---

[21]Compare C.S. Lewis' famous book *The Screwtape Letters* (1942), letters from Demon Screwtape to his young nephew Wormwood, about tempting a Christian (the patient).

Theory-U has developed the big picture well. In fact, the theory is entirely about a change from the small to the big picture, our global crisis. With our industries and markets we are collectively creating results that nobody really wants. Our crisis can only be solved if we start thinking from the heart instead of only from the head. This means a shift from an ego-system awareness to an eco-system awareness, a focus on our *oikos* or the whole house we all live in (Scharmer and Kaufer 2013, p. 2). Discernment requires the ability to let go of the past and lean into the future that wants to emerge through us, and an openness to let it come to us. The metaphor of the iceberg is used to describe the relationship between spiritual awareness and the disruption in our world. In each layer, from surface to depth, there are blind spots which need to be addressed. On the surface, the level of symptoms, we are confronted with the visible behaviors. They appear in three divides: ecological divide (self and nature), social divide (rich and poor) and spiritual-cultural divide (self and Self). This last one manifests itself in an overstressed society with increasing cases of burnout and depression. Beyond the surface, that which does not appear, we find the wrong structures. Without going into details of Scharmer and Kaufer's diagnosis of our world, the main point is that one finally ends up in the deeper source, the inner place from which we operate.

7.5   *Journaling and Mentoring*

Journaling is an important spiritual and reflective practice. Ignatius made notes of his observations regarding his inner life. He registered what gave him consolation and what led to desolation and, with the help of his notes, tried to discern patterns in his behavior. He also recopied his notebook regularly. A journal is strictly personal, it is our spiritual memory and a reminder of our vocation, images, prayers and struggling. In our notes, we also connect our bible readings and prayers with events in our daily life, however small. In this way the journaling has an integrating function. "A spiritual notebook or journal can be an anchor to remind the leader of her or his vocation and higher purpose. Revisiting, rereading, or even rewriting these notes on a regular basis could center the leader in the spiritual aspects of her or his leadership" (Rothausen 2017, p. 5).

Even though the journal is personal, it can be used for a conversation with a mentor or spiritual director. Ignatian reflection is not a strictly individual endeavor, it is a guided reflection. The role of the director is one of careful guidance in the process of discernment and to discriminate internal movements. The spiritual director daily provides the exercitant with material for about four hours of meditation; the next day they review how it went. The director helps to interpret the experiences of the exercitant and proposes new material for the following day. But we keep in mind that God deals directly with the exercitant and so the director must be very careful not to interfere in this process. This type of guidance is an immense responsibility and requires a special skill. Moberg and Calkins express a caution: "Guided reflection . . . is not intended to be the tool of someone looking for another technique to shoehorn into his or her consulting practice. Too much damage has been done by charlatans to allow this process to fall into the wrong hands" (Moberg and Calkins 2001, p. 266). An important principle is that discernment is very personal as well as relational; as we talk things through with our director, our ideas and feeling become clearer.

8 Conclusion

I opened this chapter with a quest for authentic leadership in a VUCA-world. Authentic leadership requires an inner compass to give us direction in making decisions. Authenticity originally means to be true to oneself. It is within this internal coherence that we evaluate options and discern. Psychologists, such as Carl Rogers and Abraham Maslow, have developed this humanistic psychology of the self-actualized personality. These models incorporate strong moral convictions and require that we are in tune with them, that we are authentic (Avolio and Gardner 2005). This has been picked up later, in a more empirical way, by positive psychologists and the importance of positive psychological capital in organizations (Luthans et al. 2007). In Theory-U, there is the inner divide between the self and the Self (capital S), the person we can become. We must drop our habitual self in order for the authentic Self to emerge (Scharmer 2016, p. 42). Successful leadership depends on the quality of attention and intention that the leader brings to any situation. Of great contribution is the way in which Theory-U creates a bridge between the inner space within ourselves, and the global ethical challenges we are faced with. Discernment spirituality, in this case characterized by presencing an emerging future, becomes a tool for social development. It is a shift from an ego-system awareness that cares about the wellbeing of oneself, to an eco-system awareness that cares about the wellbeing of all, overcoming the ecological divide, the social divide and spiritual cultural divide. This broad and yet profound framing gives us direction for discernment.

However, one may wonder if the self is able to let a better Self emerge without some kind of resourcing from a faith tradition or at least a larger narrative which confronts the self. Maybe this is Otto Scharmer's own blind spot? Are we able to overcome superficial judgments, cynicism, fear, and egocentrism by our own internal power? The answer from the Ignatian tradition is that we can't. The experience of calling and purpose presuppose a transcendental act which lifts us up beyond our own capacities and helps us overcome our selfish ego. Theologically speaking, or from the perspective of a Christian faith-narrative, the emerging Self is a restoration of the *imago Dei*, a new person able to connect and to love as Christ did.[22] This is why Ignatius's method of discernment invites

---

[22]The intimate unity between the experience of the self and God we find in the work of the Jesuit, Karl Rahner. We can't experience the one without the other and anthropology starts and ends with Christology (see especially Volume 13 of *Theological Investigations*). More practically, this

us first of all to pause and become aware of the God who loves me. Secondly to face our own weaknesses, faults, and mistakes as they cast a shadow on the present and future. Ignatius doesn't avoid the feelings of shame, but faces them head on and from there moves forward to forgiveness and healing. The source of healing is not coming from the self, but from a trust in a loving God speaking to the self. Trusting on the self is a mistake as is only seeing our own weaknesses can be paralyzing. I concur with Theresa Rothausen that these practices of confronting are crucial for all leader development (Rothausen 2017, p. 12). Discerning as an authentic person means on the one hand an experience of our failures, and on the other hand the experience of being loved and of intense gratitude. Without this real "eye of the needle," the confession of selfishness and the continuous healing of it, spiritual discernment leading to moral change for the common good, might remain an illusion.

References

Source Texts

Ignatius of Loyola (1951) The spiritual exercises of St. Ignatius: based on studies in the language of the autograph. English edition: Louis J Puhl (1951), available at http://spex.ignatianspirituality. com/SpiritualExercises/Puhl#pre01. Accessed 15 Jan 2018
Ignatius of Loyola, Munitiz JA, Endean P (eds) (1997) Personal writings. Penguin, London
Ignatius of Loyola, Palmer ME, Padberg JW, McCarthy JL (2006) Letters and instructions. Institute of Jesuit Sources, Saint Louis, MO

Other Sources

Avolio BJ, Gardner WL (2005) Authentic leadership development: Getting to the root of positive forms of leadership. Leadership Q 16(3):315–338
Avolio BJ, Luthans F (2005) The high impact leader: authentic, resilient leadership that gets results and sustains growth. McGraw Hill, New York
Bennett N, Lemoine GJ (2014) What VUCA really means for you. Harv Bus Rev, 1 Jan 2014. https://hbr.org/2014/01/what-vuca-really-means-for-you. Accessed 18 Jan 2018
Bouckaert L (2017) Spiritual discernment as a method of judgment. In: Nandram SS, Bindlish PK (eds) Managing self through integrative self-management: how to cope with volatility, uncertainty, complexity and ambiguity in organizational behavior. Springer, Dordrecht, pp 15–25
Caraman P (1990) Ignatius Loyola: a biography of the founder of the Jesuits. Collins; Harper & Row, London
Chiesa A, Serretti A (2009) Mindfulness-based stress reduction for stress management in healthy people: a review and meta-analysis. J Altern Complement Med 15(5):593–600. https://doi.org/10.1089/acm.2008.0495

---

therapeutic view on salvation as restoration of the image of God is characteristic of the Wesleyan tradition, as it is closely related to the Greek Church Fathers (Maddox 1994).

Covey SR (2014) The 8th habit: from effectiveness to greatness. Simon & Schuster, London
Darmanin A (2005) Ignatian spirituality and leadership in organizations today. Rev Ignatian Spirituality 36(2):1–14
Dhiman S (2017) Holistic leadership: a new paradigm for today's leaders. Springer, Dordrecht
Endean P (2009) Karl Rahner and Ignatian spirituality. Oxford University Press, Oxford
Fry LW (2003) Toward a theory of spiritual leadership. Leadership Q 14(6):693–727. https://doi.org/10.1016/j.leaqua.2003.09.001
Fry LW, Nisiewicz MS (2013) Maximizing the triple bottom line through spiritual leadership. Stanford Business Books, Stanford, CA
Gallagher TM (2008) Meditation and contemplation: an Ignatian guide to praying with scripture. Crossroad, New York
Gallagher TM (2009) Discerning the will of God: an Ignatian guide to Christian decision making. Crossroad, Chicago, IL
Gallagher TM (2012) Spiritual consolation: an Ignatian guide for greater discernment. Independent Pub Gr, Kindle
Gallagher TM (2013) Discernment of spirits: a reader's guide. Crossroad, New York
George B, Craig N, Snook SA (2015) The discover your true north fieldbook: a personal guide to finding your authentic leadership. Wiley & Sons, Hoboken, NJ
Giacalone RA, Jurkiewicz CL (2015) Handbook of workplace spirituality and organizational performance. Routledge, New York
Goleman D (2014) Emotional intelligence. Bloomsbury, London
Greenleaf RK (2002) Servant leadership: a journey into the nature of legitimate power and greatness. Paulist, New York
Hannah ST, Avolio BJ, Walumbwa FO (2011) Relationships between authentic leadership, moral courage, and ethical and pro-social behaviors. Bus Ethics Q 21(4):555–578
Heiding SF (2012) Ignatian spirituality at ecclesial frontiers. Dissertation, Oxford University
Heuvel SC van den, Nullens P, Roothaan ACM (2018) Theological ethics and moral value phenomena: the experience of values. Routledge, New York
Hinson EG (2007) Ignatian and puritan prayer: surprising similarities; a comparison of Ignatius Loyola and Richard Baxter on meditation. Merton Annu 20:79–92
Holder A (2005) The Blackwell companion to Christian spirituality. Blackwell, Malden, MA
Inglehart R (1997) Modernization and postmodernization: cultural, economic, and political change in 43 societies. Princeton University Press, Princeton, NJ
Inglehart R, Welzel C (2005) Modernization, cultural change, and democracy: the human development sequence. Cambridge University Press, Cambridge, MA
Johnson C (2011) Meeting the ethical challenges of leadership: casting light or shadow. Sage, London
Lafontaine R (2011) Ignace de Loyola ct Martin Luther: vie spirituelle et théologie. Nouvelle rev théologique, Tome 133(1):45–64. https://doi.org/10.3917/nrt.331.0045
Lennick D, Kiel F (2011) Moral intelligence 2.0: enhancing business performance and leadership success in turbulent times. Prentice Hall, Upper Saddle River, NJ
Liu E, Noppe-Brandon S (2011) Imagination first: unlocking the power of possibility. Jossey-Bass, San Francisco, CA
Luthans F, Youssef CM, Avolio BJ (2007) Psychological capital: developing the human competitive edge. Oxford University Press, Oxford
Maddox RL (1994) Responsible grace: John Wesley's practical theology. Kingswood Books, Nashville
Martin J (2010) The Jesuit guide to (almost) everything: a spirituality for real life. HarperCollins, New York, Kindle
Maryks RA (2014) A companion to Ignatius of Loyola: life, writings, spirituality, influence. Brill, Leiden
Meissner W (1994) Ignatius of Loyola: the psychology of a saint. Yale University Press, New Haven, CT

Moberg DJ, Calkins M (2001) Reflection in business ethics: insights from St. Ignatius' spiritual
    exercises. J Bus Ethics 33(3):257–270. https://doi.org/10.1023/A:1017574904755
Neal J (ed) (2012) Handbook of faith and spirituality in the workplace: emerging research and
    practice. Springer, New York
Northouse PG (2016) Leadership: theory and practice. Sage, Los Angeles, CA
Nullens P (2011) Dietrich Bonhoeffer: a third way of Christian social engagement. Eur J Theol 20
    (1):60–69
O'Brien KF (2011) The Ignatian adventure: experiencing the spiritual exercises of Saint Ignatius in
    daily life. Loyola Press, Chicago, IL
O'Sullivan MJ (1990) Trust your feelings, but use your head: discernment and the psychology of
    decision making. Semin Jesuit Spirituality, St. Louis, MO
Otto R (1959) The idea of the holy. Penguin, Harmondsworth
Pargament KI, Mahoney A (2011) Spirituality: the search of the sacred. In: Lopez SJ, Snyder CR
    (eds) Oxford handbook of positive psychology. Oxford University Press, New York, pp
    611–620
Quick CJ, Gavin JH, Cooper CL, Quick JD (2000) Executive health: building strength, managing
    risks. Acad Manag Perspect 14(2):34–44
Reave L (2005) Spiritual values and practices related to leadership effectiveness. Leadership Q 16
    (5):655–687. https://doi.org/10.1016/j.leaqua.2005.07.003
Richter F (1955) Martin Luther und Ignatius von Loyola: Repräsentanten zweier Geisteswelten.
    Schloz, Stuttgart-Degerloch
Rosenthal SA, Pittinsky TL (2006) Narcissistic leadership. Leadership Q 17(6):617–633
Rothausen TJ (2017) Integrating leadership development with Ignatian spirituality: a model for
    designing a spiritual leader development practice. J Bus Ethics 145(4):811–829
Sankowsky D (1995) The charismatic leader as narcissist: understanding the abuse of power. Organ
    Dyn 23(4):57–71
Scharmer CO (2016) Theory U: leading from the future as it emerges: the social technology of
    presencing. Berrett-Koehler, San Francisco, CA
Scharmer CO, Kaufer K (2013) Leading from the emerging future: from ego-system to eco-system
    economies. Berrett-Koehler, San Francisco, CA
Vaughan F (2002) What is spiritual intelligence? J Humanist Psychol 42(2):16–33
Verstraeten J (2014) Spirituality as source of inspired, authentic and innovative leadership. In:
    Nullens P, Barentsen J (eds) Leadership, innovation and spirituality. Christian perspectives on
    leadership and social ethics. Peeters, Leuven, pp 49–58
Waaijman K (2007) Spirituality—a multifaceted phenomenon: interdisciplinary explorations. Stud
    Spirituality 17:1–113. https://doi.org/10.2143/SIS.17.0.2024643
Wakefield JL, Ignatius (2006) Sacred listening: discovering the spiritual exercises of Ignatius
    Loyola. Baker, Grand Rapids, MI
Warner L (2010) Journey with Jesus. IVP, Downers Grove, IL
Wigglesworth C (2014) SQ21: the twenty-one skills of spiritual intelligence. Select, New York
Zohar D, Marshall IN (2001) SQ: the ultimate intelligence. Bloomsbury, London

Patrick Nullens (Ph.D.) is Full Professor of Systematic Theology at the Evangelische Theologische Faculteit, Leuven (Belgium). He is cofounder of Institute of Leadership and Social Ethics and member of its steering committee. Furthermore, he is Extraordinary Professor of Theology at North-West University, South Africa. During his career, he has been mostly involved in different leadership roles. Innovation and spirituality are two core values in his personal journey. He is convinced of the importance of theology in practice. Therefore, he regularly preaches in both the Netherlands and Belgium. He publishes regularly in the field of theology, ethics and leadership.

Correction to: Leading in a VUCA World

Jacobus (Kobus) Kok and Steven C. van den Heuvel

Correction to:
J. (Kobus) Kok, S. C. van den Heuvel (eds.), *Leading in a*
VUCA World, **Contributions to Management Science,**
https://doi.org/10.1007/978-3-319-98884-9

This book was inadvertently published with the incorrect affiliation for the editors. The affiliation has been updated as below:

Steven C. van den Heuvel
Department of Systematic Theology
Evangelische Theologische Faculteit
Leuven, Belgium

Extraordinary Researcher at the
Faculty of Theology
North-West University
Potchefstroom, South Africa

Jacobus (Kobus) Kok
Department of New Testament
Evangelische Theologische Faculteit Leuven, Belgium

Extraordinary Professor, University of Pretoria, South Africa

Research Associate (Classical Studies) at the University of the Free State, Bloemfontein, South Africa

The updated online versions of the chapters can be found at
https://doi.org/10.1007/978-3-319-98884-9_1
https://doi.org/10.1007/978-3-319-98884-9_11

© The Author(s) 2019   C1
J. (Kobus) Kok, S. C. van den Heuvel (eds.), *Leading in a VUCA World*,
Contributions to Management Science, https://doi.org/10.1007/978-3-319-98884-9_13

Printed by Printforce, the Netherlands